Small Boat
Against the Sea

G000271540

Small Boat Against the Sea

The story of the first trans-world rowing attempt

DEREK KING and
PETER BIRD

 Paul Elek: London

First published in Great Britain 1976 by
Elek Books Limited
54–58 Caledonian Road, London N1 9RN

Copyright © 1976 Derek King and Peter Bird
Photographs copyright © 1976 Peter Bird

All rights reserved. No part of this publication
may be reproduced, stored in a retrieval system
or transmitted, in any form or by any means, electronic,
mechanical, photocopying, recording or otherwise,
without the prior permission of the publishers.

ISBN 0 236 40013 4

Made and printed in Great Britain by
The Garden City Press Limited,
Letchworth, Hertfordshire SG6 1JS

For Maggie with love / For Mummy Bird, family and friends

Contents

Illustrations

Acknowledgements: The drawings on pages 67, 109, 120, 135, 162, 185 and 209 are by Lesley Fallows; the diagrams on pages 38, 39 and 196 by Alec Woollard; the photos on pages 25 and 28 are copyright Epoque Limited and London Express respectively and are reproduced by permission of the copyright owners; the remaining photos are by Peter Bird.

Acknowledgements

We are sincerely grateful to the many kind and generous people who were lured, one way or another, into our project. Without their encouragement, support and sympathy we could not have got as far as we did.

So thank you to: John Fairfax and Sylvia Cook; Peter Tappenden; Alec Woollard; Mrs J. Bird; Keith and Tina Kirkby; John Halmshaw; Lt-Commander David Baird; Fleet Chief 'Robbie' Robinson; Peter Bell; John Cotter; John Newton; Dr Wootliff, MB, CHB; Miss D. M. French; Tony Dixon; Major John Edwards; 'German Mike' Migge; Frankie Lombard; Geoff'n King and Juicy; Dave Laughton; Victor Boddiss; La Comtesse M. Apraxine; Pierre Lampe; John Payne; Peter Hogg; David Goddard; Alec Gardner; René P. Jeanneret; Peter Ayling; Frank Selby; Joe Huband; Jim Maurer; Ernie Stanton; Pepe Rossado; Geoff Dunn; 'Black Bob' Pugh; Denis Henly; Dave Johns; Slim Simpson; A. W. A. Poole; Leslie Pullen; Edwin Phelps.

In addition, very grateful thanks indeed to the following firms who gave or loaned us their excellent equipment and stores and gave up so much of their time and advice: Airbourne Industries Ltd for three solar stills. Andrew Lusk for a food cache. Antifyre Ltd whose lifeboat extinguishers saved Britannia from being destroyed. E. Ayling Ltd for our fine oars which must have done four million strokes! Bio Strath (UK) for the elixir which kept us going. Bland Lines of Gibraltar, Both Worlds Hotel and Southern Ferries Ltd for first class accommodation and travel. Bourne and Hollingsworth for helping Carol so much. British Petroleum for the cash, telexing facilities, emergency radio, sextant, oilskins and jerrycans, and the collection of charts and Pilot books; also for the valuable public relations. Burndept Electronics (ER) Ltd for the loan of the SARBE Flotation Beacon. Driclad Ltd for the inflatable splints.

Geest Ltd for transporting Britannia back from St Lucia. The Gibraltar Tourist Board for all their help. Gladding International Ltd for the Sealey fish hooks, Intrepid reel and lures and Gladding line, which caught fish. ITN for the film and cameras which enabled us to make a unique record of the voyage and also for their advice and help and for restoring our faith in the news media. Liptons Ltd for tinned food that gave us our weekly treat. Lyle and Scott for a fine selection of pants, shirts. vests and sweaters. Matt Wood of Putney for the strong rowlocks. Optimus for the stove and lamp. Pegasus Freight Ltd for flying our stores to Gibraltar. Prestige Ltd for the skyline pressure cooker. Rolex of Geneva for the two superb chronometers (GMT Masters) and one Submariner watch. Ronson Products Ltd, whose Windmaster Lighters proved so successful that they should be renamed Storm Masters! Rowe Decorations Ltd for cash. Sailsafe Co Ltd for the loan of a highly reassuring liferaft. Sigma Coatings for the fluorescent orange paints and the cash. Sony (UK) Ltd for their all-weather radio ICF 111L which certainly lived up to its name. Swel Foods Ltd for the beef and chicken pieces which provided varied nutritious meals. The Tupperware Company whose containers kept all of our stores and valuables safe from the sea. Watts and Fincham for so much chandlery. Wiggins Teape (Mill Sales) Ltd for supplying us with Tyvec 10 waterproof paper, made by Dupont of Delaware; the remarkable paper used in the Log survived hundreds of dousings. International Paints Ltd for their fine assistance. P & O for the return of Britannia II from Australia to England and a marvellous trip to Tangier. Judy Bird and Benson & Hedges for the tobacco. Courtaulds for delicious Kesp and comfortable clothes.

Thanks also to Carol Lampe (neé Maystone) for kindly allowing us to quote her words from interviews first published in the *Evening News*.

To the Court Line crew who flew us back from St Lucia on the last eventful flight before the company folded—to Peter, Chris, Danny, Annie, Rosemary, Jacquie, Jill, Avril, Marie, Janet, Linda, Julia; and finally, to our long-suffering editor, Tony Wood—very special thanks.

He was with you when adventure filled the vision of your youth
And He stopped frustration turning to despair,
He clothed your dreams in wood and glass and gave them to the
    waves
And in farewell days He shouted from the shore;
    But you weren't surprised to find Him already on the boat
    Steering courage forward to the open sea,
    And He never let dissension mar the purpose that He gave
    And Jonah had to go to set you free.

He was with you in the danger when the fury of the storm
Threatened angry death to project and to crew;
He kept you from the crushing of the midnight tanker's hull
And the whirlpool of that threshing deadly screw;
    And He led you through the inner storms of anguish and
    fatigue
    And renewed you for horizons yet unknown
    And in days of calm you saw him in the multicoloured life
    Of the creatures that He sent to cheer you on.

He saved you from the timelessness and kept you moving on
And He gave you precious images of home,
Of the life you stood to forfeit and the love you stood to lose
If you left His way and went on on your own.
    Lead me on, Precious Lord, lead me on,
    Guide and keep me all my days, lead me on,
    Turn our dreams into reality and keep our eyes on You,
    Lead me on, Precious Lord, lead me on.

John Bayes, 1974

BELFAST PUBLIC LIBRARIES

1

Intentions

September 1971–24th March 1974

Derek
Can't be more than a thirty-yard swim, I thought. With the
water as rough as it was, against the tide and holding a bag
of clothes above my head, I reckoned it would take about ten
minutes. It would be worth it. I needed to get off the boat,
go for a walk, talk to people. My body ached from the cramped,
soaking existence. My mind was beginning to ramble. For seventy
days I had been alone, struggling to row round Ireland's
magnificent and brutal coastline. Just over half-way, I felt that
the nightmarish events which had occurred with terrible regul-
arity must be over. I'd had more than my share of gales, headwinds, adverse tides, collisions, injury, swamping, even whirlpools.
So a short trip ashore would be a little reward.

I stripped off, bundled my already damp clothes into a nylon
bag, and after checking the anchors, slid into the chilly water.
I kicked off from the weed-slimy hull and began to swim strongly
—with one arm raised to keep the bag dry. Suddenly the wind
gusted and knocked it into the water. The rhythm of my strokes
went wrong as I tried to lift the bag up. It was wet and became
heavy. A spiteful bitch sea slapped me in the face. My eyes
stung. 'Keep that bag up. Keep swimming,' I repeated to myself.
Again the bag blew down. I got worried. I glanced back at the
boat. The wind had taken her away from me, in an arc around
the mooring.

I gauged the distance to the shore : 15 yards. I was growing
weaker, the bag was sapping my energy. What a fool I was to
attempt such a swim ! A startling mouthful of burning salt water
made my heart jump. Waves hurtled over me. Filthy salt
scorched my throat. I sucked mucus in as I gasped for breath.

The bag got heavier, I got lower. I thought I should rest—

a few seconds only. Very low in the water, I stopped swimming.
The hissing of the water around me abruptly stopped as I sank.
No spray or slaps, but a quiet, pressing sensation around my
ears. My eyes opened and I saw a green void. My mouth was
open, a cold heaviness flowed into my body. Then a calmness
took over all my feelings. A perfect peace for one long second.
I wasn't frightened, rather extra-alert and curious. I felt part of
the watery emptiness. 'What's happening?' asked the inner
voice, the surviving instinct. 'I am drowning!'

My thoughts cleared. I kicked my way to the surface. My
head nearly exploded after the quietness below. I re-entered the
world of gurglings and bubbling sounds. Coughing up foulness,
I cried for help—but there was no one, just rocks one way and
my boat the other. I threw away the bag of clothes.

My eye fixed on a rock as I crawled through the evil sea.
A wave humped and obscured the black rock, then foam
cascaded off it in white ribbons. 'I—must—make—it,' I told
myself as I dragged myself on. Five yards to go; three, two.
Crunch! The turbulence of the backlash jarred me so severely
that I didn't know if I had hit the rock at all. I groped in the
seething foam and felt sharp limpets and solidness. The next
wave spewed me out of the sea and my body scraped over the
sharpness. Sprawled over the rock, legs dangling in the sea,
naked, I was shaking, vomiting—absolutely terrified.

'This must be the final warning,' I thought. 'It is now time to
give up. I've tried my best. I mustn't push my luck any further.'

But my life continued its run of contradictions. Later on that
day I swam back to Louise, and set off rowing again. On 3rd
October 1971 I arrived back at my place of departure—
Donegal: 113 days and 1,500 miles later. Even my near-drowning
hadn't been enough to stop the crazy voyage. Sharks, reefs, surf,
a Killer whale and savagely painful salt water sores added themselves to the list of horrors. I really thought I meant the next
day's *Daily Express* headline: 'Never again, says first-time
oarsman'.

How strange then, a few months later, that I drew up a
detailed prospectus of my new plans entitled 'British Trans-
World Rowing Expedition'. Why could I not settle down to my
trade as a chef and continue a very promising career? I wasn't
really cut out for such hair-brained physical ordeals. Basically
I loved the soft life, a country lad with a passion for animals,

food, comfortable beds and pints at the local. I hated driving, travelling and meeting new people. Where did my peculiar itchy-footedness come from?

For I had a terrific desire to row off again. This time, The Big One! My decision was made while John Fairfax and Sylvia Cook were still rowing across the Pacific: there could be only one voyage to cap that. I thought I could do it; I was young and strong and daft enough; I could row a good stroke; I could survive the life. And someone would surely sponsor my effort. I could think of no reason why I shouldn't have a go. So I got organised for the trip of a lifetime. Why? What for? asked my friends and family.

The frequently voiced but nevertheless dubious clichés rolled off my tongue: 'Because it's there!' 'Man's desire to better himself,' 'Because I'm British!' But I wasn't sure about them. Perhaps it was far simpler—selfishness, egotism, escapism, shirking my responsibilities. But I knew what was involved. It would demand more of me than I had ever given to anything before.

At twenty-four I had time and youth on my side—no ties, and the doggedness to transform dreams into realities. I had also nurtured an insensitivity to other people's comments. Ever since the Atlantic rowers came into the limelight in the Sixties, 'rowing round the world' has for many come to be a jocular expression of impossibility mingled with pointlessness. I certainly needed all my ability to ignore those who told me what not to do with my life.

After six months of initial planning I began to look around for two companions to make up a team; one of them was to be a girl. After Louise had been destroyed by a fire in Northern Ireland two days before she was due to be shipped to England for exhibition purposes, my idea of raising money to build a new boat quickly fell through. I had therefore to make quick money to keep up with the planning costs while I tried to raise finance elsewhere.

'Heads and freaks—daily bread. Call Wendy on . . .' pronounced an advertisement I saw in a paper. With visions of easy cash I investigated further. As I suspected, the job was selling. Chalk drawings on velvet-type backgrounds were certainly not my style. I collected a bundle of the horrible things and waited to be allocated to a group who would be driven out of London to pollute the artistic atmosphere of unfortunate suburbia.

'Derek, meet Peter Bird, your supervisor,' said the sales
manager. A bespectacled character, over six foot tall, topped by
a huge mass of curls and ending in bright blue boots, swung
towards me. He proffered a great ham of a hand and said :
'Hi man!'

Pete

The reason why I was standing in an office surrounded by
twenty or so hairy salesmen was because I was a refugee of the
times at twenty-six years of age. I had left school at fifteen and,
completely unqualified, gone straight into an advertising agency
as tea-boy-cum-production-assistant. Happy and independent,
I had then begun my education. Nearly a year later, the agency
went bust. I snatched the opportunity of this sudden freedom,
bought a sleeping bag and hitched off around Europe. Like
many of the young of that time, I had been influenced by Jack
Kerouac's holy book for misfits, *On the Road*. It was the beginning of a way of life—travel. Any time the urge came I dropped
whatever I was doing—from advertising to photography and
scores of jobs in between—and went : driving, hitching, walking, sailing. I made two round-the-world trips as a ship's photographer. My horizons extended.

Always I kept my one creed—never to be committed. Com-
mitment, I saw, was a ball and chain. It meant responsibilities
and ties that would make it difficult to stick two fingers up at
the boss if he got unreasonable.

Why not work for yourself? I tried it. Peter Bird Photography
came and went. For unreasonable boss read unreasonable Bank
Manager.

I felt totally unemployable, so the only answer was to duck
and weave more quickly—in, out and away. My wanderings
brought me back home to London and the velvet painting
business. I was soon promoted to Supervisor and financially I
was doing quite well. I intended to stay in the job for the summer
of 1972 and with the proceeds hoped to build a catamaran and
become even more mobile.

Then I met a tough, compact-looking man who wore a black
leather jacket and smoked a cigar. He didn't look like the rest
of the casual types assembled around us in the sales office. In
fact, he appeared to be the odd one. As I shook hands with

Derek King, a searing pain shot up from my fingers. I hoped he wouldn't shake hands with a customer before trying to sell!

As we drove up the M1 I began the 'get the newcomer comfortable' technique by asking a bit about him. With three others in the car I tried to make him feel part of the family. He told us he was doing some writing.

'Like what about, man?' asked a voice from the back seat.

'About a trip I made last summer.'

'Where to, man?' came the back seat.

'I rowed round Ireland,' came the nonchalant reply.

I was astonished. I asked questions. How long? What boat? He certainly didn't expect so much enthusiasm from me. As I plied him with pints of Guinness ('My training,' he said) in a wayside pub, he dropped another bombshell.

'I'm planning to row round the world,' he declared with the greatest conviction.

'What in?'

'I asked Uffa Fox to design a 40-foot row-boat, based on the lines of Britannia II. You know, the one that—'

'Yes,' I interrupted, 'the Pacific rowboat.'

'Well, last week Uffa sent me the blueprints. She's going to be a beautiful boat.'

He stared into his pint and smiled.

'What route?' I was intrigued.

'I think the best place to start from is Gibraltar. You can't row against the headwinds farther north, if you leave from the U.K. for example. Gib is the nearest British colony to the beginnings of the north-east trade winds which will be in my favour across the Atlantic. Then through the West Indies, Panama, the Pacific, North Australia, Indian Ocean, Red Sea, Suez and back to the Rock.' He downed his drink. '26,000 miles. Probably take about three years in all with stopovers for repairs, food and water.'

Surely he'll need a crew, my mind raced. He won't go alone. Not in a 40-footer.

'Er—who's going with you?' I ventured.

'Well actually I haven't got a crew together yet. I'm hoping to find another bloke and a girl.'

I heard a tiny alarm bell ringing in my head. A girl. Two men.

'Why a girl?' I enquired. I didn't fancy the idea of sharing.

'Why not,' he laughed. 'I don't like the idea of all that time

at sea without a bit of female company. And there's the personality difference which I think is important. If three men went—
well, I think there'd be more problems. Limited subjects of
talk, possible rivalry for leadership, and so on.'

'Why not a twosome then?' I suggested.

'Three people can work more efficiently than two. Don't
forget it's not like sailing. If you stop rowing—you stop moving,
except for a wind-drift. So the boat's got to be moving most of
the time, or it'll take years. And there's so much to do on top
of the rowing. There's cooking, navigating, sleeping, maintenance and all that. With three people, all the jobs are looked
after without affecting the performance of the boat.'

Derek sounded very knowledgeable. It was obvious that he'd
put in a lot of research. The route was unusual for round-the-
world voyages—but then, this wasn't a usual voyage. As rowing
can't be done against winds, it was the obvious choice. The well-
known routeing by clipper ships and, more latterly, eccentric
yachtsmen would I knew be impossible for a rowboat—the seas
would be too rough, the weather too cold for an open boat, and
there would be a lack of suitable landing places in the Southern
Ocean—the arsehole of the world, as Derek succinctly put it.

'But,' he added, 'don't think I haven't considered that route.'

I admitted that he must have considered everything.

'As far as I can see, there is only one weak point in the route.
Suez,' he said. 'But I reckon that by the time I'm up the Red
Sea, it will be open, officially. Though I've heard of small boats
going through already.'

The two days that followed were drastic as far as selling
went. Derek and I yarned for hours about his venture and the
more we spoke, the more I wanted to join him. Derek set the
ball rolling by talking about the qualifications needed in the
crew.

'Neither of them need know how to row—they'll get enough
practice. They've just got to be keen, with plenty of stamina
and nerve, and be totally uncommitted.'

'I'm your man!' I blurted out.

'I think you are,' he said.

Would we get on for three years? I thought. I thought so—
but obviously there would be a few arguments. Yet it seemed we
complemented one another. The big question was the girl. That
alarm bell still rang. But I felt confident in my ability, both

mentally and physically. I also had a very real need to go; call it a need to fulfil, I don't know, but it was the first time in my life that I had committed myself for more than a month ahead. From that day on, the sales of velvet paintings plunged.

Derek suggested we work on a demolition site to toughen ourselves up. As great steel roofs crashed around us, I couldn't help thinking 'What on earth have I let myself in for?'

Derek

As soon as we started talking, I decided that Pete Bird sounded very much like the man I was looking for. It was obvious he would have a go at anything, and his traveller's tales convinced me that he would appreciate the experience. I thought that what he would go for would be the journeying rather than the achievement. He certainly looked fit enough; I could think of no argument against him. And that outrageous sense of humour: very useful for the long, long days on the ocean.

Both of us set out to find our number three, though I detected Pete had certain reservations about a female being involved in such an enterprise. Nevertheless, he thought it proper for both of us to have a crack at her on the casting couch before any decision was made! I was totally aware of the possibility that there would be a sexual problem: namely, the old familiar of 'Two into one won't go'. Pete just saw black and white on this point.

'Either she takes us both on,' he said, 'turns each as it were, or she should say no to both of us.' Then he reflected and said: 'If it's the latter, we would be the ones with problems. The old tropic nights—full moon—warm breeze—and her looking gorgeous as she clamps her chastity belt on and drops the key overboard!'

I laughed but understood him well. These were credible disadvantages but, I thought, less complicated than a three-man crew.

'We might even turn queer!' I said.

'Oooh! Ducky!'

But this relationship business was serious. We decided that over-involvement would be treading on dangerous ground.

'And another thing,' I said. 'Don't get involved with girl friends and things. That will be absolutely fatal to the trip.'

My fear was that a distraction on the domestic side would

surely make our plans flop ... Yet scarcely a month later, I
struck up a rather close friendship with a girl called Maggie.

There was another reason for the inclusion of a girl in this
project : pure publicity. We needed publicity to pay for the
voyage; it was as simple as that. If I'd had several thousand
pounds I'd have gone off quietly and got on with the job in hand.
But such money was not available and the expedition had to
arouse a lot of interest before any company would come across
with the hard cash so desperately needed.

But I was aware of the very real problems that publicity can
bring. Pressure in many forms can force one's decisions or make
the pace faster than it should be. I vowed I would never be
pushed out to sea by publicists. Yet I had to be very tactful
and offend no one. There was a lot of good-will to build up.

The first pressures came from the press, sponsors and friends :
'Where,' they asked, 'is the girl?' We desperately needed a girl.
Of the few who asked to join the team, all were enthusiastic
and certainly would have been physically able to endure the
rigours of such a voyage. Unfortunately, these fine women were
built like Charlton Heston and did not possess the feminine
charm that I wanted to live with for three years.

One evening, in Dartford, Kent, I met an old college friend
of my younger brother's. I had known Carol Maystone slightly
and we chatted. She asked what I was doing for a living and
I told her about the voyage. Jokingly I asked her if she'd like
to come. Her dark-brown eyes looked serious. She thought for a
minute and said : 'Tell me more.'

Carol was a very attractive twenty-year-old. She was dressed
in a track suit that evening as she had been playing badminton
at the local YMCA where she worked. She told me she had
left the Army after her basic training to get married—but later
she had broken off her engagement. She wanted to travel and
she appeared genuinely enthusiastic about the voyage and said
she understood the dangers and problems of the trip. She wanted
to think about it for a week.

Three days later she rang up and said she wanted to go. I felt
excited. I phoned Pete and told him the news. We arranged to
meet in a pub in Greenwich.

I thought Pete warmed to her and felt sure she was the right
person. Carol made it clear that she knew what she was about;
that she would be willing to learn first aid and boat cookery but

would have to be given the most elementary tuition in seamanship, rowing and so forth. This, Pete and I agreed, was fair enough.

We argued the pros and cons. Carol was attractive, enthusiastic and she looked as if she could handle interviews quite well—thereby promising to add plausibility to our image. She was a sweet, pleasant-natured girl, giggly, cheerful and self-confident. But would she really be able to cope with a boat, the sea and two men? How could I be sure she wasn't kidding herself and us? Indeed, how could I be sure about Pete or even myself? The answer could only be—try it.

We decided to accept Carol as a member of the crew. A few weeks later she excelled herself. The Red Cross had generously offered to take her on a first aid course and she passed the exam at the end with flying colours. To make the success even more impressive, Pete failed his radio examination! We both congratulated Carol warm-heartedly, relieved at our choice.

Maggie expressed some concern about the third member of the crew. The idea of my rowing for three years with another woman, just as a rather beautiful friendship was being made, did not appeal to her. However, once she met Carol, her mind was put at ease in one respect. She knew Carol was not my type.

I had given long and careful thought to the question of what craft to use for the voyage. Thirty-five-foot Britannia II, the gallant rowboat that John Fairfax and Sylvia Cook successfully crossed the Pacific in, had a haunting 'rightness'. It seemed that the design was ideal for the type of work expected of her. Uffa Fox had designed her for John, so I approached him and asked him to draw up some blueprints of a similar vessel but capable of providing the bare necessities and stores for three people instead of two. The wonderful old man took the idea to heart. I went to see him and he knew just what was required.

'You want at least a 40-foot craft designed on the lines of Britannia II.' He was intrigued by the idea of a mixed crew and said he would incorporate three rowing positions—'So that you can all row together—then go below and all sleep together!' Three weeks later the blueprint was sent to me—'Pay when you can.'

But our disheartening conclusion was soon to be that no

individual or industrial company was going to oblige us with
the necessary financial aid. It appeared that despite our massive
canvassing efforts, we were not going to get started this way. It
seemed that our plans for the voyage and the impeccable backing
of the boat's designer were not enough to swing our credibility.

Then in April 1973, following a talk with Peter Tappenden,
our contact at British Petroleum, John Fairfax phoned me. He
had heard from Peter that we were having no luck trying to raise
the money to build the boat. Would we like to borrow Britannia
II for the project? She was on exhibition in Australia at the
moment but would be coming to England in June. Very gratefully we accepted. And then everything began to slot neatly
in place. The attitude of potential backers warmed at the news
of the expedition's latest asset, namely one boat.

The three of us, John Fairfax and Sylvia Cook, together with
a bevy of pressmen, met the P & O ship Manipoori at Sheerness.
Out of the bowels of the hold was hoisted a tiny, damaged and
sorrowful-looking boat. I was shocked. The last time I had seen
her had been in London, prior to transportation to America to
begin the voyage across the Pacific. I looked at her in despair :
faded orange paint; chipped; four holes in her side caused by
incorrect chocking during transportation over the roads of
Australia : cracked frames, and she was half-full of rainwater.

John and Sylvia were upset too and began pressing for insurance money. Poor Britannia was taken to a boat-builder who
estimated a renovation cost of around £600. To get that boat
fit for the sea again, it was decided to plug the holes and sandwich the existing wooden hull, on the outside with fibreglass,
using cloth and epoxide resin, and on the inside, after stripping
the deck off, with atomised polystyrene foam. This would
strengthen the boat as well as make her watertight and the
method, though seldom employed, was straightforward. The
epoxide and the fibreglass were supplied to us free of charge
and Pete and I spent many hours removing the old paint in
between the frames and ribs inside, in order to keep the rebuild-
ing costs down.

After much haggling, we received a cheque for £700 claimed
on the insurance. A very generous gift came from British
Petroleum, who in addition supplied all charts and Pilot books,
an emergency radio and a great deal of other assistance. Some
cynics believed that this gesture was a publicity stunt by BP to

back rowing power in view of the current fuel crisis. Peter Tappenden, however, said that BP was an adventurous company and encouraged adventure, particularly among young people. To have such a splendid back-up from this company seemed the end of our problems.

The cash we had was in fact written off as soon as we received it. We had to have more put by for easy access once we were en route so that any emergency in our ports of call could be dealt with immediately. So we sent out another large batch of begging

Derek, Carol and Pete, October 1973

letters to millionaires, Stately Home owners and anyone else we thought might be interested. Thirty replied, all said no.

We pressed on. Gradually equipment, advice and encouragement flowed in and every day brought more good news than disappointment.

The Gibraltar Tourist Board were right behind us and promised to help us with accommodation and flying our stores out. Southern Ferries would ship us and the boat to Tangier while Bland Lines would get us across to Gibraltar. Watts and Fincham gave us most of our chandlery and Andrew Lusk supplied the food. Tupperware and Bio Strath plus many other companies donated equipment and stores. Rolex fitted the expedition with chronometers. All this generosity was overwhelming and without it we would never have managed. But again—it was hard cash that made the project viable and our financial status would no doubt crumble if something untoward happened.

Contrary to popular belief, newspapers do not lay out large sums of money (or any for that matter) to purchase news rights. However, Independent Television News were suitably impressed by the work already done and agreed to take on the story and supply us with cameras and film for use at sea and to send back. And they would send a film crew out to Gibraltar to televise our departure.

Alas, each time our spirits were lifted by something like this, another piece of news brought us back to the ground. Problems with the boat, unobtainable equipment, the forced extension of our deadline . . . It was clear that we never would resolve all our worries. But being an incredible optimist, I just pressed on, eyes front.

I hadn't noticed the summer of 1973 go by. So much was happening and I poured all my time and concern into the project. Sometimes I felt that it just wasn't worth it. But my relationship with Maggie took an unexpected turn. I had fallen, classically, head over heels in love with her. But my fears that such an action would undermine the project were unfounded. Indeed, she did not try to prevent me from going but backed me up all the way.

Philosophically we agreed that with such powerful affection for each other, two and a half to three years' separation was going to be hard, though it could be endured. She wasn't going to sit at home and wait. Maggie wanted to be actively involved in the organisation and she took on the unpaid, unrewarding task of trying to sort out the mess of accounts we would no doubt leave in our wake. Also she would, in addition to being the trip's land-based secretary and contact with the team, try to drum up a supporters' club and keep all involved informed of progress by issuing bulletins from time to time. It was an act of courage, for we both knew how great the wrench of leaving would be when it came.

Pete
'Don't get involved with a woman,' warned Derek.

No sooner were the words out of his mouth when wham! he fell for Maggie. I decided it was a good thing for him to have someone he could share his thoughts and worries with. He could hardly share his problems with me. An initiator and leader of the expedition it would not do for him to come to me with his reservations. If Derek and Maggie could fall in love knowing that they could be apart for three years, then good luck to them. My relationship with Silla was simpler—we were good friends. I would miss her very much. We would keep in touch when possible and review the situation at each stage. If I got a 'Dear John' letter at Panama, I would be upset, but I could hardly expect an attractive girl to sit at home each night knitting—after all, I didn't have to go on this expedition.

We all agreed that Derek's original planning had been impeccable. But even the best planning can go wrong. It all began with little disappointments, promises of money or equipment that weren't forthcoming, hold-ups and so on. Then the boat-builders asked for more time. The plan to leave for Gibraltar in October was put back to November, then December. P & O were beginning to get understandably fed up with constantly changing our tickets. Although we told the builder to take his time and do a good job, we had to have a deadline. A final date was mutually decided. Britannia would be ready by 6th December 1973.

By 27th November, Derek had paid the original estimate of £600 to the builders. They were still fiddling around with her. It seemed to be a pretty rum affair, with all our gear ready and still no boat. But more fun was to come. The builder announced that it would cost a bit more. We reckoned on no more than an extra £200 and just about budgeted for it, but that would be our emergency money gone.

I drove down to the boat-builders to meet Derek who had gone down to settle the bill on the last day. I found him in the local, bracing himself with double whiskies.

'Look at that!' and he flung the bill at me. I stared in disbelief. Labour: £998.25. Materials: £250.42. Total: £1,248.67. 'I sometimes get the impression that we're not meant to go on this trip,' he said miserably.

After a lot of heavy haggling, Derek paid up another £100 and with helpful advice from our bank manager, post-dated cheques for the remainder. As we drove out of that wretched boatyard for the last time, broke and exhausted, we had one consolation. Britannia was ready.

After a final fortnight of organised panic, Britannia was delivered in time for our press conference at St Katherine's dock by the Tower. I learnt one thing that day—enjoy the attention and glamour while it lasts but don't believe what the press say about you. If someone treats you as a hero, the danger is you may behave like one.

Britannia II at Tower Bridge, 7th December 1973

The next day we gathered at Southampton. I find goodbyes sad on any occasion; it's ten times worse saying them on a ship. I could just imagine how our families felt on seeing Britannia lined up amid the lorries and cars. She looked so small, 35 feet long yet no wider than a Mini, and very frail-looking.

A last drink with families and friends. About thirty of them turned up. Carol's mum was sobbing; I realised they would all have to go quickly or we'd all be dropping tears into our gins and tonics. Thankfully the announcement came: 'All visitors ashore please.' Very sadly we waved goodbye from the cargo ramp.

I stood on the stern of the Eagle watching the lights of Southampton fade into the murk of that December evening. I was pleased to be off at long last yet wondering what I was leaving behind. A good family and real friends . . .

My thoughts ran on to my future relationship with my fellow crew. I felt a basic affinity with Derek. But of Carol I felt less certain. Derek's first mention of her had been no less than 'I've found our girl!' This fait accompli had made me apprehensive from the start. My first impression had been of a very pretty girl, younger than her twenty years. She seemed somehow incomplete, to have too many people to meet, too many parties to go to and boys to go out with. She was on occasion unpunctual for appointments.

My negative attitude towards her seemed to be taken by Derek as a hesitating affirmation of his choice. After all, we needed someone quickly : he was not to be held up by indecision.

'What do you think of her, Pete?' he had asked me once in front of her.

I didn't have the courage to tell him outright. I hoped he would understand my reticence. 'Hmmn—yes,' I had mumbled, trying to concentrate yet not wanting to be involved.

I tried to gauge the reactions of others towards Carol. They were not specifically for or against. A general non-commitment made me wonder; it was what *wasn't* said that struck me most . . . Someone suggested to Derek that *I* was the weak link in the team. (I found out about this much later at sea.) All this demonstrated the need, in a situation such as ours, for complete honesty and confidence in each other.

The short restful trip on the Eagle was just what we wanted. Eagle was a happy ship. At Lisbon we went for a trip ashore : amazingly Derek's first time in foreign parts. I watched him closely, trying to measure his reaction to every strange sound, sight and smell. Although he enjoyed himself, he appeared to have the detached look of someone who could have done without. His mind was elsewhere. For him, it was the great adventure, the greatest of adventures. The fact that we had to go to other countries was incidental. Never had he had the urge to travel, he told me, unless it was to get somewhere and do something specifically. He and I were totally different on that score.

Algeciras and untypical Spanish weather greeted us. Through the rain and mist, I peered across at the Rock of Gibraltar, rising out of the sea, far enough away to make it appear detached from the Spanish mainland. This was the bone of contention, as any

Spaniard knows, that obliged us to go on to Tangier, then take a ferry across to Gib from a 'neutral' country.

Tangier's sights and sounds smelt foreign to me. Labourers lazed in the sun waiting for something in the air that made one suspect they were waiting for nothing. They had that quality which unfortunately we Northern Europeans have never had—the ability to lie around without feeling guilty and more important, not looking guilty. An admirable trait!

Britannia was unloaded by forklift truck amid a gaggle of gesticulating Arabs and Derek and I ran off to a quiet bar. That night was spent in the city. On arrival at the docks next day we found to our dismay that the port and handling charges for Britannia were double what we had understood them to be the day before. Derek grudgingly paid up—muttering 'Bloody foreigners' to every local thereafter.

While we sat waiting for the ferry, the Mons Calpe, Derek was scrabbling around underneath Britannia, looking to see if the rubber chocks were in position.

'Oh no!' he said.

I crouched down and saw for myself: a small tear in the glass cloth, below the waterline.

'We'll patch it in Gib—won't take long,' I said lightly.

What an understatement that was.

At Gibraltar the Tourist Board, BP agents, the local rowing club and the Governor of Gibraltar, Sir John Grandy, met us off the ferry. We were welcomed and whisked off to the rowing club while a strong-arm team manhandled Britannia along the wharf. We all felt flattered to be treated like VIPs. John Halmshaw and Keith Kirkby from BP soon made us feel at ease and before we left Gibraltar were amongst our closest friends. Peter Bell, manager of Both Worlds Hotel, offered to put us up free of charge in the self-catering flats on the east side of the Rock and we humped all our baggage and equipment into Arcadia 8.

The Gib Tourist Board had located the fibreglass expert and asked him to look at our boat. We met him the next day: an East German who had escaped to the West (by rowing boat, aptly enough). We said hallo to Captain Lothar Migge, otherwise known as German Mike. He didn't mince words. Grabbing me by the arm he steered me over to the boat. Pointing at a small area of damage, he said in cracked English:

'Look here, zis no good—der glass iss not rollered down—I don't vould believe—vot a load ov sheet.'

So saying, he pushed his penknife between the glass and the wood and tore off a great loose piece. He flexed it between his fingers, saying :

'If you set out in zis you vill die.'

Derek didn't speak. I tried to defend Britannia. I asked Mike if he would patch the area.

'I vould not do it—I don't vant the responsibility. I vill give der materials for free but I don't vould touch zat boat.'

Derek and I whispered together.

'Slap a patch on her—let's get away,' I said. 'We can get her repaired in Panama if necessary, but let's go.'

Derek hesitated for a minute.

'We don't know what facilities there are in Panama. It's obvious the skin has not bonded to the wood. Supposing it lifts off at sea?'

We decided to get a quote from Mike for relaminating the whole hull, and an unbiased opinion from the Port Surveyor.

'£600 and yes—get it done.'

Just one day in Gibraltar and there we were back two months. We owed money to the boat-builder—soon we would owe more to German Mike. Where would it come from? We had already squeezed our sponsors for just about every penny possible. Desperate telexes and phone calls back to London began mounting up. Soon we wouldn't even be able to pay our phone bill.

Part of the deal ('Zat iss vhy iss cheap!') was for us to scrape the old fibreglass off. It took us six days and we found that there was a noticeable absence of help from our rowing chums at the club, who only a few days before had smothered us with every promise of help. But I didn't blame them. It was a dreadful job.

Time slipped by. Silla and Maggie joined us for Christmas, bringing chandlery unobtainable in Gib. Alec Woollard, Maggie's father, also joined us and everyone got busy varnishing tins or charts or packing food into Tupperware.

German Mike had nearly finished Britannia.

'You vill pay, zen you vill get her.' How could we find £600 cash? Frankie Lombard, our taxi-driver and friend, suggested the Casino. Not quite what we had in mind.

Then during a little at home at the Governor's, while we stood and chatted about our British Spirit, my mind went down one so far unexplored avenue to our financial redemption. In the last months of preparation in London, I had taken a job as chauffeur/dogsbody to a millionaire friend of a friend, Graham Rushworth. I felt he would be just the man to risk £600. Hearing that he was on holiday in the Seychelles and realising how bored he must be lying around in the sun, I composed a telex asking for £700 and offering every security imaginable.

The reply:

TELEX MATEOS GK 262.

GIBRALTAR

FOR PETER BIRD.

RESPECTFULLY SUGGEST ABANDON VENTURE WITH DIGNITY IF DOWN LAST SEVEN HUNDRED. MONEY IS SMALL. LIFE IS VALUABLE. YOU'RE TOO YOUNG TO DIE. GET ME ON TELEX. REGARDS GRAHAM.

So no deal. But at length we were saved by Alec and my mother who between them loaned us £600 to pay Mike. Sigma Coatings flew out our fluorescent orange paint and we finished off Britannia's hull with good antifoul.

We had one more job to perform. BP asked if we would like to try a new technique they were developing. The idea was to spray the hull, below the waterline, with a thin coat of special wax over the antifoul. They had been doing this to their tankers and the theory was that the wax minimised the drag of the hull through the water, thus giving greater average speeds. If sprayed on thin enough, the antifoul would seep through the wax and none of its properties would be lost. Surely Britannia would be easier to row with wax on her bottom? We liked the idea at first and when we found that BP could not lay on the special spraying equipment, we wondered whether it could be painted on while molten. Yes, it could—but thinly!

So foolishly we undertook the job and after much scalding, the final effect was likened to a dozen altar boys going berserk with lighted candles.

One month and a day after arrival in Gibraltar, Britannia was relaunched. With the Minister of Sport helping on one rope and a priest on the other, Slim Simpson of the *Gib Chronicle* uttered the immortal words:

'God help those in the middle!'

Derek

The launching saw Britannia into the water again—but her seaworthiness was quite another matter. We weren't content to push off until we had thoroughly checked her. So we called in an experienced small boat carpenter. Together with German Mike and a recommended surveyor he examined every inch of Britannia—and at the end of the day had come to a horrifying conclusion. She was still not ready to go to sea! No less than seventeen faults had been found, concerning the sheath bonding, the joints between the hull and the buoyancy blisters, the bearers under the deck, the water tank fittings and pump hole, drainage through the deck boards, hatch toggles, and various bolts, screws and cleats.

One month later we were still in Gib. Our spirits were at the lowest of the low. Our problems had increased—our finances disappeared. And still there was no sign of getting away. I was emphatic that we would not leave until the boat was right. Time flashed by. Pete's morale was as low as mine. Carol wisely kept well clear of us, consoling herself with a boyfriend. We worked steadily and hard and eventually began to see light at the end of the tunnel.

After the rectification of everything faulty, we took the opportunity to make improvements as follows: (1) Fibreglass tanks built, with baffle plates and adequate pumping system; (2) a slot board to peg a U bolt over the tiller to keep a desired course; (3) a compass well cut into the deck; (4) strengtheners on the foot plates and toe grips; (5) two extra outer spray dodgers rigged; (6) two steel cables running the length of the deck for lifeline clips; (7) steel strips screwed around footplate pivot; (8) more bearers placed under deck; (9) a grabrope, 12 in. high off each gunnel and secured by lugs bolted through the buoyancy blister.

Pete

On 5th March we donned oilskins and rowed out for a sea trial. A good spell off Europa Point in a fully fledged easterly gale proved that Britannia was fit for sea. It was up to us three now.

But a sour note. Whilst coming back to our berth, I misjudged the speed of our drift. Realising we were coming in too

Rough weather sea trial off Gibraltar, March 1974

fast, Derek scrambled along the forward blister in wet oilskins to fend the bow off, but slithered off and fell in, catching his hand between the bow and the iron jetty. I yelled at Carol to hop ashore and help him while I tried to get the stern closer to the pontoon. She stood, not moving a muscle, looking at the two-foot gap between us and the pontoon, while Derek swore and muttered as he swam ashore.

I shouted: 'Move—hurry up!' But nothing. I had to push past her and reach Derek myself. Carol's verdict: 'Peter panicked.'

'You can't be serious, Derek,' I said later. 'For God's sake, if she freezes up in a bloody harbour, how can she be any use at sea? She's told us she was once a PE instructor. She couldn't jump two feet!'

'She did a good calm job bandaging my hand,' defended Derek.

Geoff'n, Derek's younger brother, arrived in Gib. He soon had a steadying influence on us as he knew us all well. 'Cool it against Carol,' he said when I complained that she hadn't tried the cooker yet. 'Don't be too hard on her.'

That evening a friend gave me food for thought. 'Two people on their own,' he said, 'can take a lot of crap from one another. Their egos would never allow it with a third person present.'

Derek

So that Carol would feel a real part of the crew, I left her to supervise the storage completely by herself. I could have done it quite efficiently myself as I'd already done the job and knew exactly what foods to have in the same hatches so that several meals could be produced on the opening of one hatch—which was an awkward procedure in itself. I stressed this fact to Carol, and she told me to leave it all to her.

The first time I checked I was furious. The storage was so higgledy-piggledy that even to make a cup of tea two hatches had to be opened—one for the dried milk, one for the teabags. I tried to remedy the problem. When Carol discovered what I was doing she exploded. Couldn't I let her do a single thing without looking over her shoulder all the time? A major row followed; I was a good deal more angry than Carol.

I strode off for a walk over the Rock to cool off. I sat on the

Mediterranean Steps, looking over the shimmering Straits to
Africa, thinking of Maggie and Britannia and Carol. For the
first time, doubts entered my mind about Carol being a member
of the crew. It was unquestionably an ordeal that we were asking
her to undertake—something quite outside her experience,
whereas I had been thoroughly tested by my row round Ireland,
and Pete, not without experience himself, showed every sign of
having the natural qualities for a rough, tough, prolonged expedition that was at the same time a pretty specialised business.
People who possessed the necessary qualities for it all were not
exactly easy to find, as I had discovered . . . But Carol had been
selected, and I was responsible for welding a crew together. It
was up to Pete and me to make the most of the qualities Carol
did have—that every one of us had. I had to give her her chance.

I returned to the boat to find Carol kneeling in the galley
doggedly sorting out her mistakes. She was really trying. My
heart melted; I apologised to her for my outburst, and made
an appreciative comment on her efforts.

It became evident that an awful lot of pressure was being applied
by agitated people involved with us for an immediate departure.
Pete and I could understand their doubts. We had told all concerned (before we knew all our difficulties) that embarkation
would be in about a month's time. In all good faith they had
given money or help in some way with the prospects of seeing
the expedition go off with a great shout of publicity for them.
No such departure had happened—all that had was that we
asked for more money and remained as vague about leaving as
before. It was now almost three and a half months since we
had left England.

In our self-catering flat at Both Worlds, the atmosphere was
one of gloomy determination. I wearily tried to perfect my
navigation, Pete tried to learn the Morse Code and Carol had
started using our ship's stores for meals. Thoughts of all those
months of rowing ahead were pitifully depressing. As I looked
out of the window across the ruffled grey Mediterranean, my
silent misery screamed. I was thinking about my fiancée Maggie.
How stupid to search all one's life for a girl like that and then
leave her for an indefinite length of time. And rowing of all
things.

Pete

D Day would be 24th March, weather permitting. We telephoned ITN and the camera crew arrived, bringing more of our
equipment than theirs. Among the gear was our liferaft. This
liferaft was a sore point with me. I'd mentioned it to Derek
in the planning stages and he had said bluffly :

'What for—a self-righting, self-baling, unsinkable craft?'

'Fire,' I answered.

Derek had to fall in love before we took out insurance!

The ITN team, Mike, Hugh and John, whisked us off for a
slap-up meal and we planned our weekend of filming and
interviews.

On the eve of our departure after the 'last supper' at the
Bayuca, Derek turned to Carol and said :

'Are you ready, Carol?'

'Of course I am,' she answered.

'Are you ready, Pete?'

'Yes,' I replied. It then occurred to me that someone should
ask him, let him voice his thoughts.

So I asked. 'Are *you* ready, Derek?'

A little taken aback, he said 'Yes', then shrugged and smiled.

Derek

I stood looking at our finished boat, ready and loaded at last.
Britannia II sat low in the water with the near half a ton of
food, water and equipment. She looked less streamlined when
fully loaded—her long, narrow, canoe-like hull had lost its
elegance and the two ungainly rounded buoyancy blisters gave
her an even more awkward profile. But like the blue spray
dodger and large radar reflector on the bow, they were absolutely
essential. Uffa Fox had explained the simple but ingenious
theory of self-righting. In a capsize situation the weight of the
stores below deck would twist against the pull of the buoyancy,
thus righting her. The water on deck would then drain out via
the centreboard slots. To hasten the flow of water off the deck
we had had four scuppers cut into the hull; John Fairfax had
had difficulty draining 'deck-sweepers' out through just the
two centre slots.

In the ratholes below each blister, less than two feet high and
three feet at their widest, we should be sleeping. In the tiny

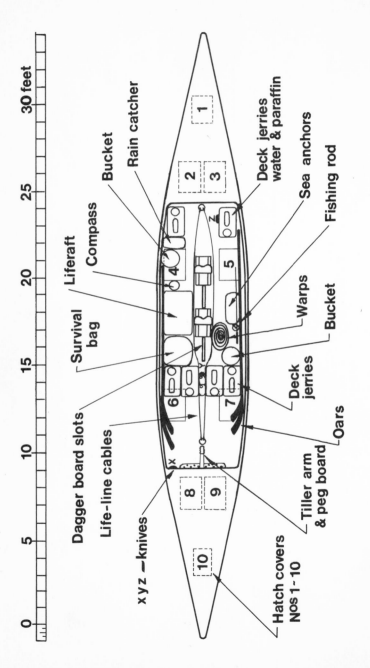

30 feet
25
20
15
10
5
0

Dagger board slots
Life-line cables
x y z — knives
Liferaft
Survival bag
Compass
Bucket
Rain catcher
Deck jerries water & paraffin
Sea anchors
Fishing rod
Warps
Bucket
Deck jerries
Oars
Tiller arm & peg board
Hatch covers Nos 1-10

Britannia II : above-deck layout

Britannia II

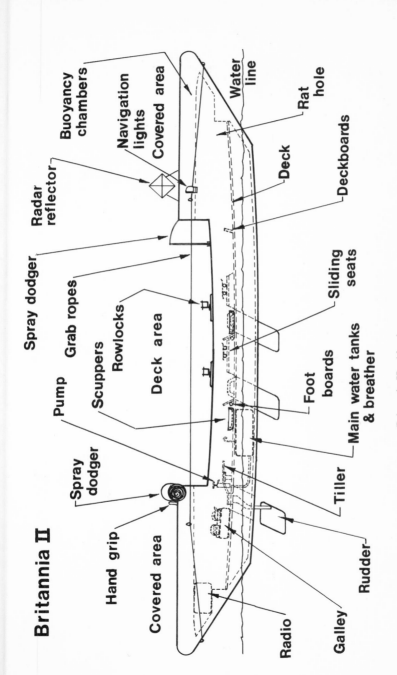

Britannia II: side view

hole forward, Pete and I would sleep with the sextant, charts
and cameras. In the rathole aft, Carol would sleep alongside
the galley, the radio and water pump. Britannia, being built
for two, was overcrowded with three people, so the rule of
'everything in its place' had to be strictly observed.

On the 15-feet-long open deck were lashed a liferaft and
survival bag, two buckets, four pairs of oars (two pairs of 9-foot-
six and one pair of 10-foot, and one pair of 12-foot for two-up
rowing), fishing tackle, sea anchors, life jackets and six five-gallon
jerrycans—four for water, two for paraffin. Two sliding seats
took up a lot of space and we should have to be very careful
where we stepped—always holding on to the grabropes stretched
between either blister. In case of an emergency and the liferaft
and other gear had to be cut loose, I thought that three or four
knives, strategically placed around the boat, would be an
adequate precaution. I had arranged three knives along the
length of the boat and promised Maggie to wear a diver's knife
always.

I watched the strange bright orange boat, plastered with the
stickers of our sponsors, bob gently alongside the float. She
really looked as though she would be going places.

Pete

The great day dawned grey and windless. The forecast was
unsettled and any wind around would certainly not come from
the East. We chased around in the Mateos Landrover saying
goodbye and returning borrowed books, records and so on. We
moved out of our flat. Our last bundles of clothes were shoved
into the wagon. We thanked the manager and staff for all their
kindness and consideration (and for giving us a few months'
grace to pay our £120 phone bill!). Then we drove down to
Coaling Island.

With the last job of flushing the water tanks through to remove
the tang of plastic, we were ready. John Halmshaw in the
Mateos launch Philippa-Ann towed Britannia round to Water-
port where we were to have an official send-off.

What a shock! There were thousands of people lining the
wharf and North Mole and scores of small craft buzzing around
waiting to escort us. It seemed the whole of Gib had turned out.

Carol and I started saying our goodbyes. I turned and saw Derek making off down the quay with a chart under his arm.

'He's gone to check on the Mons Calpe chart,' said Keith Kirkby.

'More like the booze,' I said and scooted after him. Twenty minutes and a few cans of lager later we were back to face a grumbling crowd who wanted to see us off soon.

Frankie Lombard, tears rolling down his face, handed over his Mamma's cheese flan, my favourite, and kissing me on both cheeks, said: 'Keep the tin.' Mamma gave me a plastic Holy-water-filled Madonna.

Horace Zammit, Minister of Sports, held up the starting gun and fired. With Derek on stroke, me on bow and Carol on the tiller, waving serenely like a carnival queen, we pulled away.

Hundreds of car horns, sirens and the thunderous hoots of Mons Calpe drowned the cheering crowd. The flotilla of small boats jostled dangerously around us, some a bit too close. As the hooting died down from cars all over the Rock, the sound of applause took over.

What had we done to deserve it all?

2

Reality

24th March–19th April

Pete

At a stately two and a half knots, Britannia pulled away from
Gibraltar. One by one our escorts, after a shouted goodbye,
turned for home. A special wave for Philippa-Ann—and we
were alone at last. We were pleased with Britannia—a boat of
breeding; Uffa Fox knew his stuff. Britannia was far happier
at sea than most of the other boats in the flotilla that escorted us.

Closing with the Spanish coast, we saw two Spanish fishing
boats heading for Algeciras. We were beginning a voyage while
everyone else was going home. By 1930 hours we had cleared
the lighthouse. The wreck of a freighter on the rocks beneath it
served as a warning not to get caught on that lee shore, and as
that thought was in my mind, Derek announced :

'Time we started looking for an anchorage.'

I was appalled. An anchorage on a lee shore with all those
rocks? All my sailing instincts were against it. Why? Derek had
rowed around Ireland. He had anchored each night off shores
as bad, if not worse than this. 'Stick around, you might learn
something.'

With night falling we had to find anchorage quickly. To
go on would mean rowing in one of the busiest shipping lanes
in the world, and in the dark. Derek piloted us through a group
of islets. He stood there with his shooting cap clamped on his
head, peering with a fixed look of concentration, teeth bared,
chart under one arm and his thumb in his belt—very intense.

'OK. Just here,' he said.

Using both the Danforth anchor and the grapple, we held.

Diary

2100 hrs. Anchor's holding. Feel a bit tired having rowed

continuously except for one pee break since starting from Gibraltar at 1630 hours. Derek asked Carol for a meal, but I don't think she's in a fit state to cook and I am in no condition to eat, so Derek goes without.

Derek took the first watch—three hours, Carol the second, me last. Almost asleep when Derek called 'All hands', I leapt out and couldn't find my specs. Carol couldn't find her trousers. Both anchors were dragging. We rowed out, about turned and rowed back to just about where we had started. Tried again—seemed OK. Wet noisy wind, force 4–5.

Derek had steered, using a torch, right out of the group of islets and back. I was glad I'd lost my glasses, though I suspect my imagination conjured up a far more dangerous incident than the real situation. At 0530 hours on the 25th, Derek hauled up the Danforth and then turned to the grapple, but no go—she was stuck fast about 20 feet down. I joked : 'John Fairfax would never cut an anchor', implying that Derek should dive for it. Derek, either mistaking or understanding my meaning, said :

'Do you want to dive for it then ?'

'Cut it,' I replied.

Striking out across the Straits, our first obstacles were the overfalls. Having heard so many hair-raising accounts of these tidal cataracts, we approached them with some trepidation. Once into them, Derek and I enjoyed it. Carol, who was sitting aft, staring, did not look so happy. We tried to enthuse over the delights of rough weather boating, to no avail. The waves were very short and very steep, each one looking as though it would immerse the stern, and Carol. It was a good thing she didn't turn round. In the midst of my enjoyment Derek said something I was to hear a lot of :

'This is nothing to what I've been through !'

Then we were clear. The overfalls finished as abruptly as they had begun. Although we were still rowing strongly, I felt very tired. I was sure I'd been rowing for longer than the others and I began grumbling to myself. We hadn't established a set routine.

Diary
Rowed yesterday from 4.30 to 9.30 pm—now today from 5.30 am until now (11.30)—and there's Carol sitting on her

backside doing nothing. Derek stops to look at the charts
every few minutes . . .

I was exaggerating of course—but that's the way rows
could start.

We rowed hard. Our westgoing tide seemed to have dis-
appeared. We noticed first that the land between Gibraltar and
Algeciras was opening up when it should have been closing.
Then we started to see more of the Algeciras side, then the
Gibraltar side of the bay. There was no doubt—we were being
swept back into the Mediterranean.

Our attempt to get across the Straits ended when Mike
Edinburgh, in his yacht Hazy Days, having taken the day off
work, came out to give us some encouragement, so he said,
though I suspect he knew better. I know it took a lot from
Derek to ask :

'D'you think we should go in Pete ?'

'Yes,' I replied.

'Carol ?'

'Yes, I think we should,' she answered quietly.

Hazy Days, with her auxiliary engine and sails up, was making
four knots across the water towing us, but the speed over the
sea was one knot. We had been fighting a three-knot current.
If we had tried to make it straight across, we should have been
swept right into the Med.

I sat forward, smoking a ciggy and looking at Carol and Derek
sitting aft. Their faces were cold and white, tired, and above all
disappointed. As Hazy Days let go the line, Mike leant over and
said to us : 'Whatever they say, I know you did the right thing
—I was there !'

His words encouraged us.

Philippa-Ann took up the line. Her more powerful diesel
engine towed us back to Coaling Island. We had been at sea
for just 22 hours.

Derek
Keith Kirkby half-filled a glass with whisky and topped it up
with sweet vermouth. The mixture soon warmed me up as I sat
back in the calm surroundings of his flat. Pete munched sandwiches and Carol floated in a hot bath.

Within an hour we had all stopped shivering and feeling miserable. I heard the window pane shudder as the wind whistled up and felt glad that we had taken the initiative and come in rather than flog ourselves to death against wind and sea. As expected—it was not long before the press were ringing up.

'What happened?' 'Is it true you have given up?' 'We've heard you have been quarrelling.'

My only pet-hate in Gibraltar had been the alarming inventiveness of the gossips. Rumours spread amazingly fast and became more confused and inaccurate as they sped about the small enclosed Rock. So it came as no surprise to hear this latest batch of tales.

Pepe Rossado organised a Press Conference at the Tourist Office and we were able to allay suspicions and tell them exactly what had happened. With great fighting talk I said: 'Even if it takes us a dozen attempts—we will get out of the Straits!'

Walking back apprehensively through the Main Street expecting to be laughed and jeered at by our now triumphant critics, I felt rather pleased with the reaction we did get. No jeers, no 'If you can't row out of the Straits how are you going to row around the world?' Just sympathy and understanding as everyone knew how difficult the Straits were. We were in fact congratulated on our presence of mind to come in.

That evening Keith and Tina treated us to a huge blowout at La Bayuca. I didn't think we had been pressured into leaving that day. Personally, we had to make a breakout attempt if only to justify to ourselves that we were capable of setting off. The three and a half months in Gib were really too long for a project such as this. It's quite true that harbours rot ships and men.

But we had been happy with the boat and she was ready for sea. Pete and Carol were as prepared as they would ever be and the weather, though far from settled, was favourable at the time. I took the decision then because I felt sufficiently prepared myself and also because I could think of no other reason for delaying departure, which had dogged earlier decisions. So we went.

I was thinking now that it was a good thing our first attempt had failed. I was most perturbed about the state of Carol's galley and the complete lack of organisation. It appeared that all the weeks she had spent trying to perfect her systems were utterly wasted. All the lists she had laboriously produced and the

hundreds of hours we had left her to manage her own business
might never have existed. But she was obviously frightened and
this might have caused her lapse of memory when she failed
to find the right boxes of food. I also learnt that she had started
a ten day premature period during the night.

Pete was great and made a fine crew. His problem in the
initial stages would be his great bulk : knees and elbows every-
where and a bit uncertain where to put them without damaging
himself or us. A few days of bashing the right places would be
the most effective aversion therapy.

I had learnt a lot about myself and the other two, the boat
and our methods during the 22 hours at sea. I thought it was
the best sea trial we had had. I still thought myself capable of
the responsibility I had accepted.

With Britannia at her old berth alongside the Admiralty's
Coaling Island, we were isolated from inquisitive onlookers and
we could leave equipment unattended. Pete made a few altera-
tions to the deck gear, trying to stow as much as possible below
as we had found in the darkness it was dangerously cluttered.

Apart from the rowing seats and the footrests which took up a
lot of deck space, the biggest item on deck was the liferaft. Contained in a rectangular plastic case, the raft had to be laid flat
on deck. To stand it upright and conserve space would have
merely added extra windage. I was at one time fiercely opposed
to taking such a bulky item of equipment. 'If a self-righting,
self-baling unsinkable boat founders,' I had argued, 'it would
be pointless to step into a flimsy rubber boat.' But Maggie had
insisted we take one, pointing out that fire was the only thing
that could destroy the boat. So she set about acquiring one for
us. It took her several weeks, since the Expedition's funds had
no spare cash. At last she found Sailsafe of London who agreed
to loan the raft to us if we put an advertising sticker on the boat.
It arrived two days before we left.

This was only a tiny part of what that amazing girl had done
for us. She was at the receiving end of all bills, complaints and
tangled business affairs that I had left behind, and still managed
to be our public relations agent, typist and supporters' club
organiser as well as keeping up her full-time schoolteaching job.
She did it, she said, not for the Expedition but because she loved
me.

Pete

My thoughts turned for the nth time to the subject of Carol. In the 22 hours at sea she had shown her one obvious quality—courage. Though frightened and cold, she had stuck with it unswervingly throughout those 22 hours. Never were her complaints directed at us personally—as previously on land. I thought, and it seemed to me Derek too, that Carol really tried. Was it going to get better after all? Would we get on? These questions buzzed around in my head. But I knew that if this trip meant as much to Derek as it did to me, we should never have been in this unsettled frame of mind. Damn it all, there was enough to worry about in rowing round the world—why should we have personal problems?

Always the negative thoughts filled my head. Anything positive about poor Carol was soon drowned by her own inimitable failings. Not that we didn't possess failings—plenty of them. But at least we were aware of them. Derek and I were continually discussing our own faults. Derek tried very hard to use the same technique with Carol—constructive yet gentle criticism. But Carol was reluctant to accept such comment. Her eyes blazed and she would often say she was being picked on, he was being superior. How could we get to her? But she had something. Most girls would have made a huge scene and stormed out. And here was Carol pressing on undeterred with the job, the elements, even her companions, turning against her. I had to admit she had guts.

Derek

I undertook a thorough reappraisal of the tide and current systems in the Straits. Captain Rickards, Captain of the Port, explained about the mistake I had made in timing.

I already knew why there is such a strong east-flowing current through the Straits. The Mediterranean is a warm sea and the narrow Straits is the only outlet to the open ocean. In the Med the surface evaporation tends to produce high saline water which, being heavier, sinks, and fresh lighter water from the Atlantic flows over it. But with all the great rivers emptying into the Med, there is a build-up of water here and to maintain levels, an outflow into the ocean occurs. This outflow, because of the heavy salt content, takes place at the bottom of the Straits, and there is still an inflowing surface current. During the war, the Italians knew about this lower westbound stream and their submarines could slide out without using their engines, consequently avoiding the highly tuned listening devices set up on each shoreline.

However, we had to contend with the surface current. The prevailing westerlies constantly brush the surface to form an inflowing current which can sometimes disappear after a prolonged blow from the East. Obviously a good easterly gale would be the solution. But there was one more consideration in calm weather : the tides.

By keeping close to the shore, preferably the Spanish side, the prevailing eastbound current could possibly be avoided. This, said Captain Rickards, had been the cause of our failure. The tidal streams across the Straits have different time lapses. Although the westgoing stream was noticeably strong inshore, the middle of the Straits had eased off to the nearest thing to slack water it could manage. We knew that we would drift a bit to the East but were sure we could compensate by hard rowing until we picked up the similar westgoing tide on the African shore. Then it would have been anchoring against and rowing with the tides until we got out into the Atlantic. We had got midway too early, when there was still a powerful flow into the Med, and rowing against this had proved impossible. On top of that, a rising wind from the South-West had destroyed our chances once and for all.

Captain Rickards told me to rethink the route out of the Straits. He reminded me of the old sailing ship directions. During westerly winds which increased the strength of the current, they found it often impossible to get out. Keith's father-in-law, Mr Imossi, remembered seeing over fifty sailing ships at anchor in Gibraltar Bay, awaiting a change of wind.

We decided to give the old clipper route out a try. We would have to work along the Spanish side with the tide until we reached Isla de Tarifa where if necessary we would anchor and await the next tide. I didn't think we could manage more than 15 miles in one tide anyway. The next day we would row due West as far as time allowed and then cross the funnel of the Straits at a much wider part than we had tried before. Then if we got involved in more wind and current trouble and drifted back, we should at least strike the African shore before Punta

Cires, after which the coasts trend into the bottleneck we had attempted to cross before. Should we fall to leeward of Punta Cires there would probably be no chance of getting back, even to Gibraltar. We prayed for an easterly.

Another two weeks passed, and although we hadn't got our wind, we were suitably compensated by the fact that we were now far more relaxed and less nervous. Keith and Tina Kirkby wanted us to stay with them; John Halmshaw and Dinah looked after Carol. With good regular meals and an easy, unstrained atmosphere, our tensions vanished and we got to the proper frame of mind that one really needs for such a project— calmness.

During the afternoon of the 6th of April, the herald of our easterly wind appeared. Wisps of cloud slid around the Rock's upper parts, and within a few hours the cake had been iced. The thick cloud hung over Gibraltar and the first puffs of the levanter began. It was soon blowing good and hard and seemed as though it would not just fizzle out by morning, as had happened a few days before.

At 0530 next day, I telephoned Maggie and asked her to come out to Panama.

It was still dark when we got down to Coaling Island. Pete had the flashlight on as he checked out water, stores and gear and clamped the oars into the rowlocks. I paced up and down looking at my watch. We would have to row our fastest to catch the tide at the other side of Gibraltar Bay. We were late.

It was blustery and drizzly. Pete dug his oar into a fender and pushed the bow out as I back-paddled. Britannia crawled sluggishly round. Then Carol corrected the course and the two oars swung together. Gibraltar slept as we pulled out of the harbour. We watched familiar houses and roads disappear.

Thanks everybody. Even the cynics whose scepticism has made us try even harder to succeed!

Our aim that day would be to clear Tarifa. We rowed across the Bay and our escort turned back. For the second time we passed the wrecked freighter and rowed just outside our first impossible anchorage.

The wind shrieked up and small wavelets tore past us as we rowed hard parallel to the shoreline. Green undulating hillsides dropping suddenly on to the rocky beaches provided a great contrast to the looming grey and white limestone heights of

Gibraltar. I felt exhilarated. We were making rapid progress—
the sea was lively, the wind on my face invigorating. The
strength of my arms travelled down the oar and I could feel
Britannia surge forward. She felt eager to get away to the open
sea. She had been in harbour too long.

Gibraltar crept behind a hill on the Spanish side and was
swallowed up whole. I turned my head and saw the distant
lighthouse on Tarifa Island become clearer. We were really
racing.

Carol smiling, Pete singing. I knew it would get better once
we were at sea. The church service on Gib radio included an
apt hymn. Strains of 'For those in peril on the sea' rang out
above the creak of oar and swish of sea. The long white beach
of Enseñada del Tolmo gleamed in the sun and we drifted along
off it while we paused for a soup and beef sandwich break.
Then back to work.

I was amazed at our speed. With combined forces of good
rowing, tide and wind, we were moving at about three and a
half knots. Pete turned round :

'Hell man, we're almost there.'

'Right Carol,' I shouted, 'steer us well out now so that we
take the point by about a quarter mile.'

We swung out sharply. Wind and sea were abeam and steeper
waves lunged into the boat. Tarifa Island is joined to the mainland by a causeway which has a fishing port and a naval base
on its eastern side. It was not politic to go in, however. Already
we had had to black out Visit Gibraltar slogans. So Britannia
aimed for the leeward side. The waves became suddenly huge.
We slid into a great overfall where they lost their regular motion
and sizzled and leaped in crazy directions. Carol gasped as a
white wave crashed over the stern. She struggled to hold the
tiller and hang on to the gunnel. The sea seemed to be going
mad. I couldn't row.

I clung on to the side of the boat as we bucked through hideous
walls of water. I heard Pete groan and splutter as a wave
drenched him. Carol disappeared in a cloud of hissing spray. In
a second we were all leaning out to bring the boat back to an
even keel.

'Keep her away from the rocks !' I yelled to Carol. Weed-
draped slabs were only yards away. She swung the tiller arm to
starboard and Britannia changed her heading. The riverlike flow

of the current accelerated us round the rocky outcrops and swept the boat into smooth water in the lee of the island. But we hadn't made it yet. While we were relaxing on the oars, breathing sighs of relief, Britannia drifted out of the sheltered calm and the greedy fingers of the wind caught her broadside and pressed her further out to sea.

'Quick. Grab the oars again. Carol, steer over there.' I pointed towards the causeway.

Straining on the oars, Pete and I brought the unwilling boat round. We heaved and heaved but it was useless. The wind gusted even more fiercely and the harder we rowed, the faster we seemed to be going backwards.

At last we realised we could not go on until the tide turned, so sleep seemed to be the most sensible thing. We anchored close to a huge sandy beach. After a few hours, the battering wind awoke me. I nudged Pete who was snoring alongside me and said : 'Listen to that.'

He grimaced. 'It sounds bad.'

I stuck my head out of the rathole and into the whirling air and called out—'Carol, are you OK?'

Her reply sounded as though she were a mile away.

'Yes, but I'm a bit lonely.'

'Come in here then.'

White-faced and trembling, she crawled out on her hands and knees and wriggled in to take Pete's place beside me. Pete went aft.

After a while we heard Pete's faint voice :

'I think we should have something to eat . . . The last supper.'

Bravely, Carol staggered aft and with the galley open to all the wind she tried to cook a meal. An hour later she piped out that it was ready. I clambered aft and collected our two dog bowls piled with a hot beef hash.

'I'm really surprised that she could attempt a meal in all this,' Pete said, looking out at the stormy sky—'I couldn't manage it. Well done Carol.'

By 1800 hours, I estimated the wind to be force 10. The waves, speeding from the beach just 20 yards away, were reaching us at about two feet high. I had never experienced a wind like it. The invisible force was unnerving as it screamed down from

between those hills. Grains of sand stung my face as I looked
out to the North. Spray half-blinded me and my ears buzzed
with the incredible and frightening roar.

Pete and I alternated watches. Carol remained in her rathole
and I heard her squeak with fright every time Britannia jerked
violently at the anchor line.

I had just glanced at my watch at 0225 when there was a gust
of wind that clapped like thunder. Britannia heaved against the
terrific pull but she was no match for that strength. With a slight
bump the anchor slipped out of the sand and in a trice the wind
shoved Britannia away from land. I leapt out and tried to feed
more line out but there was no holding. I remembered the
Cabezos rocks, a group of deadly underwater pinnacles. They
had claimed many ships. As long as the red danger lights on
Tarifa didn't show, we should be in the safe sector.

I retrieved the anchor, put out the drogue and then went
forward to wake Pete and tell him what had happened. As I
resumed my watch I glanced at something to the East. I stared
in horror. Two red lights by now in the distance of Tarifa
grimly denoted our plight.

As Britannia drifted towards the unseen rocks I could only
pray. For an hour I stood up, ears pricked, eyes searching the
blackness. Gradually the wind pressed us away from the red
warning and soon the tiny pinpoints of light were swallowed
up in the night.

We must have gone over or very close to the Cabezos. I told
Pete the news when I roused him for his stint.

'Ah,' he said, 'my Holy-water-filled Madonna in the bow did
that!'

Pete
At last the grey light of dawn served to rouse our spirits a little
—and how we needed it! Britannia was uncontrollable, even
with the two sea anchors, wallowing in the heavy seas. We were
all sick, tired and for most of the time cold. I had got over
my homesick feeling which was thankfully not to return in quite
the same drastic way as it had on that first night off Tarifa
Point. Strangely, it had only been then that I had realised I was
more than a jet-ride from home and those I loved. I had felt
so removed from them. I was close to tears—not the stuff heroes

are made of! Thinking of home made me see just how different our life was—the day to day running of a home as compared with the chores essential to the running of a boat at sea.

We took a three-hour watch each. I would awake from a fitful sleep, dress in my oilskins and sit for three hours—three hours that seemed everlasting. It was important not to doze off as there was shipping all around us and it would be very easy in that weather for a vessel not to notice us until it was too late.

Once I came out on watch with my throat sore from sea-sickness. Taking the small pump I unscrewed the cap on the deck jerry, shoved the pump in and put the other tube in my mouth. I squeezed the bulb. My taste buds were expecting water—they registered paraffin. The water pump had been used for paraffin! I ranted on to myself for a few minutes and then I felt it coming on. My stomach protested—I was sick.

We slipped into a kind of dazed efficiency, not seeing much of each other except at the changing of the watch. Carol stated that she wanted to get off in Tangier or on to the next ship. When I looked at the miserable expression on her face, I was moved to pity. She looked totally beaten. Now she knew what the sea could do and what life on a small boat could be like. Derek was against Carol leaving, in fact he was angry—more at himself than Carol probably. I tried to joke about it, saying I'd join her if she paid the air fare home. If she really wanted to go, I didn't think Derek or I should influence her decision in any way. After all, for her to carry on in that frame of mind would be dangerous for her and us.

Our brains were numb, and I don't think we took much notice of what she said or took it too seriously. 'She could change at the first sign of good weather', was Derek's comment. I think that was our only conversation in 48 hours. Smelly and dirty, sleeping in our oilskins, we were not sociable.

Later that afternoon, the weather having cleared a little, a small Dutch coaster went by, a figure on the bridge waved and we returned the greeting. As he passed, Derek yelled for a position.

'Fifteen miles due West of Cape Trafalgar.'

Surprise! We had cleared the Straits.

Carol complained of a stomach rash, caused by wearing a sweater next to her skin. So bad was it that the skin came away as she removed the offending garment. I had warned her two days before to wear a vest.

I think Derek and I had made the mistake of being too superior in our attitude towards Carol and consequently she tended, by natural reaction, to ignore our advice with the result, in this instance, of a very sore stomach.

Some miles to the South-East Derek spotted a lighthouse which we took to be Tangier. The position the Dutchman gave us, plus our afternoon rowing stint, meant that it must be Cape Espartel with Tangier lying just east of it. With our wind now swinging round, pushing us East, we unanimously decided to go in.

At this point I had better explain that Britannia was not run on the committee principle. Derek was the Captain—but on questions of expedition policy, under which heading came problems of crew welfare and the condition of the boat and stores, our individual opinions were voiced. In none of these matters was Britannia in prime condition. She still had her leaky hatches and the food storage system was a disaster. Tupperware containers were dotted about in six hatches and for some meals all had to be opened.

Just before we reached the town, dusk fell and as if by a signal, the wind and sea got up, closely followed by a violent hailstorm. By the time it cleared we could see by the number of lights that the town was too small to be Tangier. As we approached we could hear the roar of surf on a beach. We scanned the surfline, looking for an entrance to the harbour, but there were no warning lights and we came to the alarming conclusion that there was no harbour. It would seem either that we had been swept off course by a stray current or that the ship's positions had not been reliable.

That night we alternated watches with the roar of the surf ringing in our ears and a force 7 near-gale cutting into us. We took turns holding the anchor line, trying to detect any drag. For me, these lee shores were a nightmare. Derek did not seem to worry—he had plenty of experience of them. Carol had no experience of boats at all and so saw no danger. I remembered browsing in a bookshop along Charing Cross Road. Amongst the dusty volumes was a copy of *Callingham's Seaman's Jottings for the young sailor*. Flipping through it, one passage had caught my eye : 'Perhaps the worst plight of a vessel is to be caught in a gale on the lee shore. In this connection the following rules should be observed. 1. Never allow your vessel to be found in such a predicament . . .'

Next morning Derek, with disappointment in his voice, said : 'Well, we're still off Spain—the town is Conil, the light was Cape Trafalgar and the nearest harbour is Barbate.'

There were just seven miles to Barbate although between us and it lay the dangerous reef off Cape Trafalgar. We built up our energy on a lunch of Ryvita, luncheon meat and cheese. Then in bright sunlight on a calm sea we rowed. The combined efforts of the fair weather and the calm sea transmitted themselves to us and we rowed smartly and efficiently. We rounded the reef safely and with great sighs of relief. Although tired, we had time to appreciate the beauty of the sandstone cliffs, capped here and there by vegetation. Carol and I rowed while Derek spurred us on, reporting our progress and describing the scene unfolding behind our backs. The cliffs gave way to a harbour wall behind which lay the town of Barbate, world-famous for its sardines.

A sea-angler's launch passed us. The occupants waved, turned and offered us a tow, which of course we accepted. Once we were moored, a customs official and a policeman came out. Our worries over our recent connections with Gibraltar were unfounded. We had spread a pair of Levis over the 'Visit Gibraltar' sticker but the policeman lifted them, muttered 'Gibraltar' to his companion, and they both shrugged, smiled and left.

' 'allo,' said a little voice.

Looking up I saw a little girl paddling an enormous inflatable. 'Do yuh wanna coffee?' she asked.

In five minutes we were sitting in the cabin-cum-hold of the fishing boat Alexis. Peter, our host, lived in it with his adopted daughter Terry and his German girlfriend Biggy and her son.

Later as we left the Alexis for our beds, we saw to our horror that Britannia had disappeared. We looked up and down the harbour but there was no sign of her. Then a splash of orange appeared under the bow of the Alexis—she had come to look for us. A good omen ?

Derek had developed an ugly blister on his heel which had

become infected, so our call at this port was timely. Carol spent a lot of time sorting (under Derek's watchful eye) the stores, while I used the steady platform of the Alexis to repair one of the sea anchors damaged during the gale off Tarifa. Peter took us on a tour of the local hostelries where he had either extended credit, or in the case of Carlo's bar, carte blanche to drink on the house. I must say Pete had a way with him.

Before long Carol found herself a boyfriend, or perhaps I should say he found her. He lavished presents and clothes on her and quite soon Derek and I realised that poor Manuel was stricken with love. It was time for us to stand back and become onlookers, knowing from past experience that to interfere would be to get involved in unpleasantness.

Sure enough, one evening Carol got dressed up in the new clothes bought for her by Manuel and off she went down the quay to a car. Enter Manuel phut-phut on his moped.

'Vere is Carolina?' he asked me.

I shrugged in a negative fashion and he wandered off towards a policeman who was slouching against the fish market wall. As I watched I was joined by Derek who sat down beside me. I filled him in on the story. It was rumoured that Manuel was related to the Chief of Police in Barbate, though we had no reason to believe it, or that subsequent events were in any way connected with this incident or with Carol's behaviour.

The policeman was gesticulating. We sat in amused silence for a while. Manuel and the policeman stopped gesticulating. We stood as Manuel came towards us, and tried to become inconspicuous behind some empty fish boxes—too late. Manuel, red-faced, came puffing up.

'Carolina—she has gone off with *dos hombres*—DOS HOMBRES,' he spluttered. 'I am a very good man . . . I give her 900 pesetas clothes . . .'

He left in a cloud of two-stroke exhaust. 'Dos hombres' was added to our list of Carolisms.

Easter came. I gave Terry an Easter egg—she said it was the first she had ever received. Derek spent a lot of time walking in the pine forests which lay behind the town. He was very restless. He would have to be patient, the weather would change. I spent most of the time sewing the sea anchor or talking to Peter in the warm lamplight of the Alexis's dark cabin.

Derek

At first we were happy and grateful that such a place as Barbate existed at all. The calm waters of the harbour meant that we could rest and live in relative comfort and safety. Around us, busy fishermen, taking advantage of the foul weather, stayed in port and repaired their nets and their boats. After a few days I grew bored with hanging around the quayside. We had no money, we were again consuming valuable boat stores without getting anywhere and still the wretched weather showed no sign of modifying. And to cap it all, there was nothing we could do on board that the whole fishing fleet didn't see. I don't think poor Carol defecated once during the nine days we spent in port!

Again, gloom descended upon us and quarrelling followed. It began with trivialities such as how much I was eating in relation to my manual output. Pete got ratty with the miserable task of stitching up that sea anchor and snapped at Carol and me. Then arguments became passionate. The worst was directed at Carol when we grew really worried the night she disappeared with what were to us two complete strangers. We respected her personal life and in no way wished to be kill-joys, but pointed out that this was a serious expedition and that I, as leader of it, was responsible for her. However, she always emerged unscathed from such experiences and this time she brought back something for the stores—a bottle of liqueur, so she redeemed herself.

Whenever things got me down I found retreat in the forest. The conifers started just behind the sand dunes and spread for miles and miles. The only way out I ever found after hours of walking was always the seaward edge. Although violent hailstorms were frequent, the sun soon came out and as the firs screened me from the wind, I revelled in the warmth and security of land. The sea, it seemed, was an eternity away. Instead of raucous seagulls, the air resounded to the songs of warblers, finches, tits and even the cuckoo. Springy pine needles made a far better bed than a cold clammy sleeping bag. And overhead, instead of a vast, empty, salt-stained sky, was a cosy canopy of dark green branches, knitted together and filtering shafts of clean sunlight down to the soft ground. Dog rose bushes rustled mysteriously with lizards : pink hoopoes nodded and prodded the earth with their long beaks; rabbits scurried about; the slow silhouette of a lonely vulture high above the

trees. Was there any such thing as the cold unfriendly sea? There
was. I had to go back.

In the harbour, Britannia bobbed brightly among the quietly
painted sardine boats. There was a job of work to do—we had
to get on with it! We had been in Barbate for a week already.

We would be ready to leave on the 19th. Pete had finished the
drogue and Carol had rearranged the stores. The wind had
dropped but the weather was unsettled. We discussed the pru-
dence of setting out in such unpredictable conditions, remembering what had happened the last time we left in fickle westerly
airs. The authorities, however, finally decided on our day of
departure . . .

It was the revolting practice of the local police to harass the
family living on board the Alexis. They could not understand
an unmarried couple living on a fishing boat with two children,
long-haired, barefoot and so on. Sometimes the family slept on
deck under an old sail and the police often tried to catch them
'on the job' during their fruitless raids.

One night Peter and Biggy came rolling home from a great
evening's drinking. The rumpus they made attracted the police
who took up their spying positions on the next boat to the
Alexis. Pete and I tried to sober up Peter and Biggy with hot
coffee. Not having much luck, I went up on deck and relieved
myself into the darkness of the fishing boat alongside. There
was a strangled cry which made me jump. Suddenly out of the
pile of fish boxes loomed a tall figure. He groped for his torch
and I saw I had neatly urinated over his head and down his
immaculate tunic. He wiped his face, put on his helmet and in
a spluttering rage screamed: 'Mañana—pasaportes—salida!' I
had terrifying visions of execution—incarceration at the very
least. Then he stalked off into the night, cursing and sneezing.

Next day, with great trepidation, I presented myself at the
Harbour Office. I was given a ten-minute dressing-down by a
short fat official. At last he thrust our passports into my hand.
Now we had to go.

3
Dissension

20th April–9th May

Derek

Tuesday 20th April. Just four days out of Barbate and I knew
that the relationship between Pete, Carol and myself would soon
crack. I had to stop pretending. Things were bad on land. I
knew now that they would not improve at sea.

I was getting hot and sweaty in my oils, which I had donned
against a steady drizzle. Carol brewed up some tea and handed
me two mugs. We shipped our oars and relaxed for a few
minutes. Britannia carried on for a couple of hundred feet and
then rocked gently to a slow drift. The breeze which thumped
the hood of my oilskin had now changed direction.

'Looks like an easterly, Pete.'

'Last time we had an easterly, it veered and sent us half-way
to bloody Portugal!'

Mugs drained, we took up the oars again. The sea was becoming shorter. Both of us were missing our strokes.

'I don't fancy rowing in this beam sea,' Pete yelled.

'It would help if Carol could steer straight.'

The boat was yawing widely. I shouted to her to concentrate. She pulled a face and shrieked back:

'What do you think I'm doing?'

Pete rounded on her—'Come on Carol, you should be watching that compass like a hawk.'

'What do you think I'm damn well doing?'

'I can tell what you're not doing,' I countered—'steering us
a course!'

'If you can do better, come and try.'

'And who's going to row then?' Pete jeered.

We stuck it out until 1230 hours. The sea was not as rough as
it had been during the first four days, but it was very frustrating

to work in it. Waves were marching out of the Straits—the
great swell rolled in from the Atlantic and we were caught in
the middle of a very steep, irregular sea. Every now and then,
Britannia was punched upwards on a big trough. At the top
she would be smacked hard by a countering wave which flooded
over us. Spray stung my face, dripped down my neck and trickled
into my pants. My hands were numb from the cold. Twice,
when Britannia flinched over a switchback, my oar missed the
sea. I crashed back into Pete's knees and swore angrily. I glared
at Carol, hoping to take it out on her by blaming her steering
efforts again, but each time she put on her look of intense concentration and I could only swear more vividly. Pete grumbled
a lot from the bow as he was finding it just as difficult. On the
windward side of the boat I often swept the thin air in a stroke
whenever the wind heeled the boat over a few degrees. I knew
that Pete on the lee side would find a completely different
situation when the boat was pushed over. Once his oar had
been dipped, he could do nothing but let the weight of the boat
take it under.

The person steering had to sit aft as near as possible on the
centre line. Then whenever the sea tipped the boat and water
came aboard, a quick lean to port or starboard would correct
it and bring her back to an even keel. It was impossible to row
properly when heeled, with single sculls. Poor Carol always had
to be told which way to lean—she just hadn't got the feel of
the boat. Sometimes we would watch amazed as she actually
leaned the wrong way and dropped the gunnels even further
under the surface.

While I felt sorry for Carol, I was also very annoyed with
her performance. So at half past twelve I suggested that we
pack it up for now. No one argued with that.

I asked Carol to knock up some soup and Ryvita. I slung
the sea anchor over the side and paid out plenty of line while
Pete lashed the oars along the top of the gunnels. I couldn't
help smiling as I noticed his glasses. They were completely
steamed up.

'Can you see anything?'

'I am on the QE aren't I, young man?' he grinned.

I thought it was taking Carol a long time to produce such a
simple meal. She had opened three hatches.

'For goodness sake, Carol'—she was making me wince—'we only want soup and Ryvitas.'

Her pale face suddenly flushed. The brown eyes, ringed with salt, blazed. 'You let me do my job. I'm the cook and I do things my way.'

That Carol was close to tears was plain to see, but I made no soft comforting noises. Deep down I was furious that we had deceived ourselves in our assessment of her air of assurance. 'I can do it.' 'Of course I can manage.' 'Yes, I want to go on.' I asked her : 'Do you want to get off, Carol ?'

I was gazing at a Royal Navy supply ship ghosting eastwards about a mile away. 'If we hailed that ship, you could be back in Gibraltar in a couple of hours.'

With an air of sufferance, she said : 'I'll stay.'

Pete shrugged his shoulders.

I wasn't happy about the way Britannia lay to the wind. The idea of the drogue was to keep her head to the wind but she would not respond. Instead we had to put her three-quarters beam on to the weather. She shipped waves regularly and I hated the dreadful rolling. I despised the unending drizzle. Dripping onto my oilskins it sounded and felt like a hundred leaking taps. The soup left a greasy film in my mouth. I was cold, wet and upset.

'I'll take the first watch, you two get some kip.'

But Carol didn't wriggle into her galley as fast as I wanted her to. She was watching me as I felt my stomach heave. I had a hot flush. There was a burning sensation travelling up from my bowels, up, up, over my throat and eugh! . . . I spewed violently over the side. My mouth was on fire, I felt cold. I gripped the gunnel and chucked up again. I looked to see if Carol was still watching. She was—sneering.

I scooped up a handful of seawater and swilled my mouth out. Within a couple of minutes I was glad that Carol was retching. All over her legs where she sat. I turned and Pete poked his head out of the rathole, caught a whiff of the bile, and threw up noisily over the deck. We looked helplessly at each other as though the same thought had occurred to us all.

I had decided that four-hour watches would be enough in this weather. They were. I was soaked and freezing when Pete came out to relieve me at 1630 hours.

Four hours later he kneed me in the face as he came to bed after his watch. The cold air blasted over me as he tugged the dodger zip up.

I asked blearily, 'Is Carol all right? Is she on watch? Did she put her lifeline on?'

'Yes, I made sure.'

The sea was still lunatic, but I dozed off for a while. Sleeping was difficult for me with this crazy new movement. Seas crashed into Britannia and I heard the roar of breaker after breaker cruelly slamming our little boat. As soon as a wave struck, all I could hear was a seething sound like frying chips. Water slopped across the deck. Pete moaned as a cupful splashed into his airhole. Listening attentively, I heard Carol above all the noisy water, whimpering as the bullying waves sparred with the brave little boat.

'What have I got her into?' I thought.

'We'll lose her.'

I unzipped my side of the spray dodger and peered out. She was huddled in the aft spray cover. I couldn't see her face but the lamp lit up her hood. 'Carol, are you OK?'

Her head moved slowly and I saw her face. I would never forget it. The dye of the dodger had run and smeared her cheeks and nose. Her eyes were wild and staring. I thought that she didn't really know what was happening. I yelled :

'D'you want me to take over?'

'Yes.' She sounded like a little child, lost and bewildered.

The darkness had almost broken her. She didn't say anything else. I crawled out of the warm dampness into the night, hating my chauvinism. I should have had another hour. When Carol slunk off to bed, I sat aft and arranged the stiff canvas around me. The sea, I noticed, had quietened a little and I began to feel easier. I looked up at the sky. A gap in the clouds showed a couple of stars. I pulled out my pipe and lit it. Then I sat and watched and froze.

My four hours went by with intolerable slowness. I could see nothing, other than the dark shapes of ships rolling by, bursting with green phosphorescence. At last the hands of my Rolex came round to 0330. Pete's watch.

At daybreak Pete and I counted five ships around us as we pulled on our oils ready for another day. Pete crawled over the rowing seats to rouse Carol while I logged the latest situation. I could see that the weather was changing; the barometer was climbing and the wind, slackening slightly, had backed to the North. The day certainly looked promising to me but deep down I felt that out here I should not expect anything to be promising.

Carol appeared and we watched her vomit. She stumbled around, untied her own green bucket from the grab rope and squatted miserably on its flimsy rim. I knew that Pete, like me, was trying desperately to think of some funny remark but the pathos of the situation checked us. I didn't want to watch her performance but I really thought she would go over the side.

'Hold the side of the boat, Carol, not the bucket.'

'Hell's bells, Carol, not in the galley!' groaned Pete as the bucket momentarily toppled against the tiller. She saved it just in time. Pete and I both breathed sighs of relief when the contents were at last hurled into the sea and she pulled her knickers up.

'What do you want for breakfast?'

We asked for coffee and dried porridge oats with fruit. We both knew it would be too difficult for her to cook. I looked on helplessly as she struggled to light the Optimus stove and then turned it out after remembering that she needed the oatmeal from the hatch below the stove. Twenty minutes later, I heard the homely whistle as the kettle boiled and soon I was sipping beautifully hot coffee. Pete passed my green dog bowl and I dug into the oatmeal dampened with cold milk.

When I had finished breakfast I took a shaky sunsight and worked out a position line while Pete and Carol rowed. We switched around every couple of hours and I really thought that things were going to improve. My noon shot gave me a very encouraging position 15 miles south-west of Cape Espartel. I told the other two that we had cleared the most difficult stage and they made happier noises. Then I knew it was all going to happen again. Within an hour the wind, which I could feel quietly backing further westward, had suddenly strengthened. The squabbling began again as we struggled to work the oars. I was sickened to think that we should never be able to get on together in times of stress. The bickering went on and on and I felt the expedition falling about my ears.

Pete's diary

Only four days out of Barbate and already Derek seems to
have lost some of his bounce and confidence. He now spends
more time writing—writing about what? Like me, probably
of his doubts and fears. With no one to share them with, the
diary is his closest friend and confidant. I'm not much help
to him. Why am I not more positive in my attitude towards
Carol? I feel very sorry for her, but that does not stop me
from making life difficult for her by encouraging Derek in
his verbal attacks on her.

I'm sure Derek is thinking of putting Carol ashore. He must
be. I realise it will be Derek's decision. I could easily provoke
a situation to bring that about, but that would put a strain on
my relationship with Derek later on. No, I must hang on
and let him make the decision.

I never realised just how nasty I could be. I felt quite
ashamed at the thoughts I had last night when Carol took
over the watch from me. As I left her I took a mental note
of her clipping on the safety harness. It was a nasty night,
she huddled under the aft dodger as the wind and spray
whipped across the deck. I went forward, slipped off my oilskins and slid carefully into the forward rathole trying not to
wake Derek, to no avail as he was awake anyway.

'Did she put her harness on?' he asked.

'Yes,' I replied, then added : 'I made sure.'

Liar! I happened to notice but I hadn't checked.

Derek

That day, the 21st, we packed up rowing after a mere 13 miles.
Pete streamed the drogue while I slumped against the forward
bulkhead and gazed out at the jagged horizon. I was pretty
close to despair. Then, as changeable as the weather, my mood
abruptly ended. Looking around me I saw thousands of little
By-the-Wind Sailors. I had seen a few of these little creatures,
tiny drifting jellies, during the morning; now they were so
numerous that they were being swept into the boat every time
a wave came over. I thought they were very attractive. A delicate
fan-shaped bladder, veined with pink, resting upright on an oval
platform; below its base a fringe of purple tentacles dangled
down. They weren't more than two inches long. I watched them

bobbing up and down engrossed. Whenever a breaker sluiced through them, I could see them tumble and capsize but right themselves immediately. I saw them sometimes in such a tight mass that it looked like an oilslick.

I reckoned that the coming night would be like the previous one, but with one exception. The wind was blowing hard from the West. I knew that the nearby Moroccan shoreline, though I couldn't see it, was a very dangerous stretch of coast with miles and miles of surfline. If Britannia was blown back to land, that would be that. I paid out the spare drogue from the bow. I was definitely becoming nervous again as land got closer.

Pete and I agreed that Carol did really well with the supper. Lasagne, apricots and coffee. We told Carol so, thinking that a bit of encouragement would help, though I did find it very painful to watch her producing the meal. She was not thinking ahead and couldn't keep her balance in the tossing boat at all. But I enjoyed the meal and, like Pete, kept it down. The poor girl didn't.

After a furious night of constant soakings and lonely hours on watch, I was only too happy to see the sunrise and a clear day. The wind was only a breath on my face but I wasn't too happy about a nagging cross sea which was running, a legacy of the westerly the night before. After a good morning feed we all buckled down to work. Carol, when not rowing, would cook and sew; Pete read and I poured over the African Pilot volume and charts. I followed Pete's lead by stripping off my clothes until both of us were in our underpants. It was a glorious new feeling to have the sun on my skin but the dreadful pulling on the oars spoilt any enjoyment. I decided that as we were still fairly weak from the buffetings of the last few days we shouldn't row for more than three hours without a decent break. But in spite of the rigid hours we were trying to maintain rowing, Pete and I were swines for the little breaks. Lemonade breaks, treating blisters breaks, photographing and navigation breaks, toilet breaks. The most numerous were 'bum' breaks, when we just had to stand up and let the air circulate below. ·

My noon fix put us 48 miles SSW of Cape Espartel. I felt happier as the sea settled down and noticed that Pete and Carol were looking a bit more contented. By mid-afternoon I saw land 21 miles to the East and above the grey smudge of the hills I watched the heavy cumulus clouds build up. A gannet circled

over us, then glided up a useful thermal and slid into the distance.
How wonderful to be as free as that, I thought, looking around
our floating prison.

At 1730 hours I felt the first gusts of a sea breeze. This was
something I had feared but if we kept at least 20 miles from the
coast, the breeze should not affect us. For three hours, into early
evening, we rowed and cursed, feeling the westerly steadily
pushing Britannia shorewards. Later when the land cooled, the
breeze gradually died and I hoped the reverse would happen.
(The land air redresses the unequal heating at night by flowing
into the space left by the rising warmth of the sea.) It wasn't
very noticeable and I doubt if it gave us any distance out to sea.
I worked out a course to steer the next day that would give us
our southing. Before the late afternoon breeze we would have
to row two hours due West. I didn't want to go too far out into
the ocean at that stage. For one thing we might have got out of
the north-east trades and then got tangled up with variable
winds.

During the night Carol had a bad nosebleed. Pete had a short
row and I had a miniature Drambuie Maggie had thoughtfully
included in my ditty box. When we all mustered on deck the
next morning I explained what the course was and why I thought
we should head West for two hours. No objections were raised
so we got down to work. Rowing became hot and despondent
and for the first time, Pete had a go at me. I had mentioned
something trivial about the weather as I sat aft working out a
sight and Pete who was rowing suddenly blurted out :

'Why don't you keep quiet ? You've got a boring voice.'

I was most upset. After this surprising outburst I realised how
Carol must have felt when we got on to her. I let them row on
together and damned if I would relieve Pete after that. Sitting
aft with a book in my hand, I began to nod off—the slow
splashing rhythm of the oars made me drowsy.

I heard Carol muttering about a fin. I saw she had stopped
rowing and was gazing aft at the blue water. I stood up and
noticed a curious round fish flapping heavily at the surface just
by Britannia's stern. I recognised it as a sunfish. It had been
basking on its side but as I asked Pete to film it, the fish sank
a little and rolled over to the vertical. As it swam upright around
us I thought how like a dustbin lid it appeared—flat and round,
except for the high black dorsal fin situated almost above its

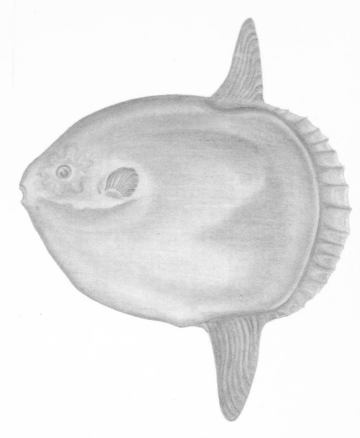

Sunfish—seen off Morocco

tail. Before Pete pulled the cameras out I watched it disappear.

When I took my stint at the oars for the row due West, Britannia went through something particularly nasty. Tons and tons of oil. I was quite alarmed at first, thinking that the slick would thicken and we should be stuck in the middle of it. I saw that the light brown lumps which ranged from pea to orange size looked rather fresh. There were no visible living organisms attached to them such as barnacles or sea lice, so I presumed that the slick had been discharged recently. We must have rowed for two miles before the slick thinned. I saw some older lumps of oil, almost grey and encrusted with tiny barnacles. These were bigger than the other lumps I had seen, maybe weighing a stone or more.

At 1730 hours I felt the sea breeze. It didn't take long to whip up a short choppy sea. Pete began haranguing Carol to pull harder. Then they both started on me to keep a straighter course. My temper flared. Pete roared and Carol extricated herself by weeping again. I asked Pete to alter course and go more South to 248°. Britannia felt better, I thought, once round, but we rolled a lot. After an hour I started timing them. Twenty strokes to a minute—hardly ramming speed. I could see Carol, red-faced, begin to flag. She gasped and winced with every pull. Though Pete couldn't see her face I knew he could see her round back stooping lower and lower. My prediction of what he would say to her was bang on :

'Come on Carol—you're supposed to be the PT fanatic! Pull woman—PULL !'

It was supper time. Carol leaped up thankfully and scrabbled around in the galley. Pete and I sat against the forward bulkhead while we ate our bacon and mash. Carol cleaned the pressure cooker and kept as far aft as she could get from us.

I loved the sunset and watched it dip below fluffy cumulus while I smoked my pipe. I was trying to forget the quarrels of the day when Pete struck up again at Carol.

'Don't hang that cooker over the side without tying it on to something !'

'I won't let go of it.'

I looked up and got very angry.

'You better not,' I chimed in, 'otherwise you're going overboard to get it.'

And I believe that at the time, had she let it slip, I really would have thrown her after it. I think she sensed my thoughts, which even alarmed me, and didn't answer back.

I spotted the first whale. He was the bull of a school of six Blackfish (Pilot whales). They splashed and blew and slapped their tails. They didn't stay long, and after they had paid their respects to us, Pete and I watched them as they romped northeastwards. Pete said to me quietly :

'You know, it's a real waste her coming with us. She wasn't interested in those Blackfish, was she ?'

'You'd think anyone would at least have looked up and stared,' I said. 'Do you think she's cracking, Pete ?'

'I don't know, but I bet I know what's half the trouble.'

'What?' I leaned closer to him.

'She's emotionally isolated . . . ,' he whispered.

He cut himself short as she came forward with two mugs of coffee.

At one o'clock in the morning, Pete and I got up and rowed while Carol slept. I fixed our course by keeping two stars over the stern. It was the quietest night I had experienced so far and I thoroughly enjoyed the stint. It was cool, the night sky clear and starry and Carol was not on deck. Pete began to talk about his snapping at me earlier. He said he was sorry; it certainly wasn't normal for him to be so sharp.

'It seems to me,' I said, 'that the three of us together bring out the worst in each other.'

'That's it,' Pete agreed. 'We never behaved like this when there were just two of us working on the boat and preparing everything.'

'She seems to be a catalyst,' I said. 'She doesn't seem to start anything maliciously, damn it all, we're guilty of that, but she always has such an extraordinary effect on us, on our own behaviour.'

'For me,' said Pete, 'it's not what she says, it's how she looks. I mean, her face seems permanently miserable. I can't stand looking at it any more. Sometimes I want to hit it just to change it. That's why I have to row in this seat so that I can only see you and not her.'

I laughed but I knew he was serious.

We carried on rowing and talking quietly. I felt so much more relaxed with just the two of us. A snort interrupted us.

'Hey—look!' said Pete excitedly.

I turned my head and saw two streamlined shapes picked out in the phosphorescence. The dolphins blazed a green trail behind them as they swam under my oar. Then I heard a last whoosh and they were gone.

I knew it was too good to be true. After an unbroken row of two and a half hours, gusts of wind from the North-West chopped up the flat calm. We couldn't see the short waves slapping into us so Pete suggested for the sake of our oars that we pack up.

When I heaved myself out of my sleeping bag at dawn, I donned my oilskins right away. I felt cold and there was a slight

drizzle. I thought I'd attempt to use the loo rope for the first
time so I tottered aft and dropped my pants. I leaned well over
the gunnel and clutched the knotted rope fastened to a cleat
on the other side. It was an astounding success. My bucket and
chuckit method immediately became obsolete.

By the time Carol had cleared up breakfast, the clouds and
the wind had gone. Strong sunlight dazzled me so I wore Polar-
oids and peaked cap for the first time. And just a pair of shorts.
Pete and I took the oars and rowed strongly. By 1000 hours the
heat had beaten me. As I squinted East, the horizon quivered
in the blaze and the oily blue flatness of the sea looked molten.
Sweat was running down my body and stayed trapped around
my groin. The sponge cushion I sat on was soaked and the
palms of my hands made the oar handle drip. I turned around
and looked at Pete, also sweating profusely.

'Let's have a break,' he said.

Carol poured some lemonade and we rested in the shade of
the dodger. When I felt better I took a sight and worked out
a position line.

I noticed, while the chart was across my thighs, a rash of
tiny whiteheads all over my legs. I showed Pete who thought
it might have been an allergy to the moisturising cream I'd been
using. He examined my back and said there were the same
spots there where I had spread the gunge the day before. I felt
leprous so I had my first wash since Gibraltar and sponged
Savlon over my skin.We picked up the oars again and rowed
off through a new concentration of oil lumps.

I envied Carol, lounging, pink-bikinied, in the shade of the
stern. While I watched her rubbing sun tan lotion over her
white flesh, I noticed something.

'Have we used that spare gallon of water?' I asked, pointing
to the spare water bag lashed over the blister.

'No,' said Carol, looking behind her.

'Well, why is it empty?'

She got up and peered at it.

'It's burst.'

We had lost a gallon of precious water.

It was a bit too quiet. None of us had said much all morning
but by noon when it became too hot to work, the old aggro

started again. Pete and I both agreed that the tins in the forward hatches were not stowed properly. We could hear them clanging together. If their coats of varnish got chipped, the tins would rust and their contents might be ruined. So in the nicest way I asked Carol if she minded interrupting her sunbathing for an hour and sorting the hatches out. She frowned, trying to think of an excuse for not doing it, but Pete and I had already vacated the rathole and were rapidly making tracks aft. Admittedly, it was a lousy job, but I felt quite justified in asking her. After all, she had stowed the tins originally. She rolled up our rubber sleeping platform and kneeling down inside the rathole, unfastened the clips. Then I heard a loud and quite unnecessary clanking as she threw tins out on to the deck. She was blowing like a dolphin for an hour and a half, and at last, thankfully, I watched her close up the hatches. Then it happened. Somehow she had broken a pair of Pete's glasses—they were even in a case. If she'd apologetically told Pete about it and been a bit tactful, I'm sure he would have forgiven her. But I was shocked when she swung around, dangling the shattered glasses between her fingers, and said :

'Look what I've done now. It's your fault for leaving them there.'

I saw Pete's eyes flash. Then he gave her the biggest mouthing I'd ever heard. Carol blanched. Everything had come to a head and this was Pete's safety valve. It had been bottled up for so long. And it finally convinced me that our relationship just wasn't going to work after all. Either Pete or Carol would have to go if this project were to succeed.

After I had worked out our position on Tuesday afternoon I reckoned that the sea breeze was responsible for putting us 11 miles off the coast. The current marked on the charts did not have any landward tendencies along that part of the coast. And before late afternoon when the breeze began, a north or northeast wind direction was definitely in our favour. So our steady drift towards Africa was inevitable. When that breeze blew, at 1730 hours every day, rowing was sometimes impossible. I thought that being blown four miles a session would be a fairly good guess. I showed Pete the chart and pointed out the miles of lee shore we'd face if the wind remained from the West. He asked where, if necessary, would be a good port to hole up in. Rabat or Casablanca seemed to me to be the obvious choices.

Yet neither of us wanted to go in, resenting any further delay.
The hurricane season would soon begin.

'Let's press on,' I said. But I was thinking about Carol and the
opportunity she would have of leaving if we did land. It was
another decision to make. I prayed. I didn't have a lot of faith,
but I had to talk to someone. 'Whatever is best for us?' I said
to God.

We ate a clam risotto for supper. I looked around at the sky
and the sunset, greenish and sickly. The barometer had dropped
and I told Pete and Carol to check lashings on all the gear and
batten everything down. The sea breeze developed into a steady
westerly by nightfall and I looked out towards land. There was
an orange glow over Casablanca way. Pete streamed two sea
anchors and the two of us alternated the night watches.

I peeped out after Pete came back in just before dawn. Rain
spotted my face as I stared at the grey smudge of Casablanca,
miles to the East. The westerly had not abated, it was still force
6. The waves, I noticed too, were running more steeply as they
always do near land. I saw three ships heading to port. One of
them, a Chandris liner, the Regina, towered very close to us. I
thought of the passengers lying in warm dry cabins. In an hour
they would be walking on land.

While Carol kneaded some wholemeal bread under the green
awning, I explained the situation to Pete.

'We're about 20 miles from Casa. This westerly is pushing us
in to the shore, and after Casa—there's no shelter for maybe 50
miles at El Yadidah or somewhere. The weather's getting worse
too. I think we should go in.'

'Me too.'

I then felt everything was going to turn out well after all. At
1.45, in stair rod rain, Peter and I pulled the first stroke for land.
The wind had strengthened considerably and had backed to
South-West. My hood crackled as the gusts struck. Gone was the
royal blue sea. Now it was greyish-brown, flecked with white
spray. I looked up at the dark clouds; it was still raining hard. To
the South I saw the almost black sky rapidly spreading our way.

Within minutes the squall was whipping Britannia. I could
hardly get my breath, but screamed to the others to hold on to the
boat. Britannia was blown down to port. Water flooded over the
gunnel. Pete and I leaned out on the other side to counteract
the roll. I saw Carol skid off the galley step and crash against the

What to do if you can't row

anchor on deck. I heard her cry out. At the same time, my oar groaned in the rowlock. I thought it would snap so I let go. We got Britannia on an even keel again but short, tearing waves slammed across the deck. I half stood up and frantically got my oar in. Wind-driven spray stung my eyes and I felt runnels of cold water down my front.

'Are you all right, Carol?' I asked, after I had made sure I was. 'Yes.'

'Lock the bloody tiller arm with the U-bolt then.'

'I can't find it.'

'Look for the damn thing then!' shouted Pete.

The squall didn't last long but I reckoned it had knocked us more than a mile back. When conditions had settled a little we took a ten-minute break. I asked Carol to get some of the bread she had made and to open a tin of jam. During the rest I watched a flock of magnificent gannets soaring towards us. They came closer. One of them suddenly folded its wings and dropped like a brick. The bird spiralled slightly to level up on a fish and then disappeared in a spurt of spray as it hit the waves. I counted over thirty of them. Half, I noted, were mature birds, snow-white against the dark-grey sky. The rest were younger, still in a mottled chocolate and white set of feathers. Six or seven hit the sea together, plumes of spray shot up and then I saw them beating hard to get their heavy bodies airborne again. They were all round us, very close. I even saw the fish kicking in their throats. The beak, like a dagger, was already closed, I noticed, in flight; they never held the fish in it so I supposed they swallowed them underwater.

'What a fantastic sight,' said Pete.

But I knew the wind wouldn't let us sit here birdwatching for long. We resumed the painful grind into the wind which had increased to gale force. The heavy swell running in from the South-West bounced Britannia up and down and I began to feel gippy. It seemed to me that the land was getting further away.

My back, arms and hands hurt like hell. Pete told me he felt knackered too, so we had another rest. The weather was foul, the day was ending and my nerves had almost frayed. During the break I read the Pilot on Casablanca. The cream lighthouse on Pointe d'El Hank, where I originally told Carol to steer for, was, I discovered, too far South. I had to make for the end of Jete Delure, a wall one and a half miles long. Once round it we could row into quiet waters, perhaps to the yacht basin. But it was still a long way off yet—probably about ten miles. Ahead of us was the open roadstead where I could see over twenty ships at anchor waiting to use the harbour. Behind them I could see tall buildings and sprawling property. The wind blew harder and we had to pull harder in order not to be beaten back. I felt shattered. Carol was still standing up steering with her feet.

'We're about a mile from the first ship now,' she said. 'It's a green one.'

'Nice,' said Pete sarcastically.

'Can you see the jetty wall yet, Carol?'

She peered through the binoculars.

'No.'

'Well, let's row to that ship and ask for a bearing.'

The murk of the drizzle had made the scenery fade. I had no large-scale chart of the port. My only guide was the small-scale chart of the coast between Cape Espartel and Cape Ghir. The Pilot was useful but only up to a point. Verbal is not as good as visual.

As we neared the ship, Carol pointed out a great shoal of dolphin galloping north. I could smell their evil smelly breath as they cheerfully pranced by us. I saw the green ship was called

Germa Gloria. She was flying the Norwegian flag and the yellow Q flag. ('My vessel is healthy and I request free practique.') I told Carol to steer round her stern. I could hear the engines throbbing 200 yards upwind. The sea had lost a lot of its kick as we were then just in the shelter of the land. I called up to a crewman as we rowed round to her lee side.

'Hallo, hallo. Where is the harbour?'

They waved at me in a friendly manner, grinning. Then an English-speaking mate showed us the way by pointing. I took a quick bearing. We thanked them and rowed off on the new course. The ships at anchor were all lit up by then. Dusk had fallen and I still couldn't see the light at the end of the jetty because of the mass of illuminated advertisements ashore. As we went further I really got worried. I was going in blind, except for the rough bearing the Norwegian had given me. What if we missed it and ended up on a rocky beach or something?

Just before total darkness, Carol spotted the low dark shape of the breakwater and pointed it out to us. We began to row towards its southern end. At 2000 hours a small trawler came very close to us. Pete quickly grabbed a flashlight and signalled to the Moroccans. I said 'No don't' but it was too late. The boat immediately swung off course and slowly circled us. The wind was still strong enough to make Britannia's steering erratic and just as I feared, the trawler crashed into the forward blister. I felt the shudder go right through the boat. Fortunately the Plastazote blister absorbed most of the bump and Britannia was not damaged.

The fishermen threw a thick filthy rope and I made a quick join to our forward mooring line. They asked in French if we were ready and when I yelled 'Oui' the trawler throttled away. The line twanged taut and I fell back into Carol's arms as Britannia took off at speed.

Presently I saw the light on the end of the Jete Delure. I felt the trawler slow up and I pulled the tiller over so that Britannia wouldn't run up her stern. Then my senses reeled.

Civilisation hit me. The roar, clank and throb of machinery and the hum of voices assaulted my ears. Hundreds of lights made my eyes blink. Coal smoke and petrol fumes invaded my lungs which for a whole week had breathed nothing but pureness. My body began to vibrate with this bombardment of sound and smells and light. I called Pete, who was finishing a quiet fag in the rathole. He came out, looked around and inhaled deeply.

'Ah!' he breathed with relish. 'People.'

And Carol remarked, 'What a stink!'

The Moroccans' boat gradually glided to a halt and I sprang forward to ask where we could moor. I could see that we were at the head of the harbour, in the fishing boat area. But before they answered my question, two younger men bawled down to me: 'Cigarettes? Whisky?'

In the lamplight I thought they looked positively menacing, dark eyes glinting and all. I knew they would not let us go until they had a reward but I explained there was no whisky, no cigarettes.

'Whisky!' they demanded impatiently.

'Carol,' I said, 'have we got any fags?'

'No.'

I saw Pete furtively slide his last precious packet into his trousers.

'Well, give them the brandy,' I said to Carol.

I knew it was our only bottle but the fishermen had done us a big favour. She handed the bottle to me and I passed it up to the men.

'Merci bien,' they said smiling. And then hopefully, 'Un autre?'

'Get stuffed—bonsoir Messieurs.'

4

Twosome

24th April–18th May

Pete

Rain ceased for the few moments it took to row from the fishing boat to the nearest free pontoon. Tired, hungry and smelly, we staggered on to the wobbly platform, the different motion un-settling us momentarily. It looked pretty quiet for a Saturday night. Our pontoon was attached to a yacht club, very dark and closed-looking.

After a lengthy search we turned through a door and—fantastic, a café: warmth, soft light, smells of coffee and Disque Bleu. In the corner sat an aristocratic old lady wrapped in a fur coat, reading. She smiled as we squelched towards her. Then a younger, just as aristocratic lady appeared. She spoke in English with an American accent. We introduced ourselves and explained what we were up to. She introduced herself as the Contessa Apraxine; the old lady was her mother. We sat down and in no time we were sipping tea, munching eggs and fruit and puffing on cigarettes. We talked until 2 am, joined by Masha's two beautiful daughters, Anna and Helen. After twenty cups of tea and as many cigarettes, we trooped off to Britannia and bed.

Breakfast in old Casablanca soon became a delightful daily event that I always looked forward to—especially the walk from the port up through the Archway wall of the old city to the café in the square. I half-expected to see Bogey sitting at one of the pavement tables. Derek and I sat and talked of the trip, of friends —and of Carol, our relations with her, our faults and hers. We both realised that it wasn't on to continue with her, but how to tell her? And deprive her of a fantastic opportunity? Or was it a fantastic opportunity? If only she could see how different we were, our humour, even if we were just sitting in a dirty café with half the customers smoking joints, looking out at ragged kids kicking a half-inflated football around a dusty square.

The answer to our problem came in the shape of one Pierre Lampe, a friend of Masha's family—wealthy, good-looking, generous, and although his English wasn't that good, great company. He took us out for meals, to discothèques and on a trip to Marrakesh. It wasn't till the trip to Marrakesh that I realised Carol's relationship with Pierre was more than the female equivalent of a 'girl in every port'. On the way home Derek and I, squashed on the rear seat of Pierre's coupé, couldn't help but be aware of Carol and Pierre exchanging looks, hands clasped over the gearstick, only letting go for a gear change and then only at the last moment with the engine almost leaping from its mountings with over-revving.

We saw even less of Carol after that day—she gave up sleeping on Britannia II. Derek and I tried to earn our keep at Masha's doing odd jobs, Derek in the kitchen showing the French how to cook French-style—even the customers were impressed. One thing I do like is to watch a professional at work, and Derek with his napkin over a shoulder and a bowl of mayonnaise under his arm took some beating. I did some repairs around the place, doors, windows, locks, whilst Carol gave Masha a new hair-do. But more and more time was spent on Britannia. Pierre came to our aid financially with a 30 quid everlasting loan of which Carol used ten on much needed provisions. I spent most of my time on Britannia making small repairs to the gear, trying unsuccessfully to plug leaks in the deck hatches. Our finances at the time were at their usual all-time low—we owed money to just about everybody. Nobody was safe from the little aside from Derek, 'I wonder if you could possibly see your way . . .'

Our problem at this stage was the stove. We had decided early on in the planning that paraffin would be the safest, cheapest, most readily available fuel, so we had approached Optimus who very kindly supplied us with an excellent stove, clean, quite reliable and good to look at. But we had not reckoned with polluted Gibraltar paraffin (not BP) which, to put it mildly, gunged up the works with a tar indistinguishable from the Trindad Lake variety—great for roads but the kiss of death for our stove. Hot food was a must, and more important still was Alec's salt water still which needed a stove capable of producing boiling water. Good old Pierre. Told of our problem by Carol, he promptly rushed out and bought us a gas stove and three refills which according to him contained forty hours each. This would give us 120 hours' burning, quite enough for cooking and condensing water. The new stove was soon installed and we looked forward to many fine meals with no problems.

Derek's diary
The relationship between Carol, Pete and me has almost broken down. Let's try to analyse it. First, I have been stubborn and tried to convince myself and Pete that the girl would change once we were at sea. All the glamour, posing for photos, TV, etc, would no longer distract her from her job. Pete, now it seems quite rightly, refused to believe this would happen. The situation between those two soon became very strained— especially on the Barbate-Casa run. I soon found I was in total agreement with Pete. It became apparent that Carol's seamanship was inadequate to our tasks, despite our laborious instruction in even simple things such as knots. She realised this inadequacy and then seemed to get worse. And when she smiled for the first time when I announced we were going in to Casa, I realised that ever since the idea of the row had been suggested to her she had been completely deceiving herself on her capabilities.

The gales are still blowing—we'll no doubt be here a few days more. I think I know what will happen, but I do baulk at losing a crew member.

Pete understood well and said it was my decision. He, like me, agreed that the cooking would be a hated job if we had to do it ourselves. And something else that both of us didn't fancy doing —the awfully painful job of telling Carol we didn't want her.

On 5th May, Carol returned after vanishing for nearly two days. I was sitting in the boat repairing a broken foot board. Pete crouched on the pontoon next to the boat sawing a piece of batten. Carol sat down between us. The problem of who would tell her to leave was resolved. She looked me in the eye and said :

'I've decided not to go on.'

Pete

I confess I almost felt a breath of fresh air pass over Britannia as
she told us. I felt sorry for her. Still, I hoped she would turn the
experience into something positive. Derek felt more responsible
for her than I did, and previously he had defended her short-
comings, but now with her resignation he felt so relieved that he
seemed to overreact and poor old Carol became the butt of our
humour in her absence.

As Carol left Britannia for the last time, Derek handed her
personal effects to Pierre who stood on the pontoon. Derek
hugged Carol as I, heartless bastard, filmed the sad little scene.
Derek was visibly upset as his conception of the trip had steadfastly included a third person—a girl.

Farewells to Masha. No sign of Carol with our lighter. She had
promised to get it back to us before we left. It was very calm, with
hardly a ripple inside the breakwater. Feeling very professional
we let go fore and aft lines—I pulled hard on my oar, reverse
for Derek, helm hard over and Britannia turned slowly. The
question was : could we row in a straight line without Carol
steering ?

*To be fair to Carol, we feel we ought to give something of her
side of the story at this point. She returned home to Dartford and
was in great demand from the press. In newspaper accounts she
commented thus on various aspects of the expedition.*

Derek and Pete

On her role

. . . to be fair to them, they told me how really rough it could
be. My job as we battled through the seas would be to hang on
at the back of the boat, acting as cook, chief bottle-washer,
housewife, pretty distraction and mediator to Derek and his
boatswain. I knew it was not going to be easy, because I was
going to be involved in the menial tasks. I had to cook all the
meals, opening tins and turning dehydrated foods into reasonably attractive meals in gale force winds. I had to wash up and
keep the two boys happy, and act as mediator when there was
a clash of personality.

On loneliness

At first I thought the problem was that one of the men thought the other was paying me too much attention, but I felt strangely that this seemed to unite them and I was the one left out. I became very lonely, dreaming of home and thinking of the sort of life I had left behind. At times I thought I was the odd one out but our journey was bedevilled with trouble from the start.

I couldn't bear the loneliness. It may seem silly that I could feel so terribly alone, cooped up with two men in a boat only 35 feet long. But the isolation developed into a stomach-aching feeling which overwhelmed me. I began to ask myself : 'What am I really doing here? Are these really the same nice men I left home with? Are they turning against me? Why am I always the only one who gets picked on?'

On our first emergency, the first night out:

We had stopped near the shore for a sleep, and I woke at 3 am to Derek's screams that the boat was being pounded by a heavy sea. 'We are being driven on to the rocks,' he said. The anchors were not holding. And I realised that despite all the books I had read, by people like Sir Francis Chichester and Robin Knox-Johnston, I knew little about how terrifying the cruel sea really was.

In the panic, Peter lost his glasses. As I scrambled to get out of my sleeping bag I lost my clothes and I had to row with Peter as the freezing rain lashed against my half-naked body. I think we all believed we would be drowned. I was trembling with fear, and for the first time I felt very close to death. Then an anchor was thrown over again and instead of slipping it held fast.

I felt a wonderful moment of elation as Derek put his arm around me and said : 'Don't be scared, we're all in it together.'

Exhausted, Peter and Derek slumped to bed. It was my turn to be on watch . . . alone. The vast emptiness, the pitch black, the awful loneliness and not knowing what was all around petrified me. It was the most terrifying moment I have ever experienced. I shall never forget it. But my joy at being a wanted part of the team shone like a light. I had been needed by them and had not failed them. They were grateful.

On tension and strain

If Derek and Peter get into a mood they take it out on me. I
am what is known as the buffer. I can take so much, but when
they start making personal comments ... that's when I feel
really bad. According to them I haven't got any imagination,
am incapable of organising, am immature and can't row or
cook. That's what they say anyway but when I ask Derek to
give me examples of my faults he can't. They have never once
complained about a dinner I have dished up. One day I just
broke down under a barrage of accusations. I can only try,
and my goodness I have tried like nothing else in this world.

On leaving the expedition

When we put into the harbour at Casablanca, I decided I
could not get on that boat with them again. We were waiting
for the right weather and could have set off at a moment's
notice—any time, any day. I knew I could not go on waiting
any longer. It was better to get it over with. They were repairing the boat when I finally plucked up courage to talk to them.
I walked up, sat down on the jetty next to the boat and said :
'I'm sorry, I've failed—I am no longer able to carry on.'

They both looked up, but seemed to show no emotion at all,
neither remorse nor pleasure. They began asking me to show
them how to work the pressure cooker and where the various
foodstuffs were packed.

Carol's epilogue

... I was like most single girls of twenty. Clothes, books, men
took up a lot of my time. I had fun. My philosophy is still what
will be, will be. But I am much more serious. Having a good
time is not the most important thing any more. Before I was a
girl. Now I am a woman.

So happily the experience did Carol good. She went back to
Casablanca and married Pierre Lampe. Peter and I got invita-
tions to the wedding.

Pete

There was a light headwind as we rowed round Jete Delure but the tide was with us. One should cancel the other. We rowed almost in a straight line; Derek moved the tiller across another notch from time to time. We glided past the ships unloading. A seaman leaning from the rail of a coaster shouted : 'Good luck, English.' Sailors scuttling round the French warship Jeanne d'Arc paused and looked down as Britannia moved quietly by.

It was a long haul around Jete Delure before the open sea. Rounding the Jete Delure we had a few anxious moments as the wind threatened to put us on the rocks below the Point but a little extra effort at the oars and we passed them. Relaxing a little we could take in the skyline of Casablanca.

I noticed my oar handle had a splinter out of it. I fell into my abstract way of deciding on a solution—plastic padding, sand it down or ignore it. I would see how long it took to become unbearable. What a hero! Only a few minutes later I moved my hand up the shaft out of blister's way.

We stopped for a cuppa. I managed most of it, but the last gulp finished me off, and I hung my head over the gunnel making what must have sounded to Derek like the most awful croaking, spewing noise imaginable. I felt terrible—mouth dry, with the horrible taste of the previous night's dinner. Luckily I never suffered very long with this complaint and always felt better after a good throw-up. I glanced at Derek between my deliberations. He concentrated his gaze very hard in the other direction. Seasickness is one of the most catching conditions I know of. Derek looked decidedly queasy, but I knew he would hang on and only let go when his stomach lining threatened to come up with the offending residue.

The steep onshore swell didn't make for ease of rowing. We seemed to stop at each wave. Gradually the swell moderated after we passed the El Hank light—almost as if we had passed a little test and this was the reward. Send us the tests and keep moderating, I thought, and it should be a millpond by the Canaries. We could still hear the sound of waves on rocks—it reminded us not to rest on our . . .

Soon my bum had a hundred per cent claim on my mind. I wondered what it looked like—red raw by the feel of it. What should the ideal rowing bum be? Not too skinny or the bones would come in too much contact with the seat, not too fat either or the fat overlap would rub on itself. It might be an idea to have a castration job done as well; not only for the obvious reason—

lack of women, but it did rather get in the way and I was terrified
I might get things caught in the sliding seat runners. Not boasting,
it was possible, I worked it out . . .

Through the ships moored in the Roadstead . . . under the
stern of a tanker . . . under the bow of a freighter. No sign of life.
Even if they had heard us the creak of oars was such an unfamiliar
sound at sea these days I doubted whether even a seaman would
recognise it for what it was.

We rowed until we felt we had enough offing and at 1600
hours we rested; there was no point in trying to fight the onshore
sea breeze which had started again. The breeze before Casablanca
had been stronger than this. Perhaps it knew that there was no
reason for us to be pushed ashore again. Streaming one drogue,
Derek set about cooking tea. Rice pilaff with salad followed by
half a tin of peaches each, finished off with coffee and a cigarette.
We dozed—sleep wouldn't come to me, I was not yet used to the
different motion at sea. At 2000 we started once again at the oars.
My seat runners had been jamming intermittently, putting unnecessary pressure on my backside. I tried a liberal dose of grease
which helped for ten minutes or so, then bang, I was sliding
down the runners without the benefit of the seat between me and
the stainless steel. I had to dig out the spare seat. I noticed too
that the wheels had gone flat one side, causing a nasty vibration.
After two and a half hours we decided to call it a day, quite
pleased with our performance, having covered some 18 miles
estimated from landmarks ashore, more or less in the direction
planned, but we were exhausted as we packed the oars away and
streamed the drogue for the night. It was obvious that we had
lost our pep in Casablanca. Two weeks of the soft life and back
to square one.

We talked about our performance as though we were not involved—as if we were a couple of machines set to do a task. Our
minds, having decided what should be done, had set our bodies
to full ahead. It remained to be seen how our bodies reacted;
perhaps they could be conned indefinitely. Sleep came without
trouble this time. I didn't wake once.

Diary: 0700 hrs, 10th May
We were up and drinking coffee in double-quick time. Decided
to get underway and make the most of it, and eat later. As we
gulped our coffee, we took in our day—wind North 2–3—good

sea, a bit choppy but on our course it would be on the beam, not so good for rowing but not insurmountable. We were about five miles offshore; we had drifted in a bit during the night. Palms and sand dunes were plainly visible in the clean air, even a few buildings on the barren landscape. I brushed my teeth while Derek cleaned up the galley. Heave ho on the drogue line, muttering to myself, 'I thought we put out the drogue last night, not an anchor!'

'What's the matter?' came Derek.

'Stuck—must have caught on some rocks as we drifted in during the night,' I replied.

I heaved at the wet line, we both cursed at it. We tried waiting until Britoo was down in a trough, making the line fast on a cleat, then a wave to lift her, hoping the drogue would come with us—not so. It was well and truly stuck. All I succeeded in doing was squashing two fingers and bringing half the ocean aboard. Bitterly, I thought of all those hours spent in Barbate wearily sewing in a new panel, and I had been so pleased with it; so unlike me to be that patient with an inanimate object. All that well-deserved praise from Derek and now the bloody thing was stuck on the seabed. The next try was to row back along our guessed direction of drift, then a sharp tug on the line hoping it would come away from the same angle it got caught at. After an hour of heaving we were still attached to the seabed. Only one thing for it. With John Fairfax's words ringing in my ears—'Drogues are one of the most important pieces of equipment you have'—Derek cut through the line as low as possible to reduce the possibility of fouling a propeller.

'Never mind, it probably prevented us from drifting ashore.'

Derek didn't look convinced but it consoled me. This left us with just two drogues, one small in good condition and one large, partly rotted but repairable.

Hallo—only two days out and Derek was going funny!

'What a beautiful bird,' he said.

'Crumpet! Where?' I said, jumping about and looking around, thinking I must humour him.

'Up there—look.' He pointed at a bunch of flapping feathers. After my initial disappointment I agreed it did look nice, dipping down to the wave tops, sometimes disappearing behind a wave, appearing from behind another inches from the water. Derek was ecstatic.

'Look at its delicate pink breast—gorgeous.'

'Yeah.'

'A Roseate tern,' he said.

'Fancy that,' I said.

We used the directions from the African Pilot Vol. I like an AA road map—looking for palm trees and houses as if we were taking a run in the car. 'Ah! That must be Azemour.' Very quiet, very calm—nothing to distract our thoughts. We aimed for a town a day at this stage. After Safi we would run out of towns as the coast tracked off south-east and we carried on south with a bit of west.

The sea was turning green now, a sure sign of shallowing water —it was getting rougher as we approached the shoals. More muscle power was needed as we pulled round away from the shoreline. We moved quickly down the coast of dunes behind which lay barren country, hilly, uninviting, but to me very attractive. I had heard it said the desert is like the sea. I was beginning to understand that.

The wind was a fresh force 5—the sea was just about rowable; above force 5 it got difficult. In shallow water like this the waves were shorter, choppier, making for an uncomfortable ride, hard and bumpy.

I now understood the term 'crude oil'. Great clumps of the stuff floating semi-submerged, turning the sea into a giant cesspool. We both decided it couldn't belong to BP. On closer examination we could see marine growth proliferating on the underside—barnacles, weeds. Nature had once again found a use for our waste. I hoped that the saline water would eventually break it down. 'The sea doth clean all man's impurities.'

Our next landmark was the tower of 'Tit' on Cap Blanc du Nord which we immediately renamed 'Bristol City', but it was too far away to see clearly. The following day the land was no longer visible—at last we felt we were properly underway. I felt we had passed our test. Everything since leaving Carol in Casablanca had gone without a hitch. I knew Derek was a bit nervous of this stretch of coast, but he looked happier when we woke up and saw just sea. Now we had good vibes and Britannia was a friend not a problem. It was a fine sunny day. I thought I saw sharks but they turned out to be sunfish. Sights at sea of ships, wildlife, even a paper cup floating by, fascinated us, so the sight of a freighter moving very slowly held our attention, then our scrutiny. As she came closer we could make out a tug with a line aboard her. Strange, though, we couldn't make out any detail on the freighter, and as she came closer we saw why. She had been gutted by fire from stem to stern, blackened by soot; she was obviously for the scrap heap. We stared in silence as the funeral procession went by.

That evening, in a contented mood, we sat in the stern munching spam fritters and a great treat of Boxty bread to go with our posh Lipton's Tea. With a tea toast, we wished Silla good luck with the new job we'd heard about in Casablanca. I didn't like the idea, I suppose because I couldn't identify with her in new surroundings. Lighting the lamp, we congratulated ourselves on clearing a dangerous coastline.

Derek

The following evening we found ourselves again in a contemplative mood. Hard, bruising work on the oars in a rising sea had left us aching and glad to stop for our meal and a chat. Pete applauded my culinary effort of beef goulash and noodles and both of us sat back belching contentedly. Although the breeze had died after blustering activity all day, a high sunset denoted more wind. As I puffed on my pipe I watched the grey cloud streaks darken to charcoal as the sky turned coppery green.

I felt a bit disappointed when, as darkness fell, the bright beam of light from Cape Beddouza swept the sky to the East and reminded me that land was still pretty close although we had not seen it all day. As I opened a miniature whisky, Pete remarked that he could see another light beam.

'Must be Safi,' I said, and went forward to take a look at the chart. I did a bit of DR and took rough bearings from the two sources of light.

'How far today?'

'About 30 miles.'

'Bloody 'ell—is that all?' said Pete, wincing from backache.

'It looks as though that may be our average,' I told him.

'What was all that balls about 50-60 miles a day then?'

'Salesmanship?' I answered hopefully.

Pete grinned and rolling a cigarette said :

'Still, I suppose we could possibly make that if we had reasonable seas—and worked 25 hours a day!'

We discussed how we could keep the boat rowing longer yet still get our rest and keep abreast of the chores. In choppy seas Pete suggested we should stow the big oars and have one man using a set of nine-footers. The previous day had proved that two-up with the big oars was really a waste of manpower. Long oars in rough seas are more difficult to handle than short ones, but neither of us cared for one man rowing. The arms grew tired quickly, entirely because of the firm grip that had to be exerted on the oars. The grip was minimal on a single 12-footer, because of the great in-board length and the comfortable balance in the rowlock. But we decided to give one-up rowing a trial over the next few days if it remained choppy.

Another thing that inhibited mileage was Britannia's disinclination to lie stern on to the sea if our course required her to. Recently it had, and whenever a wave broke under us, Britannia slid off and slightly changed her heading. Then the wind would catch hold of the blisters and slew her right off course. No amount of fine adjustment to the tiller rectified the problem. It was up to one of us to stop rowing and the other to bring her round again with quicker and more powerful strokes to prevent losing way. By bitter experience we knew that back-paddling was not helpful at all. The boat lost momentum very quickly and the effort of getting her going again was considerable.

The 13th of May began bright and fresh. Pete struggled with the short oars all morning while I tidied up the galley and took a noon shot. A huge tanker, Brunaire, passed close by, and the little dots of crew on board waved. Scarcely had Brunaire disappeared when another great shape broke the flat rim of the horizon. This time, I noticed she was heading directly for us. The Canadian Pacific tanker T. Akasaka slowed, began to circle aft of us and drifted round towards us. I was amazed at the incredible neatness of the turn as this great ship came closer and closer. Looking at her bulk bows on was I thought an eerie experience, but her bow wave was by now a mere ripple. Oriental seamen scampered from the bows to her port side. Britannia bobbed along at the foot of the great steel wall. A rope and fender were lowered and it was obvious the captain wanted us alongside. As Pete shipped his oars and caught the line, I steered towards the ship.

'Hallo. Do you need anything?' called out an officer.

'Bread and beer?' An inspired request!

'And ice cream,' put in Pete, not believing his luck.

While we gazed up at the cluster of crewmen, a beautiful woman, an Australian I think, talked to us. Pete kept whispering 'Gawd!' to me every time the breeze lifted her loose skirt.

'You are 35 miles west of Safi,' the officer said, confirming my DR estimate.

Presently, a cardboard box with six litres of Japanese beer, a gallon of ice cream and a loaf of fresh bread came swinging down to us.

'Put it on BP's account,' quipped the captain to the officer.

'Watch out for the women in Panama,' advised one cautious old salt.

Five minutes later we pushed off with an oar and when we stood a respectable distance, the great screw began to thrash the water.

'Goodbye—good luck,' they cried. Everyone waved.

T. Akasaka wasn't half a mile away when we'd each finished the first tub of ice cream.

When we left the lee of the tanker, I found the sea had really roughened up. The sun, the ice cream and the woman had gone to Pete's head and he went to bed. My rowing session was thwarted anyway so I streamed the drogue and sat aft, making a start on the beer. As the blue rollers sped by, some creaming, others peaking, I looked over the water and thought of home. That ship would be in England in a couple of days. I wouldn't be back for two and a half years. Would I stand it?

I was just beginning to get sentimental over leaving Maggie when, true to form, the sea shook me out of my meditations. A tremendous breaker caught Britannia's full length and knocked her down. In the seething foam I blindly grabbed something to save myself going over. As our incredible world righted itself again, I found the loo rope in one hand and the bottle of beer in the other, my thumb carefully over the top. The water drained out and I inspected the deck and galley. Everything was intact and Pete hadn't got wet that time so there was no profanity up for'ard. I finished the beer and donned oilskins. Then I watched the sea build towers.

Pete

The mixture of beer, bread and ice cream gurgled uncomfortably in my stomach. I eased into the rathole for a quick write-up of my diary and a bit of shuteye. If I'd known then how long we should be confined, I would have spent longer on deck, but meeting with the T. Akasaka and seeing people brought home to me how much I miss People. I must be crazy.

Except for popping out of the rathole for a pee or lighting the lamp, we didn't emerge from the rathole for 28 hours and for the last six of those my back had been giving me hell. The pain in the small of my back had been constant. I couldn't attribute it to anything—bruises, dampness or a mixture of both. The sea was tremendous. Uneven pyramids of water catching us just as we had broken free from the preceding wave swept across the deck—always, without exception, dousing me on the port side. Derek slept dry on the starboard side. The canvas dodger took the brunt of the waves but at least a dozen found their way through to me. After a few hours the problem was ventilation. We had the choice of leaving the canvas open and getting soaked every few minutes or leaving it closed and generating our own private little waterfall with condensation dripping down. In the end we compromised—half salt shower and half fresh.

To maintain a watch in these conditions would have been too dangerous for just the odd ship that was around. Besides, my glasses would have got sprayed up and Derek couldn't be expected to do it alone. I snoozed then awoke with a jolt as Britannia righted herself. I was aware of Derek rearranging himself. I snuggled down again into my sopping sleeping bag, then the terrifying sound of a ship's engines reverberated through the hull.

At once our heads shot out into the spray—and there was an enormous freighter! In fact, it wasn't till it passed that we could see it was a freighter—it could have been the QE2 at oar's length as it tore by. I could see the welding on her sides, and the lights on board. Strangest of all to me were the fumes—a mixture of smoke, oil and food. We watched with relief as the ship grew smaller, then flopped back into our hole.

It was easy to see how we had nearly bought it. A ship steaming at full ahead in that sea! No radar man would be able to pick out a rowboat on his screen even with our big reflector on the bow blister and we didn't hear her as she approached from our leeside.

A nasty night, and after being thrown around so much we both felt very weak. In the grey dawn that followed, the weather was still foul. I struggled with my oilskins as they refused to slide on over my wet clothes. I sat and thought how scared I had been at the sound of those engines just a few yards away— and how we had laughed afterwards. As Derek tried to make our Bovril (hero's drink)—just heating some water in that sea was an achievement—I began to feel better. Already my clothes were drying on me; body heat trapped in the oilskins soon dried them. We decided that the oilskins, made by Helly Hanson of Norway of material supplied by BP's plastics division and presented to us by them, were the greatest invention since the wheel. We gave them all a Bovril toast.

There was no rowing in that sea, so we sat drinking T. Akasaka beer telling jokes, or rather Derek telling me jokes—I don't have a joke-retentive memory. The seven remaining tubs of melted ice cream came in useful for coffee.

Derek's diary

Gooey porridge and sultanas. A mug of coffee and a smoke. Truly a celebratory feast. The gale has fizzled and Old Sol clears away the grey fuzz. Pete crawls out of the pit and salutes the morn by peeing over the side without holding on. That sea has really settled down. It's still a bit uneven for my early morning sunshot but I tried and that position line looks as though it's not telling lies, around 10°41′ West. About thirty dolphins romping eastward to feed inshore. They really cheer me up. It doesn't look as though it's going to be a bad day after all.

Rowing began briskly soon after 0700 and a light breath of northerly wind was a great tonic until midday.

The noon sight gave me an encouraging latitude of 30°46′ North. 'That's 195 miles South-West of Casa in a week,' I said cheerfully. 'By tonight that will be an average of 28 miles a day.

'Not bad for a week of gales,' Pete said, desperately trying to convince himself that it wasn't. 'It's not what I thought we could do, I must admit.'

I tried to console him. 'Remember we're still technically on the coastline. Seventy-odd miles from land, we still get coastal-type seas, choppy and hard to work in.'

During the burning intensity of the early afternoon, we decided to rest. The heat was knackering. Sweat poured down my over-heated body and I was sorely tempted to take a swim. A couple of dorsal fins slicing through the calm soon put paid to that idea.

'I think I'll make some bread,' I said with enthusiasm. But by the time I had assembled all the ingredients and closed up hatches and boxes, my eagerness had already flagged. In that heat, the effort had been almost comparable to rowing.

'Anyway, there's the stuff, so mix it all together.'

Bread-making

Two mugfuls of wholemeal flour, a spoonful of sugar, salt and soda, which I chased round in the bucket with a pint of milk (powder). When the gunge was dry enough not to stick to hands, legs and deck, I lovingly fashioned a crude round 'cake' with much slapping and kneading. Then into the frying pan, hot and oiled, $7\frac{1}{2}$ minutes each side and it was cooked.

We opened a tin of apricot jam and smeared a knifeful over a thick hot slice. It was only superb. After our gorge and a rest, I noticed that the wind had returned. The sun shade was

beginning to flap in the breeze so as Pete stowed it again, I set
up the long oars ready for the next stint.

Our short wave radio was tuned in to the BBC World Service
and the long afternoon was pleasantly interrupted by the first of
a serial, 'The Assassination Bureau'. It was good to hear a decent
programme in English. Already the wail of hideous Moroccan
music had virtually put us off listening to the entire Medium
Wave band which it seemed to occupy.

Suddenly Pete shouted: 'Look at that! A bloody great
whale!'

By the time I had shipped the oar and jumped up the whale
had dived. I peered out on the port side where Pete was pointing
and waited.

'I'll get the camera,' said Pete, scrabbling forward.

A great whoosh from behind startled me. The vast grey-
marbled back curved out of the sea as I swung round yelling
'Quick! Quick!' to Pete. Just as he sprang up with the camera
the huge animal dived again. The next time he surfaced, he
must have been a good half mile from us.

I was entranced. That was the first Baleen whale I had seen—
Pete too. I thought that Pilot and Killer whales, which I'd
often seen, were big but this one was colossal. The beast, quietly
grazing and offensive to no one, had permitted me to see him.
I really felt privileged. But the pleasures of the sighting soon
faded when we got back to the oars.

I cursed at the rising fresh wind as the sea chopped up again
and the boat rolled awkwardly. Pete reluctantly cooked the
evening meal: fried 'T. Akasaka' bread, cubes of spam and
Parmesan cheese. Every time the boat rolled he sang 'We shall
overcome.' After the meal, darkness fell.

When I went aft to haul in the sea anchor next day, the rope
felt lighter. Pete had streamed it when the wind switched a little
to the West during the night. Now, as I retrieved the line, I
knew that the drogue wasn't there. I didn't say anything to
Pete who looked remorseful. I just wrote one accusing sentence
in the log book:

'Pete tied the knot.'

It was soon forgotten. For the rest of the day a tolerable
gale, whilst preventing rowing, at least slammed us along on
course. So we sat and chatted and fiddled and chewed dried
apricots and life wasn't all that bad. Until the night.

Log

17th May. Wind N.4. 0900 hrs.
Happy Birthday, Maggie. I wish I were with you to celebrate it instead of here.

After we had our meal last night—spuds boiled in seawater, cheese and marg—we lashed everything down as the gale was looking bad. Took one of the daggerboards out, strapped the lamp to the stroke seat and got a box of goodies out and a kettle of water to drink in case we were holed up for more than the night. Then we took off the oilies and crawled below, pulling down the outer spray dodger and tucking it in tight. The sea anchor was the bucket but not very effective in those seas. Almost immediately heavy seas broke over the deck. Still the lamp burned. About two hours later at the height of the gale I heard a roaring sound like an express train. The wave crashed into Britoo, slamming her over on her side and putting me on top of Pete. The hissing was horrible, gurgling water all around us. The boat began to take on a list and at 2400 hours I braved it outside to check the rudder and to see if the scuppers were doing their job. They seemed to be letting more water in than out. Still the lamp glowed in spite of sea sweeping the deck. We both slept for a few hours. Another night like that with this list and we'll be in trouble.

Pete

With one of us keeping a wave watch, we took it in turns to pump out the port hatches. Whenever a doubtful wave approached, the one pumping would slam the hatch closed and wait till the water had sluiced across the deck. A few hours before this would not have been possible but the wind and the sea had now quietened down considerably. Britannia, once again on an even keel, rode the waves much better. I suspect the seepage came through the compass well, although this wouldn't have caused the leak in the after deck hatch. The only explanation must have been faulty seals on the deck hatches, and with the deck almost permanently awash even in moderate seas, that problem would be forever with us.

The next day, after another bad night, the wind at last died. Derek took the opportunity to wash for the first time in nine days, whilst I looked on in some amusement at his hearty sluice down. I noticed his rash of little white spots had returned. My theory for their appearance was washing in salt water, so it was the best excuse for not washing I could think of. Derek's answer was the oilskins. Suffice it to say, my whiteheads were not nearly as prolific as Derek's. We spent the better part of an hour having a spot-squeezing session.

My back, which was still giving me a lot of pain, got steadily worse so I took up Derek's offer of a massage and it felt better immediately. Roll on the opening of Derek King's Massage Parlour, Soho, London W1. Another reason I thought for my sudden back pain was constipation. I hadn't been for three days so I prescribed some 'movers' (Dulcolax), but made the stupid mistake of reading the dosage after taking three tablets. I sat around waiting for the imminent explosion wishing Derek would take his smug grin off his face.

5
Extremes
19th–29th May

Derek

Not one but two explosions!

The first, Pete's longed for relief, came quickly and without warning. One minute he was sitting comfortably reading, the next—clambering aft, pulling his pants down and hanging over the gunnels. The contentment on his face! The second was a climatic explosion which gave plenty of warning and was obviously going to be an experience that neither of us would relish.

The initial sign came when I was stowing charts forward. I glanced up at the barometer as I lay on my belly. I noticed that the needle had fallen dramatically in the last two hours. I crawled out to tell Pete and we both looked up at the afternoon clouds. They appeared smooth and oily grey but with crisp, hard edges, a sure sign of wind. Already I felt the first breaths of air creeping over the grey ruffled sea. I prepared a hurried but filling meal of noodles and chicken pieces and filled a flask with hot Oxo. Pete meanwhile took the heaving line and began to lash down the deck jerries securely.

By the time we had finished our final mouthful, the breeze had reached a shudder. Wavelets poppled and the cross swell felt more noticeable. My eyes followed a solitary shearwater, a lovely brown-backed bird with white face and belly and a remarkable wingspan of at least five feet. He wheeled and soared and on occasions lazily beat his wings as he floated out of a thermal. Then, as he passed in front of the sunset, I quickly forgot about him. The most vile puce colour, a sickly sight with a hazy white disc that was the sun, made me exclaim in astonishment to Pete.

Pete scowled and said nothing. I watched the damp curls on his head quiver as a gust of wind caught them. The air seemed

to be growling a warning. For the first time the sound of the
wind actually drowned that of the sea.

Pete suggested that a sea anchor would slow the boat down
too much and she would be more vulnerable to big waves—not
being able to skid off before they broke. I suggested therefore
that while we retain the basics of a device to keep the boat
end-on to the wind, we should minimise the drag by streaming a
knotted rope or a bight instead of the drogue. So we made a
great U bend in 60 fathoms of rope and fastened both ends to
each side cleat on the gunnels. Thus we had a light steady drag
astern which gently checked Britannia's tendency to be caught
by the wind and dispatched at a tangent to our course.

While Pete obtained an assortment of goodies to chew on,
such as dried fruit, barley sugars, Kesp and vitamin tablets, I
drew one gallon of water, siphoning it into a small jerrycan, and
lashed it outside our sleeping rathole. Cigarettes, tobacco, towels
and a radio followed and we both slithered into the pit just before
total darkness fell. Oilskins inside with us, everything lashed and
secure, stomachs full with wholesome food—we were ready for
anything. Pete tuned in the Sony to Radio Luxembourg of all
things. We lay and waited.

Short swells tearing over disjointed swells that were themselves
probably an offshoot of another storm far out in the Atlantic
slapped us unmercifully. This was only the start of something
that was to be more than we were used to. Under the damp dark
shell, lamplight flickering through the ventilation hole, we
listened to the crescendo of seas colliding. Then it was as though
the world had turned upside down. For 30 hours we lay half
in unreality—half in over-reality.

Diary
How long can this boat, can we, survive this treatment?
Thrown against each other, shaken, twisted, one minute Pete
lying on me, the next me on him. It's like being enclosed in a
tunnel with a train going through. A continuous roar. Not just
outside, but above and below. Even in the very boat. Clattering of tins and gear under my head. Miles away in the stern,
the galley clangs and jangles as pots, tins, cutlery and boxes
break loose.

Then the comatose hours. Sleepy sensations of noise and
activity. The noise of the rolled up charts jumping back

and forth. And in the semi-awakeness, dark but distinguishable shapes—Pete's head, the barometer, the toothbrush pocket. Each object taking on its own fantastic shape in the gloom. The eerie flickering of the lamp distorting familiar possessions until they become alien and unrecognisable. Drowsiness clouds everything for a while and all I'm aware of is a smell. What is it? Sweat? Stale clothes? Salt? Farting? It doesn't matter— it's foul and it's familiar.

Those damn salt sores itching like hell somewhere around my crutch. I want to pee but don't possess the willpower—a burning around my groin and realisation that I must go out- side. My bladder nearly gives out but I manage the last-minute scramble out into the storm, slashing onto the wave-swept deck. At least it keeps my sleeping bag a little drier.

For the one dangerous minute, outside and unsafe, the air is pure and invigorating. A light grey dawn haze above, a dark, moving, swirling carpet around me. But the fresh air is far too buffeting to be enjoyed. It slaps me. Shakes me. Takes away any pleasure of refreshment. Reluctantly I rip up the dodger zip, Pete curses again and I wriggle back into the rathole. 'Try to sleep, man,' says Pete. 'Sleep and forget what's going on.'

Thirty hours in there was more than I could stand. When I crawled out, another day was dawning. I pulled on my oils and lurched across the deck to the sanctuary of the galley. I tried to ignore the sea. It was almost like snow. Spray hung over the white humps and I tried to whistle nonchalantly while I rooted out some food. After nearly an hour of painful fiddling, a pot of tapioca began to bubble. I shouted across the deck to Pete who stuck his head out and blinked.

'Breakfast!' I mouthed, tapping the pot with a knife.

He looked surprised and pleased and soon we were sitting side by side hungrily swallowing our milk pudding with raisins. I even had a kettle boiled so we could have tea. At least it proved we could cook and eat in the very worst weather.

Cheerfulness returned. Our pipes came out and for a while it was as though nothing was wrong. But each time a great wall of water curled and burst over our heads our false frivolity soon faded. Presently we were again hanging on for our lives. A day of mumbling inactivity passed. Another meal. Another night. Our trepidations returned with the darkness.

Pete

The lull came at last. By noon on 21st May the wind had dropped to a steady force 3, leaving the sea in a confused state which would remain so for some hours as the weather moderated. As the sun came out, so did the creatures of the deep. In the space of a couple of hours we saw four Pilot whales heading West, two 40-foot Sei whales which swooshed majestically past us with seeming indifference, and my favourites, a whole school of dolphin. With what seemed like military precision, about thirty of them leapt in a line together. I thought they must have been frightened by something.

Sorting out the galley became Derek's priority. After ten days or so of the find it, use it, chuck it back routine, the place was a shambles. Derek dug into the pile of dirty cutlery, broken jamjars and spilt coffee whilst I tried to sort out my photographic problems. The relief at removing our oilskins on deck after all this time was a fabulous tonic. To feel the cool fresh wind once again made the day. When oilskins are removed it's a sure sign that things are on the up and up. The sea had dropped to an acceptable rowable elevation, so we got to work with the rowlocks and our joints began creaking in unison with the unaccustomed prolonged exercise. I had just about got to my optimum stage of tripping out at the oars when Derek aroused me with 'Look Pete, a pineapple.'

Sure enough, bobbing up and down in the sea not ten yards away was a juicy pineapple.

'Back on your oar, Pete, forward on mine.'

I wondered if it was edible. As we approached, our pineapple turned into a turtle, floating quite still on the surface obviously waiting for a nosy fish to investigate—a quick snap and it would all be over. Unfortunately this time the turtle's hunting technique was its own downfall. The silly creature must have got bored and had gone to sleep. With one deft movement Derek bent over the side and picked him out. A baby turtle! I listened as Derek told me how to kill them.

'Slit the throat here,' he said, pointing to the stubby little neck. 'Drain the blood straight into a cup. It's very good to drink and we do need a change in diet.'

'Wouldn't get much more than half an egg cup from that little fella,' I replied.

As we filmed, examined and photographed him, I was glad that Derek's enthusiasm to put the knife in waned. His little flippers flapped in anticipation as we lowered him into the water, then he was gone, spiralling down at a rate of knots to deep safety.

Strange that with the improvement in weather we got ratty with one another. Why, I don't know. Perhaps it was the first time we had really relaxed enough to worry about the trivia that made up everyday life. But there was undeniably a feeling of animosity between us. I had no idea of the reason for it—perhaps a need to reassert ourselves? I only hoped it was not the shape of things to come.

Our day ended in absolute calm and tranquillity with the dodger open for the first time. I smoked a cigarette and wrote up my diary before going to bed.

Diary: 22nd May
The new cooker Pierre bought us in Casablanca makes all the difference—just turn the knob, flick the lighter. We got a new cooker, Pierre got Carol.

Derek announced our position. We were passing between the mainland and the island of Fuerteventura. We have done well —considering the weather we're really pleased. The question now is whether we need to land for anything. Once we have passed the Canaries there's no going back. The wind and current would be too much for us to fight against—we've learnt our lesson well in the Straits of Gibraltar. We are OK for food, more than enough; OK for water, we have 50 gallons plus Alec's still; no damage to the boat that we can't take care of ourselves so we have no real need to put in and neither of us wants to. We know the risks of putting into port and the difficulty mentally of leaving. Also, we don't have the time, if we're to cross the Atlantic before the hurricane season starts in the West Indies. As it is we'll no doubt have an unscheduled stop in the West Indies while we wait till the end of the season.

Our evening meal didn't go with the usual high spirits. Derek put the pressure cooker on, lit the gas, turned to light his pipe, and we both sat listening to the soft hiss of the flame doing its work. The spell was broken by Derek saying 'Bloody thing's gone out, where'd I put the lighter?'

I checked the connections from the bottle to the cooker and found no kinks or sharp bends to impede progress, whilst Derek checked the jet. I lifted the gas bottle, it felt light. I shook it, and apart from the rattle of the valve there was no sound of liquid gas.

'We can't be out of gas,' said Derek, 'after only 14 hours. It must have leaked.'

It was then we realised Pierre's 40 hours were in reality 14 hours. We were numb with disappointment, for we realised how important the stove was for our survival. We could eat cold food but we needed that fuel to run the water condenser.

'Now we're knackered,' said Derek.

He immediately plotted a course for a port in Spanish Sahara, but after careful thought it became obvious that an African landing was out. The only point in its favour was closeness, but it was a hideous coastline with little by way of decent ports. Taking stock of the situation, we had 28 hours in the two remaining bottles, three small cartridges of one hour each and 14 solid fuel packs given to us by the army in Gibraltar. Derek went into a depression and harangued himself for jettisoning most of the solid fuel to make room for what we believed to be more essential provisions. The main worry was water, with 50 gallons left, split between 35 gallons in the main tanks and 15 in the deck jerries. The water we had would not be enough to last the estimated 70 days to the West Indies and without fuel for the stove, we could not use Alec's salt water still which we were relying on. That was the crux. I consoled Derek about the unfortunate unloading of the fuel and as we talked, the gleam came back into his eyes as it dawned on us—we still had five gallons of paraffin, and with pen and paper we got busy with a design for a stove—the design of which did not really matter, what did was that we had something to burn.

We came to a unanimous decision. We would carry on and if we saw one of the Canaries, go in, but not banking on it. We had to cook our dried food but if necessary we could eat it raw, with careful rationing of cooking time, meaning no more toast or pancakes. Everything had to be cooked in the pressure cooker. Seven minutes spent boiling a kettle would have to be cut down or cut out. As we talked out our problems, the wind rose.

'Not much chance of making it to the Canaries now.'

Derek

While Pete was working out the amount of fuel left, I returned to another stunning problem discovered the day before. Navigation again.

'Will I ever get it right? OK, so it's been rough and not a lot of sun, but how am I misjudging the calculations to an extent of up to 60 miles error when compared to my DR?'

Spurts of foam shot over the chart board as I worked from it. The wind tried to tear the sight forms from the bulldog clip and the pages of sight reduction tables flicked over just as my eyes picked out the column required. Then my pencil broke. While I reached down for my knife another wave laughingly lifted the heavy almanac from the board and drenched my plotting sheet. Little wonder my navigation was out.

I gave up for the time being, vowing not to return until the weather settled. But I could not sit back and wait. Within an hour I was back, struggling to keep balance, shakily measuring the angle of the sun through holes in the grey cloud. Then back to the damnable calculations.

I checked and double-checked everything. And then I saw the cause. It was a ridiculously elementary mistake. The one minute of index error I was allowing for was down on the form as one degree! Of course, it all made sense then. A simple case of not keeping figures under their column headings had caused all the fret.

That was one problem solved. The fuel crisis was disturbing but we thought we could manage. To ease our minds I suggested a game of Scrabble. Pete had been given a travelling version of the game and we sat clad in our oils with spray lashing over the deck. With the letter counters safely inside our dog bowls which we clenched between our knees, we played for over an hour until rough seas (or perhaps it was the dubious words we made and lack of a dictionary to settle the argument) forced us to pack it in.

I stood up and held on to the aft grab rope. The wind thumped my face and I knew it had backed to North.

Pete's diary

Britannia really doesn't take to these short coastal seas. Every other wave flops on to the deck and makes life very uncomfortable and I'm now looking forward to the long Atlantic rollers. As we try to row, each wave seems to stop Britannia dead in her tracks. Like the sea and the weather around us I feel grey and unenergetic. The barometer pops up and down like a yo-yo every few hours, visibility is awful, no birds or life anywhere. By mid-afternoon we could just make out land on our starboard side and the picture in the Pilot confirmed it as the south coast of Fuerteventura. We had a try for it but after rowing for three hours aiming for that murky smudge we realised the futility of fighting the wind and the sea, then four particularly savage gusts made up our minds for us.

I dug out my flask of Rusty Nails (Scotch and Drambuie)—a few swigs each and I felt better. The thought of landing and the aggravation that went with it passed as Fuerteventura disappeared in the mist.

Derek's thoughtful face peered at me from the forward rathole, his pen poised over the log. He didn't look happy. In a moment of inspiration he placed his pen and wrote no more than two words. At that precise moment a wave broke right over his head. He looked up, dripping, and said nothing, just shook the water from the paper, wrote a bit more and held it up for me to see. In block capitals it read simply 'SODDIT! SHIT'.

As night fell we lit the lamp and in its friendly glow drank a tot of crème de cacao. The light from the lamp highlighted the deck and in so doing, cut out the sea in the darkness around us.

The wind hadn't dropped below a force 7 for three days so we welcomed the respite. On the morning of 25th May, the wind dropped and the weather brightened. We felt knackered after a ten-hour stint at the oars so our conversation was limited that evening to 'Bloody cold isn't it' answered by an inspired 'Bloody true'.

At night the ionosphere dropped, making it possible to pick up the familiar sounds of BBC's Late Night Extra. During the day we had to put up with what sounded to our ears like gibberish. To Spaniards, like Spanish. Every programme was interrupted with a word which was the source of a deal of amusement—*pantalones*! We spent hours trying to think of in what context

—an ad for trousers maybe—perhaps a radio equivalent of *Police Five* in which the thieves hived off with a truckload of *pantalones*. It didn't matter much, it was a diversion, although more and more we left the radio off as by some unspoken word we wanted it that way, not to be interrupted in our little life, though we still had a hankering after comfort, women, food, all that would seem in everyday life a necessity. I think we needed peace in our own minds. We had set out to row an ocean and all the familiar human sounds were making us uneasy and could tempt us to try for land.

Entering up the log

Our routine was broken on the morning of 26th May by Derek taking a wash. So fierce was he in his ablutions, to me looking on in the comfort of my sleeping bag it seemed almost like a chastisement. The purity of body and mind syndrome. Having finished his ordeal he stood up, beat his chest like a gorilla, took in a few deep breaths, turned to me and uttered these immortal words—'After a wash like that, something must happen!'

Words failed me. Looking up, I expected the clouds to open, a flash of lightning and whoosh, we should disappear in a puff of smoke.

It was cold and wet and miserable and I didn't feel like

emerging from the warmth of my sleeping bag. I watched Derek shivering as he swathed himself in sweaters.

'Do you know,' he said, 'just think, a few miles north of us figs and bananas are growing.'

My sullen reply: 'I expected to see three inches of snow and robins hopping around the deck.'

After a couple of hours rowing, we warmed up. The sun came out for a look and we stopped for a break with some excuse or other. I turned to reach for a cigarette and saw a white freighter making directly for us and slowing. Derek grabbed the water jerries and held them both high above his head. We saw the captain signal to the helmsman and at the same moment the telegraph rang.

'Great, she's going to stop!' cried Derek, jumping around excitedly.

The ship circled us, slowing, and the second time round a heaving line was thrown, missed and her momentum carried her forward a hundred yards. We took to the oars, pulling on them like maniacs, cursing at them for not reversing. (It was later explained to us that certain ships cannot stop their engines abruptly without causing severe damage due to excessive heat build-up in certain components, unless run down slowly—hence the two circuits and no reversing.)

Another heaving line and with shouts of encouragement from the crew we fended Britannia off. With the Nikon round my neck and letters clenched between my teeth, leaving Derek to finish a letter to Maggie and to sort out the water tanks, I clambered up the side of the 5,000-ton Polish Oreal Line ship, Gdynia II. Hands grabbed me as my wobbly legs gave way at the unaccustomed stillness of the ship. Grinning like an idiot I shook hands with all and sundry. The captain then asked me what we were doing out here.

'Rowing across the Atlantic,' I replied.

Shaking his head he burst out laughing.

'Do you need any provisions?' he asked.

'Well, er, just water, fresh bread, vegetables, anything you can spare—oh, and would you post these for me?'

He nodded, smiling.

'Will you take lunch with us? We have a little time.'

I couldn't believe it—it had to be a dream.

In the saloon, Captain Antoni Zarniewicz was a gracious host.

I felt a fleeting pang of guilt at the thought of Derek struggling with the water jerries as I tucked into the chicken and mushroom soup. It wasn't until I was halfway through the second course of chicken and chips that Derek appeared, his eyes boggling at the sight of the feast.

In between the captain's laughter and our scoffing, we answered his questions. He was clearly amused at these 'crazy English'. I chanced to glance up at the door which the captain and Derek had their backs to, and it was my turn to laugh. Two crew members crept by, holding bottles of wine and other goodies which could only be destined for Britannia II. We finished the meal with mixed fruit salad. The captain apologised but it would not be possible for us to shower as he had to get on or he would miss his berth in Las Palmas with his cargo of timber from Ghana.

We shook hands, took photographs of one another and the first officer handed us our position of 27°15′ North, 15°32′ West, about 60 miles South-West of Las Palmas. Derek smiled as it checked with his position. The last presents we received were for Derek a straw hat, and for me a baseball hat.

As I clambered down the ladder to Britannia, I noticed a great tarpaulin sack placed right in the middle of the deck. I had a peep inside, swung round to Derek, and just had time to tell him some of the delights within before the crew of the Gdynia lining the decks broke into a cheer.

I got quite emotional—they had been so kind when we had been at our lowest.

Derek

As soon as the Gdynia was underway and the farewells ceased, we both dived into the boxes. The Poles' generosity was overwhelming. So was the great thought to our needs that they had obviously given.

The boxes contained an Aladdin's cave of essential and useful stores. We began to sort it out, listing and stowing and eating oranges as we did so. For the first time in a long while Pete sang his song about the redoubtable Moriarty :

> 'Moriarty solves all our problems, Moriarty—Moriarty,
> Moriarty will give us fresh grub'

and I helped with the harmony. We were both deliriously happy and Pete let out a whoop of glee after I read the list of our spoils to him : 2 large smoked sausages; 4 lbs fresh butter; 2 loaves; 2 dozen eggs; 20 lbs oranges, lemons and grapefruit; 18 bottles of Sock blackcurrant drink; 3 bottles red wine; 1 dozen tins of Mirabelles; 3 cans milk; 1 can cherry jam; 1 chocolate and vanilla cake; 1 tin sweets; 2 bars chocolate; 2 packets cigarettes; 1 carton matches; 1 bottle aftershave; and beautifully thoughtful —a hot water bottle.

When all was stowed, we set to work at the oars again. This time it was with a great deal of pleasure. I actually enjoyed the work, to feel the power thrusting Britannia along was marvellous. Blue sea and skies, singing, laughing and looking forward to the evening meal.

Several ships passed us on that busy lane and I was glad that we were crossing it in daylight. A Shell tanker diverted to take a look but the massive ship kept a healthy mile away. Then, later in the afternoon, another Polish Oreal Lines vessel, the Hel, slid by. We waved and the ship's siren blared out a dozen times as the crew waved back. It felt wonderful. Life was fine out here after all.

Rowing stopped at 1800 hours as a special celebration. I stripped off and dived into the sea, feeling in a rare mood. But the water was chilly and I didn't last long. I tried to encourage Pete to join me but he said 'Not likely—I'll watch out for sharks.'

After hauling myself back on board I cooked a simple but superb meal : three fried egg sandwiches each washed down with a bottle of fruity wine, coffee, oranges, a smoke. Listening to our favourite tapes—what more could we wish for? A dreamy sunset, a satisfying mellow feeling—total happiness. I had one more desire. I wanted Maggie to share this experience with me. And the thought that she couldn't made me a little sad.

The glorious night did honour to that day. Fine and clear, the huge band of the Milky Way stretched above us and reflected dimly in the calm sea. Lamplight flooded the deck with a pleasant glow. At 0200 hours we went to bed, and for the first time the dodger flap was left open and I could see bright stars above and feel a gentle night breeze on my face. We weren't allowed, however, to be contented and have sleep. Both of us grumbled about indigestion from the mammoth glut of food.

Ships bumbling around us all night had to be kept under scrutiny and Pete woke me up once I had got off, to say he could hear heavy breathing—probably a whale.

So not surprisingly, the sun had been up for at least three hours before we crawled out next morning. Oranges and tea for starters and rather less willingly than yesterday we rowed off. In a total calm and under a furnace sky we stuck it for just a couple of hours before collapsing with the heat. Blearily, I managed to pour some salt into two bottles of Sock and we both drank them down. It didn't taste very good but there was the danger of heat fatigue if we didn't get some salt back into our systems.

Pete, being fair-skinned, was suffering more than I was. We had both worked nude during the day, which was rather foolish considering the scorching we got. But by late afternoon, when the dreadful heat was declining and we tottered out of the rathole's shade, the groggy feeling had almost gone. Earlier I had placed the thermometer on deck. It read 45° Centigrade.

Pete's rowing seat was giving him a lot of trouble. Every now and then the seat runners would catch in a dent on the slide and he would shoot off backwards uttering streams of profanity. He announced that today while it was too hot to do much, he'd replace the old slides with our spare. I thought it a good idea and said I would have a go at making a sea anchor. Fortunately the Poles had given us some of our goodies in a large canvas sail bag. It would be ideal for my purposes and during the afternoon and by lamplight that night I worked hard.

I fashioned a 'collar' out of half-inch steel cable and threaded it through the hem of the bag's opening. Then I spliced three short nylon ropes to three points on the 'collar' and linked these to a swivel eye so that a parachute affair was formed. I sewed a heavy hemp rope to the bottom of the bag and then cut a six-inch diameter hole so that the water could flow through, thus opening the bag. I tested it before cleaning up all the splicing and ragged bits and a plump Pilot fish swam into it to inspect the job.

By late evening, when the sun's last rays petalled out of the horizon, a stealthy airflow crept from the West. Increasing quickly, it steadied at a brisk breeze, and when it was time to row, I found that we had a beam sea to contend with. Hot and fatigued, we tried to row but the sea was just too choppy.

The dawn of 28th May showed a still troubled sea. The strange

westerly wind was backing its own swell. Short cross seas flinching over the undulations of two different swells cramped any
rowing style. We rowed with increasing difficulty, then abandoned
the oars. I sharpened my knife and made a scoop net, mounting
it on a boat hook pole; I had seen some tiddlers under the hull.

As Pete sat reading, occasionally peering up over his glasses to
see if there was any action, I was becoming increasingly bad-
tempered. The tiddlers were too fast for me. I spent an hour at
it and succeeded only in netting the Pilot fish—I had christened
him Albert—who swam in to see what it was. I lifted him out
and apologised for the indignity before returning him. Those
little tiddlers drove me mad. Angry at my earlier thwarted
attempt, I also spent half the evening trying to net them. Pete
grumbled every time I cursed as the net missed and I replied
rudely, 'Well, I'm trying to catch your bloody food!'

'You can eat the bastards,' he retorted. 'I won't.'

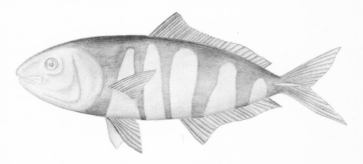

Albert the faithful Pilot fish

He buried himself in his book and I swore savagely as the
shoal darted out of range as I thrust the net down.

'Why rant and rave?' I asked myself in a moment of coolness.
'What's happening to you, man? Pull yourself together.'

Maybe I should follow Pete's lead and sit back and read or
something, take a lesson from him, relax. I tried to engross myself
in one of his paperbacks to keep my mind off the situation. But
after ten minutes I stowed the book and dragged out the sextant.
I just couldn't ignore the fact that this was a fight.

'If we're going to win we must keep working.'

I hadn't crossed a position line from the morning's sight yet. I
struggled to get my balance as the boat lurched and swore as

the image of the sun in the sextant swung in the viewfinder like a pendulum.

'You're a glutton for punishment,' said Pete, shaking his head. '24°43′ North, 16°35′ West,' I announced after completing the calculations. I was glad I took the sight and Pete was pleased too. It was important for both of us that the navigation was right. We could have said that it didn't really matter—we should still get across the ocean and find land at the other side—somewhere. If we had unlimited supplies and time—well, who would want to navigate accurately? We'd still get there. But time was not on our side. We needed to keep a tally of our mileage and our precious food and water in case we had to ration it. Navigation was vital. It didn't surprise me when Pete groaned: 'Oh not again' as I carefully checked my sight forms and plotting.

It was as well I did. Somehow, probably due to the difficult jagged horizon, I had made an error. We were nine miles further North and twenty miles further West than I had originally calculated.

'Swings and roundabouts isn't it, Pete?'

'Ah well,' he said, 'I'd prefer to see a westing than a southing.'

I agreed. 'But let's take Uffa's advice—I'm sure he was right.'

Uffa Fox had advised us to 'please head south down the African coast until you are just north of the Cape Verde Island. Otherwise you'll have John Fairfax's trouble with the variables.' And I wasn't going to question the wisdom of the grand old sailor.

As the sun sank behind piles of grey cumulus, a ship cruised towards us. Her hull was royal blue and the superstructure was cream. I could just make out her Famagusta registration and the name Elikon round her stern. One of the crew standing aft waved. I was sitting down against the galley dodger, with Pete in his usual perch. I raised an arm and gave a short wave in return. Then as the ship sped on, I sat back and continued to smoke a cigarette, thinking how friendly the sea made people.

I became aware that the throbbing engines were not fading away as the ship steered north. Indeed, they were getting louder. I jumped up.

'Hell's teeth, man, she's turned. She's coming back.'

Lights twinkled from the deck as the ship drew out of the darkness and approached.

'We could use some water and spuds if they've got any,' I said.

'And I wouldn't say no to a shower.'

'And ice cream.'

When the ship was 50 yards off our port beam it became abundantly clear that they hadn't turned round to give us showers and ice cream.

'What do you want?' shouted the captain, with more than vexation in his voice.

Relaxation in the rathole

'Nothing,' Pete yelled back.

The ship moved in front of the sunset's pink glow.

'Then why you wave?' exploded the captain.

'No,' said Pete feebly.

'You bloody fools!' screamed the captain. The ship turned about once more and left Britannia tossing in an angry wake.

'Oh no,' I croaked, slumping back. 'I only waved to someone who waved first.'

'Well, that hasn't done us much good if they report us to BP or someone,' said Pete, who was as upset as I was. 'Can you imagine them complaining that two idiots are waving down every ship that comes near them—for nothing.'

Why did nothing last? Exhilaration one moment—despair the next. Once again doubts filled my mind. Supposing all the ships that passed us complained of either our distress orange paint or our waving? There might be a long and damning list of these complaints. What would we say when we reached land? Would we be allowed to go on? My mind raced as each new guilt fantasy came to it.

By 2200 hours, the wind was gusting up to a force 6—from the West. I streamed the new sea anchor to check being blown back. I left Pete on watch. He was wrapping the canvas dodger around him as I slunk below.

6

Terror

29th May–6th June

Derek

From my row round Ireland and my experience so far across the Atlantic, I had discovered that there are two types of fear. One kind is the sudden confrontation of the unexpected; like the time a Killer whale circled around my little boat Louise. Though the brute didn't touch me, the stories of what his kind have done to small boats came to me in a very sick flash. A cold chill sinks to the pit of the stomach and a momentary numbing of the brain makes you freeze. But the involuntary spasm of trembling seems to shake the head clear, and the mind is clarified. Then it's quick-acting, and if you are lucky the danger will soon be over.

It must happen to thousands of people every day on the roads —a near-collision, a misjudgement at a corner. If you get away with it the experience is usually remembered, but not exaggerated, for it didn't last very long. Unlike the other kind of fear that begins with a whisper, then growls. It climbs to ominous heights until the mind is reeling in frightened circles. And when the roar of the danger is over, the mind retains that feeling of impending doom as it built up to its crux. You feel washed out by it. It will always haunt you—sometimes boldly on the surface—more often lurking, nagging inside your head. You don't forget it.

Such an experience happened to us one night, and by the following evening my fear, and I think Pete's, had grown to alarming proportions.

A gale was brewing, so in accordance with our usual practice we were checking all lashings and stowing the galley gear before holing up in the rathole. Pete said he reckoned we had a fair bit of water in the compass hatch but the sea was already bursting over us and it was obvious that we couldn't open it and pump out. We had to leave it.

I hadn't long got comfortable on the sleeping bag when the first of the big 'night' waves crashed aboard. They seemed terrifyingly huge when we could not see them. Probably they were no bigger than those we saw in daylight. But lying down with the sensations of noise, weight, wetness and strength all around made monsters out of them. I thought we had had worse but it seemed that there was rather more sea swilling back and forth across the deck than usual. I first became aware of the list when Pete groaned out of his sleeping bag : 'Get back on your own side— you're nearly on top of me.'

I felt below me and he was right. Lurching back to my side I tried to jam myself against the side by wedging the sleeping bag under me. I kept rolling back so I looked out. I shook Pete : 'Man, we've got a list, look at the deck.'

He poked his head out of the sodden dodger and saw for himself. The crazy angle was accentuated in the lamplight by slopping water trapped on the port side.

'You'd better lie as hard against me as you can,' I said.

He pushed against me and we both stayed like that for a few hours. It became a fearful night. Neither of us slept. Each time a wave swept in we both pushed ourselves against the pull of the list.

'It must be either the compass well leaking or the hatch cover itself,' Pete suggested.

Every time a wave slammed her from below the waterline, Britannia tottered on the edge of going over. But we jerked ourselves back to trim her as best we could. And all that night we waited for the big wave that would flick our world over and over. Dawn broke up the darkness and gave me a little confidence. It was safe to venture outside and I started shifting oars from the listing side to the other. But the sea had determined that there would be no pumping that day.

It was a day of suspense. We lay hoping for a lull of even a few minutes when the waves didn't crash in. It was not to be. By dusk the sea was even more furious. Another frightening night; every minute passing with some sharp bang or violent slap that kept the boat's side heeled over and my imaginations of disaster never flagging.

There is always a lull; a time when the vicious wind needs to rearm itself, ready for the next onslaught. Our lull came in mid-afternoon. The sea stopped breaking and flooding aboard and it was with terrific relief that we were able to get the hatch pumped dry. Britannia came up on to a safe even keel.

We'd come through another alarming situation, but never before so sickeningly long drawn out. As I sealed the leak around the compass well, I thought how far we were pushing our chances. How many had we got left?

Pete

By the evening of the 30th of May, the west wind had veered to north-east, leaving an ugly cross sea. Britannia started her cross-sea shuffle, making it impossible to work two-up. While Derek rowed, I cleaned the lamp, trimmed the wick and gave all metal parts a coat of grease. Neither of us talked much, we were still upset about the ship the previous night. Two tankers passed close by, the Esso Sara and the World Knowledge. We refused to wave or even to acknowledge their presence, though we did agree that 'World Knowledge' was an intelligent name for a ship.

I crawled to the kitchen to cook supper, pulled back the canvas, and peered in—what a mess. A pool of water complete with oil slick was sloshing around amongst the cups, plates, tins and jars.

I've heard housewives complain about their kitchens. Too small, no shelves, can't find anything! Ours was 18 inches high by four feet and tapered dramatically to one foot in the stern. This space also housed the radio, the spare rudder, the tiller, the cooker and a box of food, kept handy for bad weather. Take that space and imagine it leaping about as you cooked, your body half inside and someone throwing a bucket of water over you every 15 seconds! After much cursing and swearing I produced a stew with mashed spud just about edible. We ate quickly lest the sea should take it first.

In the lulls we took turns at the oars. I felt that every yard counted. What a way of life : cold, wet and tired. Not for the first time I asked myself what we were doing out here. At that moment Derek drew my attention to a small turtle following Britannia. He kept with us for three-quarters of an hour—he must have fallen in love, taking Britoo for the mother of all turtles. How sweet! The distraction had taken my mind off the misery and by God, I needed it too.

On 31st May and 23 days out of Casablanca our position was 24°59′ North, 16°37′ West, which made an average daily run of 30 miles according to Derek's dubious calculations. Not bad, but we found it did not do to think too far ahead. Just the thought of the Pacific Ocean being next was far too much to comprehend, comparing the meagre distance thus far covered. The thousands of miles to come was a mind-boggling thought. At times I was very keen on the idea. At others not nearly so enthusiastic—there was no apparent reason for these changes. My way of life was quite simply to live from day to day and enjoy it as it came, getting the most out of it.

The sunset turned a sickly yellow that evening, the water rough, the wind fresh. The bight streamed out, keeping us stern on to the weather. We noticed a black tanker crossing in front of the sinking sun, heading South. Silently we watched for half an hour till it dawned on us she was turning, still three or four miles away. It was the smoke that told us she had changed course. Then both port and starboard navigation lights became visible. She passed us to port, then made a U-turn and came back towards us. The shape grew and grew.

'Coming in for a closer look,' said Derek, peering into the gloom.

I was worried; the sea was treacherous, it was getting dark, and the ship must have been all of 100,000 tons. We soon heard her engines clearly above the sound of wind and sea, her flood-lights were on and we were picked out in a blaze of light. I ran forward, grabbing the torch, signalling that we were OK. Still she came. Almost against her windward side, the wind took us and we hit her amidships. Still travelling at three knots the tanker slid past as we, doing our best to fend Britannia off, bumped and scraped alongside. All I could see was a wall of black steel—strangely in this moment of fear I managed to notice stupid minute details of her hull, flakes of rust, weld lines, loading marks.

A metallic voice through a loudhailer called :

'Do you need any assistance?'

'No thank you!' we shouted at the top of our voices. We were now directly under the bridge, only a short distance from the engine room and not much further to the propeller. At that moment it dawned on me just how real a danger we were in—hearing the boom of the engines, realising that no way could she stop before we reached the screw.

'Do you need any assistance?' repeated the voice.

I don't think I had shouted so loud in my life :
'If you don't stop your engine we soon will do !'
Looking up into the glare of the lamps, I hadn't noticed how close we now were to the prop. Derek had.
'Quick, grab the oars, Pete—we're going under the stern.'
Back-paddling with all my strength, my back to the tanker, I looked at Derek facing me. Biting his lip and with one foot on the tiller, he fixed his staring eyes on a point over my shoulder— I could see in my mind's eye just what Derek could see. I could hear the great propeller and the white foaming water a few yards off. I wondered, as I looked up, where the stars had gone.

Derek

I felt sudden fear. The vast stern towered over us and we seemed to be sucked closer as the monstrous ship inexorably continued underway. Britannia's bow touched something solid and leaped back. In the feeble glow of the lamp I saw a great glinting body. In front, Pete looked tiny and ineffective as he tried to back-paddle. Engines thundered deafeningly. Explosions of green phosphorescence swirled from the unseen turning screw. The darkness below the overhang was terrifying. Violent shudders vibrated through Britannia : Pete was trying to row against the evil-sucking draw that the ship made.
'Pull harder, Pete !' I cried.
I kicked the tiller round to help him. The oars screamed in agony and protest in the rowlocks. I saw his face, a look of fear and concentration and huge effort. A gurgling noise, malicious and animal-like, came from below. Green sparkling lights sprayed out of the black sea.
'No. Not this way. Don't let us die this way.'
A new vibration, a roar. The propeller was coming nearer.
With a gut-ripping shout, Pete put his last massive push into the oars and I felt the boat instantly come free. The tanker thrust Britannia out from under her as if giving birth and launched her out into the starry night and safety. It had all taken a few seconds. It put years on us.
The bright stern lamp grew smaller as the terrible apparition disappeared into the darkness. We were both trembling uncontrollably. We stood and watched the lights melt away, for a long

time saying nothing. Then Pete spoke very softly and with the greatest conviction.

'I never want a ship alongside again.'

I echoed his words.

Pete

Sipping our cocoa we unanimously decided we had seen enough ships. I fervently hoped we should pass through this shipping lane very quickly. It was getting far too busy out here.

The next day, as a celebration feast for our survival in the dice with death, Derek cooked a special of spaghetti, hollandaise sauce and chicken. While he cooked, I tried experimenting with the daggerboards by removing them. My theory was that Britannia would not be subjected to the thump of waves hitting the extended boards, with the added advantage of the boat being drained faster, the sea being able to run unhindered through the empty slots. One thing in theory but quite another in practice. It was bad with the boards in, but without, the result was appalling. Britannia rocked wildly, just as Derek was putting the finishing touches to our meal! What a good thing Derek had a sense of humour. By way of a token I set up the Mark I kerosine stove on deck, just in front of the galley, wedged between water tanks and hatch covers. There was a pint of water in the kettle which was held to the stove with an elastic hook strap. We ate our meal, and 25 minutes later I saw a wisp of steam spiralling from the spout. I removed the kettle and held it up in triumph at Derek. I saw a black sooty face—we were both, along with the boat, covered in black oily soot. But I had been imagining the wisp of steam, for the water was only lukewarm. Mark I stove went over the side very quickly. We immediately started planning Mark II.

Diary

2nd May 1974. Silla's birthday and at breakfast we sat clutching our mugs of coffee singing 'Happy Birthday dear Silla'. We planned a special meal for her party, with a bottle of Gdynia wine for the toast, of course. As Derek sat forward writing the log, I pondered on all the things I was missing. I wished she could swop places with Derek for a day.

The flying fish put on a good show for me: shoals of them

taking to the air, changing direction in midflight and diving, all as one like a flock of starlings on a field. At midday we were both shaken by what sounded like a sonic boom—Concorde maybe? The weather is still cold—it's hard to believe we are in Lat. 24° North.

As I smoked one of my BH specials (Benson and Hedges pipe tobacco rolled into a liquorice paper) my mind once again tracked off back to London, memories of family and friends, comfort and good company, only to be interrupted by a shout from Derek—'Look! Dorados!'

Derek
I had been watching a piece of driftwood floating nearby. On it, like a miniature Kon Tiki, clung a score of brown sea lice—the sort I had seen living in oil globules. Then I noticed shapes underneath it. They grew bigger—blue and yellow fishes—our long-expected dorados had arrived. Eleven or twelve of them glided forward, swam ahead of the boat, dived, then came up astern to swim forward again. Some of them could have weighed up to 50–60 lb.

I threw over the spinner but it was snatched by a big one and ripped off before I had time to strike. As Pete hurried to get the cine camera, I dug out the speargun, loaded the lethal dart and took aim from the boat. To avoid refraction and missing, I should have been in the sea, under the water, but I thought it was too rough for that.

Pete filmed me missing for ten minutes. I fired 18 shots in all, looking forward all the time to fried fish. My range was five feet and the wretched creatures stayed five feet six inches down. Occasionally one of them turned on his side, flashing a large silver target area. But still I missed.

'You have a go,' I said to Pete in desperation.

'No way,' he said and went aft.

Again I thought: 'Why doesn't he help out? I do most of the cooking and try really hard to catch fish. He sometimes makes me think that he believes it's below him to do these things.' Troubled, selfish thinking on my part? Whatever it was, there were many times when he niggled me and I don't doubt that I must have got under his skin too. These moods never lasted long; there was always a meal which served us not only nutritionally

Wilson's Petrel

but also gave us a great morale boost. Such a meal was the Party that evening. Washed down with the wine and finishing up on Horlicks, it put both of us in a rare humour.

After much juggling with figures, I cheerfully announced that our position was 23°47′ North, 18°09′ West. Our westing was increasing and I felt it prudent not to go much further South for the next few days in order to give us a good push out into the Atlantic.

Pete staggered forward (the sea was still disconcertingly lumping) and wanted to see the good progress I had pencilled on the chart. He fingered the weaving, wavy line, looked at me and smiled, 'That's great, man!'

'See,' I said, 'it's worth all the bother of sights after all.'

As we worked at the oars, I stared at the tiny Wilson petrels fluttering and dancing over the wave crests. Dark and delicate, they seemed too fragile to be out on this hostile ocean—always on the wing, never resting but eternally searching for and picking up invisible food. I had a very pleasant surprise in the afternoon. A swallow—a good old British swallow—actually landed on the grabrope. He twittered a hallo, then soared off northwards, going home. Pete didn't believe me when I told him.

It was time to open another weekly letter from Maggie. She had made up a pack of envelopes containing letters, photographs, cards, even menus or programmes of concerts from our evenings out. Silla provided Pete with similar goodies and it really kept our sanity going. These letters from home were as important for my mind as food was for my body. Every one I read a dozen times before I stowed it again. Sweet memories of the girl I loved came to me any time I desired. It was always a poignant occasion when I opened my ditty box. I thought of all the things

The loo line

I was missing, of the girl who loved me so much that she quite unselfishly let me go and do what I thought I needed to do. Even a silly, sloppy 'Love is . . .' card meant a great deal to me.

That evening as I was eating my meal, Pete sat next to me using the loo rope. It was a good sign. I didn't mind him using the loo rope while I ate; he didn't mind me eating while he crapped. We must be getting on all right.

Pete
Silla's birthday party went well. Sipping wine after the meal I felt contented, although I did miss company, people—Derek's

company excepted of course—and all the trivia of everyday life.
I'd always wanted to find a message in a bottle, but the next best
thing was to send a message. We pressed the empty wine bottle
into service. We scrawled our position and reason for the festiv-
ities, and heaved it over the side. (The bottle was found by Frank
Sheehy at Pasture Bay, Long Island, Antigua, West Indies on
4th April 1975, some ten months after we sent it.)

Diary
Still the dreaded cross sea is with us, making one hour's rowing
seem like six. I've lost count of the times I've fallen off that
bloody seat. I feel exhausted and am covered in black grease
from the seat runners. One would think it would be a clean
life at least, at sea. Today's stint at the oars has provoked
Derek's old back, injured during his Irish voyage when hauling
in a fouled anchor. As it came free he fell back hard, hitting
his coccyx on a corner. The doctors in London told him never
to row again. Although he looks very fit and fat—I still can't
see his belly button—it could be a painful problem. Now he's
never without his personal cushion clutched in his hand as
he scrambles around the boat. Not much I can do except give
him a painkiller if it gets really bad.

I took the opportunity to film the rough sea, although I knew
from past experience that the camera has a flattening effect on
waves. Only a ninety-foot tidal wave poised over Britannia
would get the desired footage, and as our cine cameras flinched
at the very sight of water, I doubted whether the results would
present a true picture. Whilst filming Derek in a hero-type pose,
I mentioned my fears about the inability of our equipment to
capture the drama of our lives.
'Perhaps I should accidentally fall overboard, then you could
rescue me,' he immediately suggested.
That night we talked about our personal fears. I hadn't brought
the subject up, as to do so, I felt, would make my fears more
tangible and therefore more likely to be realised. But as it was
Derek who started the conversation, somehow it felt OK. Derek's
great fear was an attack by Killer whales. The danger had been
brought home by Dougal Robertson and his family when their
yacht Lucette was attacked and sunk by them in the Pacific.
My own pet fear was falling overboard to watch Britoo drifting

away faster than I could swim. Now that we had abandoned the use of sea anchors at night, my fear had become a distinct possibility. But I tried to reassure Derek and told him : 'A quick blast with the Very pistol should sort out any Killer whale.'

'Only one problem, Pete, you never see them if they attack, until it's all over, and even then you may not see them—just the feel of teeth sinking into your body.'

'Hey,' I protested, 'you're trying to frighten me—it's your fear, Derek, not mine.'

Diary: 9th June

It's not that I doubt God or the power of prayer, but with all those people praying for God to look after us, he might just do that, only his idea of looking after us and ours may be two very different things. He may decide to look after us forever, assuming I'd warrant a place upstairs. Might be nice—bet I'd get a job rowing the heavenly barge, with Derek as cox.

'Faster Bird, Big G wants to waterski.'

I find myself making deals with God, the kind I know and he knows I won't keep, like if you look after me (alive) I'll go to church every Sunday, no more dirty thoughts, words, deeds, etc, especially if they're married !

Bloody horrible gale last night, neither of us slept. Derek's back very painful and his coccyx is giving trouble still. My bum very sore and spotty. Derek says it will make a good photograph—some album.

Our second gas bottle very low, so are our spirits. Is it worth it ?

7
Doubts

7th–19th June

Derek's diary: 7th June

We have been talking about death. The horror of that tanker seems to have only just hit us. How easy death seems out here. One great rush of water wrenching us away from the boat and that's it. A ship crashing into us in the night—a shark or whale—a fall into a hard corner—losing our water. It seems almost certain that one of these things should happen, in spite of the precautions we take.

Because of the fact that there are only two of us out here, with no distraction, we must be growing 'over-aware of our situation' as Pete put it. Maybe we are bored, thinking too much. When one considers the constant threat of death in normal existence, fires, road and air crashes, maniacs with bomb or gun and so on—the antidote to all these threats is civilisation itself. The involvement and total occupation of day to day living erases the worry of when one's time is to be up. But out here, life is vastly different and death always feels present. We can't pretend to ignore it. Every great wave that thunders by could take us with it. This is a waiting game whose result will very likely be death. It's not the way of life that we fondly imagined would be our ideal. Our enthusiasm is now considerably less than when we started out. Doing battle with nature no longer grabs us so much. The odds against us are becoming alarmingly clear to see. How long can we go on?

My thoughts shot back to the time I tried to convince Maggie that I would be all right, that I knew what I was doing. Maggie told me that she knew the risks and was not going to make light of it. Throughout the voyage she would be realistic, she said—completely prepared if I died at sea. (Her faith would make this possible.)

Pete

Our conversation about death set off a chain of questions which I wrestled with as I lay wide awake in the soggy cocoon of my sleeping bag, listening to the waves tumbling outside the stale warmth of our rathole.

I had felt that a trip like this would perhaps need a special quality, a quality I hoped to find in myself? But no—there was nothing special about rowing across an ocean—once started there was no going back, and the special quality needed for such a task could be found in anyone, anywhere, who had the need to try. I wanted to pit my energy and resources against life. I realised that the real battle had been left behind—I had escaped from responsibility. Living out here, our problems were simple : forgetting to clip on a safety harness, failure to check equipment. The decisions to be made were basic : how long at the oars today —when to eat—what to eat.

But I liked it out here. It suited me in many ways. I could sit and dream and look at the sea, never tiring of it, unlike Derek who could never sit for long without leaping up and throwing out the fishing line or coiling a rope or writing for an hour. He was too restless for this kind of life, I thought.

The talk brought home to me my responsibility to loved ones left behind. What was it I had said to Derek—'the responsibility of being loved?' Was it a clever off-the-cuff statement or did I mean it? Was I just using that word love? Was it just another of those words so over-used as to lose its meaning?

My thoughts were interrupted by a sharp bang from the rudder and a shudder ran through Britannia. My first concern was that the rudder had failed. Together we pulled it up out of its slot. Still in one piece! We heaved a sigh of relief.

'No doubt there's a shark around with a nasty headache now— it couldn't have been anything else,' was Derek's conclusion.

But the shark had, in fact, damaged the rudder. The tiller had worked loose from the rudder shaft. I packed the joint between the tiller and the rudder with stainless steel strips. Tightening down the retaining nut, we resolved to inspect it frequently, for if the nut came off, the rudder would drop out and disappear forever and Britannia without steering would be impossible to manage. We had a spare, true, but if we were stupid enough to lose one, we'd as likely lose another.

Derek

Hearing Pete talk about what was in his mind took a great weight off mine. Even when I spoke I no longer noticed the bluffness of one who was superconfident and trying to kid himself. We were both being frank and entirely realistic. We had all along, of course, been fully aware of the risks and dangers involved in the task we had set ourselves. We had each been able to face the idea of death—where we ourselves were concerned. The two years of single-minded planning had hardened us to this—and, we realised now, had also hardened us *against* due consideration of the effect that our prolonged voyage and separation from our loved ones would have on us. We had each found our girls at a late stage in the preparations and the full meaning of our relationships was only now dawning on us. When you are loved, I thought, you realise the risks more.

We began to talk equally realistically about what would happen when (if) we reached land. Our debts . . .

Suddenly I noticed a shoal of dorado ghosting underneath the boat. The surface of the water was creased by the wind and I could see only the blurred outline of the fish. I thought it was time to have another try at them. They didn't seem as nervous as they had been a week before; the blue shapes were keeping close to the boat as though seeking protection. I hauled myself up by the grabropes and began to untie the fishing rod lashed under the starboard gunnel.

'You couldn't catch a cold, man,' Pete laughed cruelly—but on form so far, justifiably.

I tied a big Flectolyte spinner about two feet from a Jardine spiral weight and lowered the tackle into the water. Immediately there was a snatch and swirl of water as a dorado surged about, trying to dislodge the hook. He fought hard and fast, diving down and trying to get behind the rudder where it seemed he knew the line would snap. I let him run but reeled in a bit at a time and eventually had him at the side of the boat. 'Give me the tea towel quick' I said.

The fish was still powerful and kicking furiously. I held the line in one hand while I lifted him up by the tail, the towel providing the grip.

'There you are, Madam, couldn't be fresher.'

Pete looked pleased. 'I'll get the camera!'

I killed the fish by driving a knife through his brain. He

twitched, then lay still. As soon as he died, the turquoise blue back and silver belly turned to a dull pewter colour. I looked down at the shoal.

'Watch this,' I boasted.

I cast out the spinner again and another, smaller fish grabbed it.

'You can stuff your dried eggs for breakfast now,' I said.

I returned the smaller fish and wrapped the seven-pounder up in a rag, ready for dinner next day.

'This is really good news,' Pete murmured happily.

As the excitement died down I dug out my diary and finished the past month's general assessment, which I had begun the day before.

Diary: 9th June

We are now one month out of Casablanca plus another ten days at sea from Gibraltar. (Six days spent in Barbate and twelve days in Casa.) Our total rhumb-line mileage is 1,415 from Gibraltar to our present position of 21°45′ North, 23°30′ West. Thus the daily average mileage from Gibraltar is 34½ miles. From Casablanca to our present position we have averaged 40½ miles per day. The total distance to go (straight line) to the nearest island in the West Indies is 2,040 miles to Barbados. So we are well over a third of the way there.

Our rowing average is harder to define. Whilst some days see up to 12 hours, others see five or six and sometimes none at all. The sea state is an important factor. If the wind shifts between north and east or north-east to north a cross sea very quickly builds up and apart from finding it uncomfortable to row in these conditions it's also dangerous. A dipping oar and rolling boat could mean a broken oar or even teeth, ribs, jaw and so on. We have been thumped in all these places while trying to bravely stick it out.

In good rowable seas we use one of the 12-foot oars each and are thus able to save strength and row faster. When the seas are rougher but it is still practical to work, one of us operates a pair of nine-footers from the bow seat. This is tiring and we don't seem to last long doing this. With two up using the long oars, we stroke on average 24 per minute; in any heat or when there is an awkward chop on the water this drops to 20 s.p.m.

Speed is also difficult to estimate whilst rowing. I can only work it out from one day's position to the next allowing the number of hours spent rowing and guessing the drift. At full belt, two-up and a manageable following sea, three and a half to four knots can be no exaggeration. (Gibraltar to Tarifa proves that it can be done.) When we cannot row, the wind is usually in our favour so we are not being blown off course and the 12 miles a day current is certainly beneficial. It would no doubt be possible for us to drift across the Ocean in the trade winds belt and not row a stroke but I shudder to think of the time it would take.

Most of our equipment is proving to be first class. The Domino Gaz stove is gloriously efficient and we have no fears of leaking gas and explosions now we check all the hatches as often as possible for corroding containers, etc. There is no soot either. But we have a gas shortage and we are awaiting this penultimate cylinder to finish so that we can judge the last one even better. So far we've used seven hours of gas in 20 days and there is still a lot left.

The German storm lamp is probably the most successful piece of kit (for the money) we have. It proves its worth by being completely swamped with waves—then giving a token splutter, it goes on burning. Only severe gusts of wind extinguish it. As the casing is of corrodible metal we are taking great care to grease it regularly.

We have decided not to use the Solas II emergency radio near shipping lanes, but just for the purpose it was intended for if necessary, to make broadcasts to set folks' minds at ease. The VHF walkie-talkie was used once but without success as we tried to call up a passing ship.

Sextant errors are checked as often as I can manage but in this boat one needs a total calm for the fine adjustments. I just hope my allowances are not ridiculously out. I did make accurate adjustments in Casa, though.

Personal hygiene is pretty grim when it's too rough or cold to wash. Salt water sores are exceptional these days and layers of grime and peeling skin irritate. Generally we're rather leprous. Teeth are the only things clean round here and Pete carries it off to the extreme of brushing his gnashers five or six times a day. Blisters on hands are now a ghost of the past —great calloused pads now.

Because of the permanent damp in the rathole, the perspiring induced by Terylene sleeping bags and lack of air when the dodger is down, sleeping is still difficult. We both get fiercely aching backs and all this on top of my spinal pain (which is getting worse).

Surprisingly neither of us seems to have lost a lot of weight. We eat rather a lot of everything so it's little wonder we're not losing much. Food was one of the important items that we decided not to skimp on. But soon we'll be on the dried food. The tins from Liptons are getting dismally low and there will be quite a few weeks of totally dehydrated fodder before we land. We have half a dozen fresh lemons left. Water is holding out well thanks to the Polish ship but I can't help getting a niggling feeling that we could run out and not be able to make any from Alec's still.

One task which is time-consuming is the film we are making. Although Pete does most of it and sets up the equipment, I find it taxing to act and re-enact scenes such as fiddling with the stove until the shots are right. We film every aspect of life out here, even using the crapper line, and we hope to write off our debts by selling a full-length documentary one day. There's still plenty of film left.

Our major occupation is gazing at the sea. There is hardly any wildlife now—we haven't seen a whale or dolphins for days. Just Wilson's petrels, dancing all day over the wave tops. Sometimes one of us will point out an old oily plastic bottle or a polythene bag floating by. We both stare at it and feel that after all there is someone else in the world.

So like the boat—things can be up and down. We've just got to keep going.

I slipped the diary back into the log book and returned it to its pocket up on the rathole roof.

'What have you been writing—a novel?' asked Pete.

I told him about the assessment, looking at everything in retrospect. We had proved we were capable of working and living in a strange and hostile environment.

I turned to Pete—'Pete, d'you think we've got the freedom of the sea?'

He looked up surprised.

'Well,' he said pensively, 'the sea is free enough but we're still confined to a tiny boat. So I suppose in that respect we aren't free at all.'

Then he frowned. 'Anyway, what the hell are you thinking about now?'

'Oh forget it. Shall we break the rules and have another Horlicks?'

As we noisily sucked at the hot drink, Pete said, 'D'you know, I think we're talking an awful lot of crap nowadays.'

'Well, that's a sure sign. We do need to get off this boat.'

Pete

Derek's idea of placing one of the daggerboards across the forward dodger, allowing us to open the canvas for ventilation yet keep the sea out, worked very well. For the first time I awoke reasonably refreshed to the smell of fried fish permeating the rathole. I was up and washed in record time. The dorado was delicious; half a tail each and we saved the rest for our dinner that night.

The course was 280° True. We rowed briefly on that until Brit swung off. Derek corrected this and we rowed again but she repeated the performance, this time swinging off North. Then it occurred to me : we were using food and water stowed aft, the answer was to move some weight aft to compensate. I started with the emergency water and the kerosine lashed either side of our apparatus—five gallons each and it made an immediate difference. Brit rode higher forward, which would have the added bonus of keeping us drier at night when we moved forward. Next was the remaining canned food. This too caused an improvement when shifted. We got quite enthusiastic, looking forward to a night without getting wet or suffocated. I regarded bedtime with renewed relish, wondering whose turn it was to 'put out the cat' (last in bed).

Derek, sitting under the forward dodger, started huffing and puffing at an obstinate column of figures. The grunts were punctuated by the odd 'Damn and blast'. I tried pacifying him with a 'Don't worry—take it easy—do it tomorrow.'

He savagely tore up the plotting sheet and said angrily :

'You do the bloody navigating then.'

'Even if I could I wouldn't let it get to me like that,' I thought. Later on as we lay in the rathole listening to Radio Luxem-

bourg, Derek turned to me and said with a note of incredulity :
'I could have hit you today.'

I didn't ask why—there was no specific reason—he was fed up
and I was the only target around for his frustrations. I replied
simply :

'Good thing you didn't.'

We didn't discuss it further; just saying it was enough to dispel
the bad atmosphere that had been around all day. It was as close
as we had come to blows—ever. A punch-up out there would
not be good. Sleep came quickly.

Diary: 13th June

Finished Hesse's *Steppenwolf* at last. I found it depressed me
but made compulsive reading. I would have identified with
the Steppenwolf a few months ago. Not now. I no longer
wish to be a loner—something I'd always felt myself to be. I
don't think a man's basic temperament changes and on that
assumption I've been deluding myself for years—never mind.

On the morning of the 14th, I woke to a cry of agony from
Derek. He was standing clutching the dodger frame, his face
contorted with pain.

'My back hurts like hell.'

Time for Pete's massage parlour. After a few minutes of my
expert pummelling, he was mobile and almost free from pain.

'That's better.'

'Think nothing of it, m'boy.'

'OK, ducky,' he replied.

But we were now getting very ratty with one another. Derek,
I knew, was fed up at watching me clean my teeth, and I am
sure I had other equally obnoxious habits. At that time, however,
there was one thing especially about him that bugged me so much
I had to do something.

He had the habit of butting in on my singing. From time to
time I would hum a little ditty to myself, only to find after two
bars Derek drowning me out with his great baritone voice singing
a different tune. I thought at first I might be imagining it, so I
decided to test him.

As we sat drinking our Horlicks I began to hum very quietly.
Sure enough, in he came on the third bar.

'Do you realise what you're doing?' I asked.

'What are you talking about?'

I explained my grievance.

'Oh,' he said, 'I never realised—I must be getting the good vibes from you!'

Derek

I dressed up in oilskins as the sea was roughing up. An unsteady walk aft holding the two grabropes and swaying heavily with the roll of the boat and I flopped down next to Pete.

'Evening.'

'Evening,' I replied.

'Where are you going tonight?'

'Oh, I think I'll have a quiet Guinness at the Rose and Crown and come back to watch the Big Match on telly.'

These fantasies were important to us. We didn't feel so isolated from the world.

'What are you doing?' I asked.

'I was thinking,' said Pete, screwing up his eyes in concentration, 'of going round to Keith and Tina's for supper. They said I could pop in later on. Tina said it's nothing special. Soup with fresh bread, grilled pork chops with barbecue sauce and fried spuds. A few drinks afterwards.'

If rowing ever was pleasurable, our efforts the next morning certainly cheered us up. An angry night, weatherwise, gave way to a peaceful dawn and although an awkward lingering swell often tipped Britannia onto her beam ends, we enjoyed the stint at the oars. A morning sunshot gave a position line a few miles either side of the 27th Meridian and the thought of good progress prompted us to burst into song as we stroked out a rhythm on the long oars.

By midday the sea had become a vast flashing molten sheet. We had begun working naked but hats, sunglasses and strips of towelling over our privates had been donned for protection. We sweltered and winced in the heat, both praying for a breath of wind to cool us. My eyes ached from the glinting reflections. It reminded me of being in a discothèque when the mind-reeling stroboscopic lights are switched on.

'Come on, man—this is daft,' I said to Pete. 'Pack it up.'

Through his dark glasses I could see his eyes screwed up, with pinpricks of moisture around them.

He wearily stowed his oar and said: 'You know—I think a pair of camels would be more suitable for this job than us.'

When we stopped, Pete went aft to get our much talked about bite to eat: stale bread and lemon curd. It was delicious. I vowed never to malign a sandwich lunch at home again.

During our rest, I looked across the water and saw cats' paws moving slowly towards us. At last. Presently a breath of wind on my face began to dry the sweat and not many minutes later, a cool breeze from the North streamed over us. The wind blew our humour back and it wasn't long before we were laughing again. As cumulus cloud began to take shape and move across the sun like huge cauliflowers in a greengrocer's rack, I took a good sunshot before the clouds managed to obscure him.

Pete timed the shot as usual and when I gathered all my papers and books around me I asked him for the time, which he usually kept in his head until I had finished reading the angle on the sextant.

'Sixteen thirty-eight and eighteen seconds,' he said.

I worked out the sight and found the final intercept to be way out. I checked again—and again.

'Hell's bells, man, according to this we've done about 780 miles in 24 hours!'

I could not see the mistake in my calculations. For an hour I laboriously plodded through every move. Then I looked at my watch. It said 1650.

'You twot,' I said. 'It wasn't 1600 hours. It was 1500!'

'Oh, sorry,' he said gloomily.

Pete had the only working chronometer and I relied on it more than my Submariner, so consequently I didn't even glance at mine.

I needled him. 'No wonder we've been getting some incredible fixes.'

'OK, man—I'm sorry.' He was getting angry now.

I was still fuming when I drew a line down longitude 40° West on the chart. Then vindictively, I labelled it 'The Bird Line'.

'When we cross that next month I'll talk to you again.'

But this silliness soon passed, and around meal time I said 'Sorry' and Pete 'Forget it.'

Sunsets lately had been either heavily cloudy or slightly hazy affairs. That evening, elegant rows of small cumulus and high mares' tails gave the sky real perspective and I didn't feel so remote or small against it. Watching the last slanting sunrays fade, we settled aft for our evening smoke and chat. The best part of the day. We talked about our eventual return home. Pete tried to work out what he would do for a living when he got back—probably go back to photography. I envisaged a marriage within two months of my return; I told him where we would be married and how many would come. We must have sounded like a couple of old women plotting weddings!

Log: 16th June
1245 hrs. Up early with a delightful calm. I cooked breakfast while Pete snored on. It rained a little and we caught enough for a cup of tea each. As it was so quiet we decided to make hay etc and do the nasty job of cleaning the hull below water. We donned wetsuits and armed with masks, snorkels and scrubbing brushes, jumped in, after trailing a few lines aft. An incredible blue below.

I had a shock when I saw the thriving gooseneck barnacle colony. They were predominant around the daggerboards and rudder but fairly evenly spread from bow to stern. They apparently seemed to be feeding on the antifoul! We knew that we had a few around the waterline and thought maybe that deeper below where the light is dimmer they wouldn't be so prolific. However, the hull is not deep and there aren't many shadows so they lived happily. Until we got busy.

Pete scratched at the surface colony as he detested staying under, while I flattened myself against the hull or hooked my legs around the daggerboards and scrubbed like hell. They were very tough and I think the whole job must have taken an hour. In the end I was getting so tired through constant surfacing for air that I decided to start hyperventilating so I could stay under for longer. Not a wise thing to do but it got the job done more quickly. Pete filmed a little of the operation below, then went back on board to watch for sharks. Albert the Pilot fish nuzzled me and peered lovingly into my mask as though he really fancied me. Just before I came out I took a few shots with the Nikkor of Britannia at a distance. While

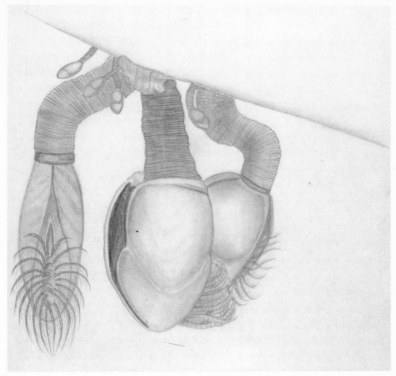

Gooseneck barnacles on Britannia's hull

I coughed up a pint of seawater, Pete made me an Ovaltine and thus ended a highly industrious morning.

1900 hrs. An even more industrious afternoon followed. We cleared the four deck hatches and the two galley hatches; cleaning off mildew, pumping out water, drying and repacking all the contents. No rowing as we were both knackered. While I took a few minutes off to fish (I caught four) we saw an incredible sight. There was a crash and as we looked up thirty or forty dorado in hunting blue were chasing a shoal of flying fish. The dorados leapt when the flyers took off and some caught them in mid-air. All the hunters must have been over 10 lb, with some up to 50 lb. They kept up the pursuit for a few minutes then vanished. But the flyers were still in a panic, soaring and skittering on and on. Most exciting to watch.

After I cleaned one of the fish for brekky tomorrow I cooked a meal and alas, the gas came to an end. We now have one more bottle left which will give us 12 hours like the last one did. At 20 minutes a day we'll have 36 days, plus two little cans giving $1\frac{1}{2}$ hours each. Then it's candles, Meta tablets and our paraffin tin can stove. We should be OK to the West Indies, though food may begin to get monotonous. We're very low on milk powder—but that's really about all. Found 3 lb of flour as a bonus in one of the hatches earlier. Everything else is sufficient to last us six weeks, when I calculate a landfall. We may also meet a ship.

A solitary Arctic tern visited today for a wee while. Nice to see him especially as he tried to come aboard.

Pete

'Look,' said Derek, 'a fin.' Following his pointed finger towards the setting sun, I saw them—a school of Pilot whales heading directly for us. Suddenly they were all round us. About twenty-five of them. We watched in fascination as they playfully charged, missing us by inches, slapping their tails, snorting and generally having a good time. Engrossed in this spectacle, we soon realised they were cleaning up our larder of dorado! The smell of fishy breath wafted over us as they ate their way closer. Some came within an arm's length, giving us a good view of a browny black sleek skin. One had the audacity to dive underneath us looking for dorado hiding between Brit's daggerboards. With a final flap of their tails they moved slowly South. I thought the tail-flapping sounded uncannily like the smacking of lips after a good meal. The big bull with a huge blunt head and mischievous black eyes patrolled the perimeter of the school —like a teacher counting his pupils. When we looked over the side for our lunch, all we had left was a couple of Pilot fish, headed by the ever faithful Albert.

The visit from the whales raised my spirits for a bit, but not Derek's—he had been in a grumpy mood. He made pointed remarks like 'I did most of the scrubbing this morning—two bloody hours' after an ill-timed remark by me about cooking. To bury the hatchet we played a tape—Elgar's *Enigma Variations*, and afterwards in the beautiful sunset heightened by the

Fire risk—open paraffin stove on deck

tiny pink clouds, the sound of Beethoven's Ninth wafted out to
the empty seascape.

The evening was marred somewhat by the cassette player
breaking down and the knowledge that the second gas cylinder
had given out. This left us with one cylinder plus a small $1\frac{1}{2}$-
hour canister. And five gallons of kerosine.

The 17th of June was quiet and warm. There were a few
rain showers but most of them missed us and having lost out on
the showers, we made up with a swim. I devised an improved
version of the tin can stove—at least a simplified one : a lighted
tea towel dropped into a can of kerosine. Very sooty but it
seemed to work. I even made some bread. One problem we
never over-came was that the wick, having burnt, went out. For
every ten minutes of cooking time we had to replace the wick.
Still, it was heat to cook with, even if it was a little dangerous.
In effect we were cooking on an open fire on an open deck—
just like the Vikings! The fire extinguisher was kept very handy.

As the days passed, the hot weather became more and more
of a problem. By 1100 hours it was too hot to row. We resolved
to get up before dawn and row, missing the heat of the day. I
made good use of the time by filming every aspect of life on
board.

An excited Derek hopping about was a sight to bring a smile
to anyone with a semblance of a sense of humour.

'Look! Look! It's a Red-billed Tropic Bird, the first I've seen
—oh, I wish Maggie could see it.'

Maggie see it!—I wished I could see it. Looking up all I
could see was a speck in the blue sky. But it came closer and
Derek's enthusiasm was justified—a pretty bird with its two
long streamers and pure white plumage. No sooner had I finished
bird-watching, my eyes temporarily blinded from the sky, my
neck with what felt like a permanent crick in it, when I felt
Derek nudge me. He nodded towards a small green crab scuttling
across the deck in the direction of the liferaft.

'Does he know something we don't?' he asked darkly.

The sea built up slowly. We kept working at the oars. Sunny
and warm, the sea was blue laced with white, like Wedgwood
porcelain. Cheese from the Army compo rations (acquired in
Gib) with bread and chutney was a delicious reminder of a
ploughman's lunch at the local—it was beautiful. Only one thing
missing—beer!

Diary

Reggie Bosanquet on ITN said that we were the best prepared expedition of its kind ever undertaken. He should see Derek now, ripping open the emergency pack. He's stowed a large tin of Kesp in it. We're finding it increasingly difficult to lay our hands on food requiring a short cooking time.

As I finished writing, the first of the evening waves crashed across the deck. Quickly putting my precious diary in a Tupperware box, I helped Derek prepare for the inevitable bashing we were about to receive. Daggerboard out, bight streamed astern. Having lit the lamp and tied everything movable down, we settled to our cup of Horlicks before turning in. I took one sip of my favourite drink and a wave sneaked up from behind and dolloped over me. I started laughing.

'What's so funny?' asked Derek.

'It's just occurred to me. When people ask what it's like out here, we can say it's like this—imagine your mum coming up to you in the evening as you watch the telly.

' "Here you are, dearie, a nice cup of tea." So saying, she hands over the welcome cuppa. As you sip, someone tips a bucket of water down your neck.'

We decided that ocean rowing was a crazy way to live.

8

Struggle

20th June–5th July

Pete's diary: 20th June
Happy birthday, Brother Tony—yukky weather for it. We sit around—bored, can't read, can't write.

Contrary to popular belief, one doesn't fight fear—one simply acclimatises oneself to it. It would be physically impossible to be frightened all the time for say two months—so if we had lasted the first few weeks of a voyage such as this, even if those two weeks had been really frightening, nothing after that could be as bad. We had made it. But I saw the 20th of June marking a turning-point in our relationship. It seemed the difference in our warty characters had never been so painfully apparent. Having learnt that patience was worthwhile on an ocean-going rowboat, I would—although having never been blessed with much patience —apply this principle by accepting whatever came our way regarding contrary weather and waiting calmly for rowable conditions. But not so Derek.

His obvious lack of patience had stood us in good stead in getting the trip accepted and moving, and it was his energy that fired the necessary rockets at the appropriate people to realise this ambition. His very impatience had been instrumental in our achievements thus far. And I didn't underrate its importance for a lot of the time at sea. But that day I saw Derek struggling with himself to keep doing something. As I sat in the stern smoking, I watched as he scribbled furiously in his diary; ran out of things to say and snapped it shut; stood and checked that the oars were secure; tightened the dodger straps; checked the water containers and realigned the compass grid. Straightening up, he peered at the sun, satisfying himself all was correct. He could not keep still for a moment. He had a per-

manent scowl on his face. It always happened—depressive
rattiness always occurred when climatic conditions made rowing
impossible. Derek's continual fidgeting annoyed me intensely,
whilst my apparent lazy sit-about attitude annoyed him.

We both became very petty-minded. We were at times totally
unaware of just how transparent we were to each other. On one
occasion, at meal-time, Derek used the very last dollop of mustard. Now Derek had a passion for mustard : he used enough
to blow the mouth off any normal man. I liked mustard well
enough but my intake was a fraction of his consumption. I
exploded.

'You used the last of the sodding mustard you greedy swine!'

'Sorry, mate, I didn't think you liked it.'

'You lying bugger. It's because of your greed that it's run
out already!'

'OK, OK. I've said I'm sorry haven't I—here.'

He scooped a knifeful onto my plate. An hour later we
laughed about it.

We had been told by some pundits that the Atlantic would
be a 'milk run'. For forty hours the gale blew. We were exhausted
by the constant buffeting and Britannia's awful rolling. We felt
no fear, we were just thoroughly fed up. We tried playing
Yahtzee. This game's played with five dice, requires no skill
but is still an entertaining game. As we played, the chances of
making a run of wins diminished and neither of us could gain
a decisive victory. As with any game of chance, I grew bored
with it.

We managed an evening meal, although lunch was scrapped
—not because of the weather, more for saving fuel, though we
couldn't entirely control our pangs of hunger at midday and
cracked open a can of Percy Dalton's Famous Peanuts and had
a swig of Biostrath each.

The waves became extra-malicious, singling me out as the
chief object of their overt sense of humour. I know what the
man meant when he said : 'I have a great affinity with trees—
dogs keep peeing on my leg!'

True, I did not sit on the weather side. I had a laugh at
Derek's expense when a wave slammed into the blister and down
my neck. Derek chuckled briefly until that same wave carried
on under Brit, leaving a sharp trough which she slid into. Not
being able to climb out of the steep side in time, the top of the

trough poured over the gunnel, soaking **Derek**'s backside. That moment christened these waves 'bum soakers'.

Late on the night of the 21st, the sea began to lump irregularly.

'What the hell?' began Derek when the wind swooped out of the North. As we sat in our forward positions the sea thumped the stern, punching poor old Brit first North, then South. Every ten minutes we went through this ridiculous cycle. We tried a sea anchor and a bight but to no avail. So we just ignored it and hoped for a ceasefire by morning.

Then the dreaded routine of the race for bed against the deck-sweepers. We decided it was Derek's turn to go in first. He removed his oliskins and handed them to me. I shoved them in the galley and waited for Derek to rush the 15 feet to the rathole. Once inside, he sorted out the sleeping bags and arranged the assorted clothing so I could dive straight into the damp haven without stopping—minimising my chances of getting wet and of the rathole getting swamped. All was successfully negotiated that night.

We breakfasted on egg and apricot jam. This unlikely combination was the most successful yet. Cheered, we settled for another inactive day, the wind having risen to a force 7. Britannia had ceased yawing and we were holding stern on to the waves in relative comfort, at times even surfing down the waves.

On the morning of the 23rd, the wind veered to the East and with it the inevitable cross sea. I decided that such seas, though awkward, should be ignored, so I went forward with the intention of repairing the ciné camera, which of late had been running only six seconds per wind, instead of the designated 15. Leaving Derek quietly reading Alan Villier's *Cruise of the Conrad*, I picked my way to the rathole. Kneeling down poking head and shoulders inside, I undid the four toggles securing the camera hatch. Just as I lifted the cover, I heard Derek shout :

'Look out!'

Then all I could see was blue and white. Then a roaring noise. I remember thinking what a strange position Brit was in.

Derek

I don't know what made me look up. My ears had become so

attuned to the familiar roaring of the breakers that I seldom bothered to keep a watch out for deck-sweepers. But something strange happened. It seemed to me that there were a couple of seconds of uncanny silence. I jerked round and saw, simply, a huge blue mountain with snow on top. At the same time as Britannia climbed the almost sheer slope, I yelled :

'Look out, Pete !'

Then the monstrous force broke as Britannia reached its summit. Blinding surf catapulted me out, over the grabrope. My hand gripped the line and I held on for my life while the terrible surge swept over me. I lay streamed out horizontally in the surf. The wave thundered on, leaving our world on her side. In the seething froth that lingered in the wake of the wave I saw a water pump float away, and a couple of boxes, a pencil and the tube of sweeteners bobbing around me. I looked into the boat. The deck jerries although lashed had been twisted loose and I saw Pete struggling to get out of the rathole and trapeze out to right the boat. I hauled myself in and immediately pulled out the daggerboards and opened the scuppers so that the water could drain out.

'What happened ?' asked a bewildered Pete.

'That bastard,' I said, pointing to the diminishing wall of white water now over a hundred and fifty yards away.

Pete scrambled back in to whip cameras and other valuables out of the flooded hatch that he had opened before the wave struck. I replaced the deck jerries and the gas bottle that had broken loose and then turned my attention to the galley. It was a shambles. Most of the water had drained off the deck and through the rudder slot in the galley and I could inspect the mess. Everything was out of place and had moved to new and unusual positions. The kettle was standing in the frying pan as though that was its normal place. The salt pot was under my cushion and Pete's book which I had been reading had been swept under the radio, stowed right in the apex of the stern.

Behind the stove back, standing fairly high, was a tall beaker. It had been empty when I had wedged it in, now it was full of seawater. It seemed that the whole galley had taken the brunt of the wave. I thanked God we hadn't been cooking at the time.

'It must have been The Wave,' I said, 'you know, the one in 300,000, supposed to be three times the height of the running sea. Law of averages and all that.'

'That must have made it over 45 feet,' said Pete, squinting at the wave tops.

Pete had stripped all his soggy clothes off and encouraged me to do the same.

'It's not cold, man. Really fresh.'

Presently we both stood there, holding the grabrope. We looked like a couple of new born babies, with beards. We were so relieved about getting over another potential disaster that we were soon singing 'The Engineer's Daughter' and whooping defiance at the tumbling waves.

'You'll never get us,' Pete shouted at the surf and gave the two-fingered salute.

'I'm going to have a wash,' he said suddenly. 'The first one in seven weeks.'

'What, with soap?'

He put on his Carol imitation and said : 'Mmmh! Special soap for my soft parts!' (based on a clanger Carol had dropped during a radio interview).

I followed suit and discovered that it was also my first wash with soap for a month. We sluiced each other down with buckets of water and hung about waiting to be rinsed by a little rain squall coming our way. It missed us by a hundred yards.

Once the sun had been covered by shapeless banks of grey cloud, we began to feel the cold and gradually cocooned ourselves in our sweaters and oilskins. We yarned and smoked till 0300 hours the next morning. Pete had a fund of extraordinary funny stories from the days when he had been a ship's photographer.

At last we decided to pack it in. Pete moved forward and fumbled with the toothpaste. Then he crawled into the rathole and I heard the Sony click on and muffled music float out.

'That's a Caribbean station,' Pete suddenly cried, hardly believing his ears.

I ran forward and swung myself in. Sure enough—a beautiful steel band! Heavy atmospherics crackled and partly obscured the broadcast. But we cheered. We thumped each other's arms for joy.

'Nearly there, man.' I said.

'Coconuts! Women! Beer!' he listed.

'Fried egg sandwiches,' I added.

The muted music finished and the next record was a calypso. We listened entranced, feeling that the 1,500 miles between us and the source was so much less now. At the end of the record a foggy voice announced 'This is Radio Antilles' before the signal faded away and the squeaks and groans of radio language took over. Pete pushed the button down and tucked the Sony under his pillow of shirts. Sleep came quickly.

I woke up at first light. Britannia was hideously corkscrewing around and Pete and I were rolling into each other as we both lay on our sides. I crawled out and surveyed the sea.

'Not breaking, just peaking, but still nasty.'

I looked down and saw a dozen small dorado swimming on the starboard side. I thought it strange that they always seemed to prefer that side. It could have been something to do with the sun and shadows. I untied the rod.

Lowering the tackle, I braced myself to strike. I saw a fish following the lure as I slowly moved it through the water. I saw him take it but it was a half-hearted attempt and as I struck I knew he wasn't hooked well. He fought to the side of the boat and just as I bent down to lift him, the lure tugged out and the fish had his freedom. Undeterred, I tried again but the same thing happened. And again and again. Four fish lost at the boat's side. I was angry but not because of my hurt fisherman's pride. It was quite evident that the fish were becoming hook-shy already. Once one fish had been pricked by the hook, his mates were very soon informed that danger was afoot. They were obviously aware by now that the little silver fish did not mean food after all.

Instead of fish for breakfast, I rehydrated some apple flakes with warm water and divided the mush up into the two dog bowls.

The wind was flukey and light, though the sea was lumping in heavily from the East. We worked naked until the sun, just before local noon, roasted us. Then it was shirts and shorts until the stint in the cooler afternoon.

At dusk Pete drew the daily gallon of water from the tanks below into a yellow jerrycan. He sniffed the top of the can and peered down the hole.

'Man! Have you seen this?' He looked shocked.

Pete

Derek staggered up to me and scowled into the aperture. Filaments of black slime hung suspended in the water. A growth of black fungus—how? We had sterilised the tanks with Milton in Gibraltar; we had topped up with heavily chlorinated water in Casablanca. It seemed unlikely that the growth could have originated in either. Perhaps the heat on the deck? Though the gap between the deck and tank top was filled with insulation—surely this would keep the tanks cool? A filter of nylon tights (inherited from Carol) removed most of it. I didn't think it harmful until I noticed Derek had been making sudden and frequent use of the loo rope.

'I've got the squitters!' he said, gripping the rope and concentrating. I consulted my medical list, running my fingers down the columns and stopping just under the heading 'Movers'.

'Oh no—it's stoppers you want.'

I handed Derek two tablets, checking as I did so that I had given him the right ones.

'Thanks, mate—they should hold things up for a bit,' he mumbled as he stuffed them into his mouth.

We were both having trouble sleeping, Derek especially, owing to the aggravating pain in his back, but through it all we kept our good humour. As there was no sign of dorado around Brit, Derek took the opportunity to cultivate a relationship with Albert, our sole remaining Pilot fish.

More time was spent on navigation. Derek took many shots and worked out a collection of position lines. Looking over his shoulder I saw the weaving line of our progress. Only pencil lines on paper marked the passing of two and a half thousand miles from Casablanca. Following this snaky route with my eye, I saw our present position of 19°39′ North, 34°35′ West. We had 1,400 miles to go to reach Barbados. Our enthusiasm sparked up when instead of counting miles, we began to count days at sea. At 35 miles a day we'd have 40 days left. Derek tried working out our speed by dropping a piece of paper overboard forward. It took six seconds to travel the 15 feet of deck. We worked out how many 15-feets to a mile, multiplying the answer by six seconds, converting from seconds into hours—answer : two and a half knots. I was a little doubtful of the mathematics and this procedure meant we had to row to a more than average speed before Derek would rush aft and I dropped the paper in, stopping the clock when it reached Derek.

Whilst I was busy inventing (a sieve attachment for an electric mixer, a sure money-maker when I got home), Derek got on with a more practical task—cleaning the gooseneck barnacles from the hull. As I sat engrossed in my thoughts, I was aware of the industry overboard. From time to time I heard Derek surface and with much huffing and puffing, take in air for his next descent. This pleasant routine was shattered by a yell. The boat heeled as he clambered back in, dripping water over the diagram of my invention. He pointed at the water :

'Look ! A bloody Portuguese Man-of-War.'

This deadly creature floated gracefully through the spot where Derek had been industriously working a few moments before.

A bright full moon that night made the ritual of lamp-lighting unnecessary. After debating whether not lighting the lamp constituted one turn or not, I was startled to see what appeared to be a bat circling the boat. Derek said it was some sort of Petrel. It flew very fast on slender wings, reminding me of bats flickering about on warm summer evenings at home. Some sailors say that a bird flying around at night is the soul of a shipmate lost at sea. I found it difficult to believe that, with my shipmate belching over his Horlicks as he sat beside me.

The sea, having settled, lulled us into a false sense of security which was shattered by one nasty little wave which sprang from nowhere. It walloped our highly regarded dodger, snapping a weld on the steel frame. We sat amazed—this magnificent dodger, having stood up to thousands of waves ten times the size, had succumbed to a piddling little sweeper. As if in ashamed embarrassment, the structure collapsed in a heap on the deck. We looked at one another and laughed out loud.

A lazy day, the 28th. Derek tried to be energetic. I heard him crawl out of bed at 0800. I heard his urine splashing noisily into the bucket, then an escape of wind. I heard the sound of the reel, a few minutes' silence, a grunt of disgust, then the clatter as the rod was stowed, and he was back in bed. We snored on till 1000, and finally got to work at the oars after a fair breakfast of apple and coffee by 1100.

I could put it off no longer. I had resisted Derek's efforts to use the radio, saying it was too rough, not enough range—anything but use it. The radio is a small boat sailor's nightmare.

With a boat like Brit it was worse. It was stowed in the galley and took half an hour to drag out and set up. The 20-foot whip aerial did just as its name suggested. So well did it whip, it snapped at the base before we had started transmitting. Derek held the remains as I cranked the handle and I tried for one hour, except for time spent waiting for the distress silences to end, and got nothing. I repeated our call sign 'Two Delta Golf Foxtrot' again and again. Our only reason for going through this performance was the knowledge that our folks had not heard of us since we'd met the Gdynia five weeks previously. Derek had made the mistake of promising to try for radio contact every 12 days and as most people assumed trying meant certain contact, they would be worried at our silence. I had told my family not to expect any radio communications at all. Families tend to think using a radio at sea is like using a telephone.

Having reached the 36th Meridian, we found that trying to steer a south-westerly course was near-impossible. The light east wind on our quarter did not have the power to hold us as we slept peacefully.

The BBC time check had become an institution with us. With one of us conducting, we hummed the intro theme as it played. My Rolex was doing remarkably well even for a chronometer, losing just six seconds in 12 days.

With the good weather came my desire for an all-over tan. However, after a couple of hours, much to my chagrin and to Derek's amusement, I had burnt my privates—so badly that it looked as though it had come from a can manufactured in Frankfurt. The next day I decided to persevere with my aim and very cunningly I converted a sleeve from an obsolete sweater. With great pride I presented Derek with my fait accompli. He collapsed in a heap, holding his stomach and fighting for breath.

'Take it away,' he said between raucous bellows. 'You'll kill me, man.'

Derek cursed his kindness in returning so many dorado to the sea.

'If we collect another shoal I'll catch as many of the buggers as I can before they get wise to the hook. Then we'll salt 'em—we'll have a real lunch.'

'Right on,' I said with as much enthusiasm as I could muster.

We carried on with our breakfast of 'dogsbody' (old Windjammer fare—rice and raisins). We spent most of the day debating what to have for supper, until Derek, out of boredom, went for a swim. I went forward to write a letter home. Trying to concentrate on my letter, I heard Derek ask for a brush. Without being aware of it I absently threw one to him and carried on only faintly aware of the sound of scraping under the hull and Derek remarking : 'Barnacles have grown a lot since last time.' It was a statement I didn't need to answer. I was engrossed in the problem of finding something interesting to write.

'SHARK !' By the time Derek's voice had died I had reached the end of the deck where the footloops hung over the side. I stood waiting for him to make those last five yards, willing him on. I had never seen anyone swim so fast, and a second after he touched the side he was lying panting on the deck.

He gasped : 'Came towards me from below—spiralling up.'

I was surprised at a shark being near us. After all, the last we had seen had been off the African coast. Derek was still getting his breath back. I noticed his stomach was badly scratched where I had heaved him over the gunnel. Then he began to tremble.

'Probably shock,' I said.

'How about a cuppa ?'

After getting some clothes on and a cup of tea inside him, Derek seemed OK. He thought that the muck and disturbances caused by scraping the hull had attracted the beast. Derek had been playing a game of dare with himself—seeing how far he could stray from Britannia, and must have attracted the shark by his movements. Lesson one—don't play tag with sharks.

Derek

A fitful night's sleep was just the tonic we needed. Next morning we fairly bounded out of the rathole eager to begin a new day. The sea was as flat as a sheet of glass, the ubiquitous swell barely noticeable.

After breakfasting on dried egg and syrup, we set about rowing and pulled away briskly. After an hour the stroke was definitely flagging. Another hour passed and it was mutually agreed—too damned hot !

Pete rigged the awning and both of us collapsed underneath, fanning ourselves with a hat or a book. While I enjoyed my second swim of the morning, Pete leaned over the gunnel and suggested that we try out a solar still while the sea was so

Topping up a solar still with seawater

exceptionally calm. As I climbed back on board, he was already scrabbling inside a hatch for the kit. We took turns blowing up the large plastic bubble and when it was rigid Pete tied the lanyard to a rowlock so that the ball floated alongside. The weighted collecting bag sank underneath it, taking the six-foot coil of polythene tubing so that the condensation could cool into drops of water well below the surface. Pete poured the first few cupfuls of seawater into the funnel at the top and all we needed to do then was to keep the reservoir topped up throughout the day.

I had mixed feelings about the amazing mirror calm which lasted for two days. While it was a change from being thumped about and soaked and rocked until we were nearly driven crazy, the calm made me feel most uneasy. I had visions of it being the quiet, eerie lull before a storm. The stifling heat was ghastly too. Rowing early in the mornings and late evenings was all we could manage. Our tempers flared for no apparent reason and even small talk became an intolerable strain as I attempted to suppress snide comments which were desperately trying to find voice. Even the flying fish dared not take off, for risk of being grilled in mid-air.

The oppressive heat brought out the worst in me. While I

baked underneath the awning, grumbling and swearing, Pete would tell me to relax and wait it out. We would start moving again soon. It couldn't stay like this for long.

But the calm had one compensation. We were able to see animals and fish that would normally be obscured by waves and foam. Right underneath the boat hundreds of small fish gathered, seemingly for protection from the sun. These fish were bream-shaped, no more than two inches long and sporting a head-to-tail dorsal fin. They were golden yellow, spotted with black. Pete pointed out to me that when one of them seized a morsel of food (grains of rice or breadcrumbs that we dropped in), he would pass it to another as if to say : 'Here ! What d'you make of this ?' And that one would present the scrap to another, and so on. It was usually the fifth or sixth fish that eventually swallowed it without proffering the food to anyone else.

Another interesting group was a party of eight mackerel-like fish, about six inches long. The strange thing about these was that the troop had a leader. He (or she) was always out in front and the others followed his (her) every move, keeping a respectful distance from him (her).

I was sure Albert the Pilot fish was pleased that we weren't making fast progress. He was portly-built, and in his silver and purple stripes he reminded me of a businessman running as fast as he could for the morning train. Whenever we were rowing well, poor old Albert was belting along, just keeping up with the stern. Now he was in his element, and with stately ease patrolled his domain under the hull putting all the newcomers in their place with no imminent fear of another breathless run.

We didn't have to peer downwards only to see wildlife. Thousands of dolphins, as far as the eye could see, splashed and leapt out of the flat water. As it was so calm, visibility was remarkable.

Perhaps the most fascinating thing we saw was early one morning when we were getting into our rowing positions. A few hundred yards away, a great whale surfaced and we saw, for a few seconds, a baby whale, the size of a large dolphin, clamped onto the mother's teat. The second time the pair blew, the babe had detached itself and was swimming along by the mother's side.

That afternoon, while Pete was swimming, I heard a crash and at the same time, Pete saying : 'What's that ?' As he scrambled out of the water I looked up. A magnificent blue swordfish sprang clean out of a panicking shoal of dorado and flyers, twisted and fell back with a huge slap. The brute didn't appear again but I could see scores of dorado suddenly leap out in fright as the fish terrorised them from below.

There were less spectacular but equally fascinating occurrences. We both became very excited when I fished out a little prawn-like animal, about four and a half inches long. The creature was found dead and floating by the side of the boat, and what startled me at once, as I looked down at it, was the huge bulbous head. I scooped it up in my mug and we peered at it.

It looked like something out of *Dr Who*. While the transparent body was familiarly prawn, the head, with two flylike eyes etched delicately onto the perspex-like surface, was something I had never seen before. Pete photographed the beast and I took notes and sketched it, thinking that it could possibly be new to science. (Dr A. J. Southward, of the Marine Biological Association of the United Kingdom, has, according to my description, identified the creature as a large amphipod belonging to the genus Cystisoma. Very few specimens have been collected, and little is known of the species. Records suggest a length of two to three inches as common, so this was a big one.)

Throughout the calm the solar stills proved a great success. In the heat of the day, 16 ounces of drinking water could be collected in about six hours, as long as the reservoir level was kept topped up. But there was one problem. If ever we really had to rely on them, how could we operate them in a running sea? The bubble would roll and spill out water and chafing against the side of the boat would soon ruin the plastic. No doubt we would think of something.

Pete made a cup of tea from the second day's collection and while we gratefully sipped, I felt a tiny disturbance of air around my face. A sweet paper on the deck moved slightly. At last the calm had ended. By dusk a refreshing breeze put new life in us and all the familiar plopping and gurgling noises around the boat gave the reassurance that the silent world of the calm no longer existed.

Log
2300. The water is blue—not reflection. I've shone my torch

down just now and the shaft of light is the same colour as the day. Curious.

I dug out another of the cigars that Maggie had packed for me. As I puffed away I remembered all the times I had smoked a cigar in her house. At the weekend I'd go up to Birmingham by train; a bus to the house; let myself in. There would be Katey bounding up and barking and licking my face— then Maggie would come downstairs. A beer from the fridge, a smoke, a cuddle . . . How I missed her. I finished the cigar and tossed the butt end into the sea. The cigar was gone, but the smoke aroma lingered on—with my thoughts of home.

'Right, man, it's ready.' Pete's voice sounded crisp and enthusiastic. I heaved myself up and staggered over the rowing seats and deck jerries to sample the 'surprise' that Pete had been planning since the previous evening.

'What is it?' I asked in disgust.

Pete stopped beaming and a flicker of annoyance crossed his face.

'Surprise, man. It's variety, isn't it?'

I knew he was trying to convince himself and my being nonplussed wasn't helping him much. So I tried to sound eager.

'Is it custard?' I ventured hopefully.

'Oh bugger you—eat it,' he snapped.

I picked up my green dog bowl and gingerly prodded the yellow-ochre stodge lying in the bottom. I brought a forkful up to my lips which trembled with trepidation. Pete's eyes followed the lump of food.

'You swine—you try yours first.' Why should I be his food-taster, I thought.

He looked down at his bowl thoughtfully; then swiftly he dug a lump of food out and popped it into his mouth. He smiled.

'Hey—it's good!'—then as he swallowed it—'Well, edible.'

My first mouthful confirmed it. Dried egg with peanut butter. I ate it dutifully and in order not to upset him, I lied how nice it was. Pete seemed pleased.

'You see,' he said, 'I've thought of all the things we've already put in with the egg. We've had jam, syrup, honey, parmesan cheese, onions and cocoa so far. And yesterday I found that seven-pound box of peanut butter.'

'That was good thinking, Pete,' I said magnanimously.

'And I've had another idea.'

'Oh—what?' He must have detected the tone of my voice drop.

'Ovaltine and peas,' he announced undeterred.

'Well—let's see tomorrow.' He might have forgotten about it by then.

When the sun reached his zenith, the hottest, most unbearable part of the day, I started nodding. Suddenly I heard something through my drowsiness. It wasn't the regular beating rhythm of the sea. Something rustling, but so quietly. I looked up. Pete was lounging across the galley entrance, his back against the port side, his feet sticking out over the starboard. He furtively passed his hand over his mouth then quickly flicked something into the water. It was a sweet paper. Then he pulled his hat over his face.

'So—he's nicking barley sugars is he?' Throughout our rest I watched him every so often slide his hand into the galley and surreptitiously take a sweet. He thought I hadn't noticed.

I became rather silly about it. I started to imagine that Pete must have been pinching extra portions of raisins or apricots whenever he offered to do a meal. Of course, I thought, that was why he had volunteered! I wondered why he didn't talk for a few minutes after dividing our prune ration—he had his bloody mouth full of 'em! In my diary I wrote :

> I realise how petty this must sound to anyone not familiar with our situation. But food is the only thing we have to look forward to out here. When it goes—or at least the little luxuries—life will be pretty miserable for both of us. Anything that could precipitate an argument out here should be avoided—so I won't say anything yet.

As I read these words the next time I opened the diary, I was horrified. Did I actually write that? I asked myself. Something as inconsequential as that? Blowing things up out of all proportion and being suspicious of my friend. What was this voyage doing to me? I had written accusingly : 'Pete is pinching barley sugars.' Well, so what? Come to think of it, I'd been taking more than my ration's worth of sippers from the water tanks. And Pete hadn't even mentioned it. I felt really ashamed.

After a nondescript risotto for supper we attempted a rowing stint, but the sea was chopping up and we were tired.

Two-up flat-out—taken with the self-timer

'I think we'd be better off having a smoke,' I suggested.

So we packed it in. It appeared that our enthusiasm to push ourselves on and on was quickly dissipating.

'What the hell,' I told Pete. 'We would get to the other side eventually without rowing a stroke.'

Next day we woke again at 0815 and unwillingly took up the oars. I didn't feel like doing much. I told Pete that navigation was a pain in the arse. He admitted that it was more painful for him to listen to me cursing than it must be for me to navigate. So for the second day, I refused to get the sextant out.

For the next 48 hours, the wind blew freshly from the East. The 5th of July began hazy but the breeze cleared the fuzz by mid-morning.

While greasing the rowlocks I looked down at the deck, between the bow seat and the life line cable, and was surprised to see two small Portuguese Men-of-War with their stinging tentacles wrapped around the cable. Obviously they had been washed in during the night and I was astonished that one or even both of us hadn't stepped on them. I unlashed the Whale dinghy pump from the forward bulkhead and sucked them up. They

shot out, tentacles and all, over the side where they righted themselves and sailed off. There were quite a lot of them about. They
reminded me of pink polythene bags as they drifted by, their
'sails', with narrow end on to the wind, bobbing and flinching
over the waves.

I was fascinated by the fish that accompanied these Men-of-
War, which are themselves a symbiotic colony of very different
but all essential cells. One, or two more usually, lived happily
in the dangling mass of tentacles to which they seemed quite
impervious. The fish looked rather like the little dragonet found
in British waters, except that the fan-like pectoral fins were larger.
These ugly little brutes remained absolutely faithful to their
protector and when I dared disturb them with the end of a fishing
rod, they withdrew even deeper into the mass of stinging cells!

As I gazed into the blue water, a dozen herring-sized dorados
appeared and I soon boated two of them for supper. The meal
over, I got the fuel diary out and totted up the number of minutes
of gas we had used during the last seven days. Fortunately it came
to 125 minutes as compared to the usual 140. It became obvious
that we had suffered a loss in appetite in the heat of the week.

I glanced at the four deck jerries. All empty except one, containing the five-gallon emergency water. It would have to be an
emergency to use it. In Casablanca we had poured the kerosene
out and filled the can with water, but it still tasted of fuel despite
the washing we gave it. Squeezed between the jerries was a one-
gallon jerrycan, containing what was left of the day's ration.
Below deck, I could hear the water in the main tanks slopping
and the sound gurgled up through the breathing tube.

I was thinking. Supposing . . . no, impossible. But there could
be—a leak in one of the tanks? I could not keep it from Pete.

'Funny you should mention that,' he said with a look of concern. 'That's just what I thought today. When I drew off our
ration I kept getting air blocks in the pump.'

'Oh no, really?'

'Yes, but then I thought that the honeycomb of baffle plates
could just have caused uneven levelling in the tanks, and perhaps
that's what it was. Anyway, why did you think that?'

'I don't know really. I heard the breather pipe and I started
thinking pessimistic things. You know, although we thoroughly
tested the tanks on shore, we haven't checked them out here yet.'

Pete got up. 'Well, let's do it now.'

There was a fairly choppy sea but only the odd splash of spray was coming aboard. Opening the hatch, we lifted the larger Tuppers out of the way and crouched down to look under the heavy fibreglass tank on the starboard side. Underneath it, between its supporting chocks, we saw a puddle of water.

'What is it, fresh or salt?'

Pete dipped his finger in, sucked it and winced.

'Yeuk—it's all right, it's salt. But we'd better see the next one . . . Salt under that one too.'

'But there may be a slow leak. Don't forget there's always sea-water in the hatches and half a gallon or so of fresh wouldn't taste,' I said gloomily. 'I reckon we have about ten gallons left—if there isn't a leak. That's enough for another twenty days. Then it's Alec's still, solar stills and so on. We could be making our own water for about two weeks before we land.'

'Well, we'd easily have managed that with plenty of gas—but now . . .'

Pete sighed. 'We don't really know how much water we've got, do we?'

I shook my head.

9
Temptation
6th–16th July

Derek

A combination of the stifling heat inside the rathole and the nagging worry of a new fear, the water situation, prevented a decent sleep. I lay awake thinking about the possibility of a leak. Then I would dismiss it when I thought of the craftsman-like work German Mike had done. But no matter how many points I could think of to indicate to the contrary, the threat that a leak could have been caused by chafing seemed a very real one.

Eventually I dozed off, only to awake not long after with Pete's arm in my open mouth. I couldn't immediately lift him off as my arms were wedged against him and the side. So I bit him. He grunted and turned over and I lay looking up at the shaft of grey dawn light coming through the airhole in the dodger.

The hours crawled by. I didn't possess the strength to leap out and face a new day. I could hear the sea crashing away and feel the boat lurch and roll and topple and slide over a thousand waves.

'What the hell if I lie here for another hour. Or a whole morning. Or forever. Rather that than face another day out there.'

Pete was calling from outside. I looked at my watch. 1046.

'Derek—come along. No slacking,' he said cheerfully.

'Good old Pete,' I thought. 'This is what a close partnership really is all about. Whichever one of us is down, the other will do his best to cheer him up—get him out of himself again.'

I heaved myself out and unsteadily peed into the bucket. I glared down at the tiny amount of liquid splashing around at the bottom.

'Want it?' I asked Pete.

'Not yet, thank you,' he said politely.

I sat down next to him. 'Let me see your arm.' He showed me.

'Why?' he asked, after I had examined it.

'I bit it.'

'Oh.' And Pete turned back to the manufacture of breakfast.

'D'you know—the wind was blowing from the South-East this morning,' he said later.

'Was it be damned,' I said. I didn't like the sound of that while we were trying our hardest to make a southing. I looked out and the sea seemed choppier though the wind was light and variable. The sky was a grey haze and an oppressiveness was setting in.

Just before midday, while we were silently toiling at the oars, I saw two huge sharks following in our wake. The humps of sea obscured them every now and then but as they came closer I could see that the brown backs were over 12 feet long. Their scythe-like tails stood out of the water and swayed menacingly

'They're definitely following us,' I said.

'What sort are they?'

'I don't know—I've never seen sharks that big—except the old basking sharks off Ireland ... Anyway, I don't think they'll bother us', I added, giving myself a crumb of reassurance. As long as I could see them, I'd know what they were doing.

Suddenly, as though they had heard me, they dived. I jumped up and looked into the sea below the stern, waiting for two great torpedoes to hit us. I braced myself and I noticed Pete had pulled in his oar and he too gripped the side of the boat. Nothing happened. They had gone for good.

We began rowing again, laughing at our nervousness and over-awareness. Whilst on the oars, I wondered if perhaps we had rowed into an extra-strong flow of the North Equatorial Current.

Log

1540. 7th July. The ocean seemed pretty lively today—loads of dorado, the two sharks, millions of flying fish, scores of Men-of-War and also the oilclots have returned.

2017. Relaxing after a superb blow-out. As it's Sunday we opened a tin of pork shoulder, made apple sauce and thick gravy, spud and runner bean and onion salad with vinaigrette.

That lot was chased down by our last tin of Mirabelles from the Gdynia.

Water in tanks getting muddy now.

The next day I took a careful series of sunshots and late in the afternoon, after plotting and transforming position lines, I obtained a fix of 18°47′ North, 41°57′ West. While the fix lay some 120 miles west of the infamous Bird Line I had drawn, I felt a bit depressed. The position the day before had been about the same and it was only at 1500, when we tuned in to BBC World Service for a time check, that I discovered Pete's chronometer had been set wrong. However, we corrected it and if the feeling of 'losing 30 miles' was acute, it didn't last long.

I looked at the considerable distance to go on the map before Barbados was reached. About 900 miles. It seemed an incredibly long way. 'Why,' I thought, 'even at a steady 30 a day, we still have another month to go.' With our water as it was it looked as though we'd have a rather uncomfortable time.

The following day brought a change of weather. Right from dawn, a spectacular cloud formation, high, middle and low clouds all represented, entranced me. By midday the high wisps of cirrus had been covered by towering cumulus, and to the East I saw tall columns—thunderheads—growing rapidly. By 1400 hours the clouds overhead had gone, but from the East threatening black banks of cumulo-nimbus moved towards us.

During the intolerable heat at local noon, I dived under the shade of the rathole and cleared out my hatch. I re-read all Maggie's letters and opened an envelope marked '9 July' to find a card with an encouraging message from her.

I dug to the bottom of the hatch, finding such treats as a tin of tobacco and a cigar which Maggie had carefully mummified in layers of polythene. Right at the apex of the hatch was a little pile of coins. I brought them out and counted them : 97½ pence.

'Enough for three and a half pints of Guinness and a bag of crisps when I get back—if prices haven't gone up,' I wrote in my diary.

My final reckoning on our 1800 hours position was 17°42′ North, 42°43′ West. We had averaged about 40 miles a day during the last 48 hours and this was not only surprising, but tremendously encouraging.

'Maybe that current we're in is stronger than we think,' I said.

Sifting through my hatch earlier, I had discovered my spare pipe, so that night I decided to give my old white faithful a rest and smoke a few fills with the new one. The briar was new and not yet carbonised but the first few smokes weren't bad. I waited up late for the waning moon to creep out of the thick bank of clouds before I put my cushion in the galley and went to bed.

We rose an hour before dawn to a fresh breeze. A zipping sound made me turn my head. Out of the sparkling water a cloud of flyers burst into the air, their bodies flashing in the sunlight. Chasing them I saw a hunting party of dorado, galloping like dolphins after the shoal. The pursuers didn't give up at the surface for they leapt after the panicking flyers and caught them in mid-air, returning to the water with a neat dive.

I whipped out a spinner and cast it over the dorado, reeling in across their path. I felt a jerk and a small one leapt into the air, the spinner dangling heavily in its mouth. He put up a great fight—so did a second one, but that was all. Two little 'uns out of about twenty.

'Ah well—makes a change from eggs,' Pete remarked as I sliced fillets from the fish.

I scraped the mess of innards and heads off the chopping board into the sea. Albert trundled up to them and seemed to go off in a brief frenzy as the cloud of blood and bits hung around him. Then I noticed, as the guts drifted away, another Pilot fish, slightly smaller, swim out from under the stern to investigate. Albert had had a bit of crumpet under the boat all the time, and I'd thought he was a confirmed bachelor!

The fish went down a treat. I still think that dorado has the most superior fish taste I know. To my palate it was like fresh salmon, with the colour and consistency of the tenderest veal. Black tea rounded off this magnificent early meal and we sat back feeling very mellow.

Swarms of Men-of-War were now littering the ocean as far as we could see. Neither of us dared go in for a swim, especially as we had seen a rather gruesome fight. I was watching a Man-of-War drift by and I noticed that it kept being pulled down. I stood up and saw the blue outline of a dorado, about four or

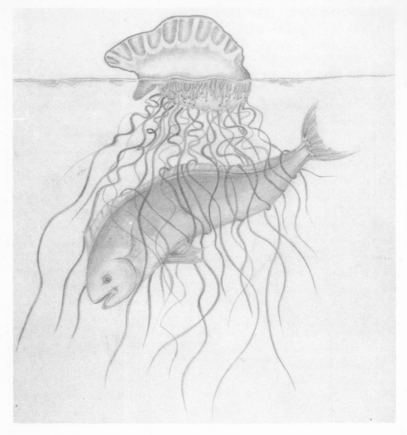

Fight between a Portuguese Man-of-War and a dorado

five pounds in weight, hopelessly tangled in the venomous
tentacles. The fish was putting up a brave fight, tugging the
jellyfish down. But the gas-filled bladder was too buoyant and
repeatedly bobbed up to the surface. We watched the frantic
thrashing begin to subside and the duel ended quietly, with
the victorious Man-of-War drifting away clutching its prize.
All it had to do then was absorb the poor fish into its community. Such was life out here.

After breakfast I went forward again and dragged my soggy
sleeping bag out to dry. I draped it over the bow blister, pegging
one end to the radar reflector and tying the other to the dodger

frame pole. The breeze blew vigorously from the East and soon whipped the pegged end of the bag off the reflector so that it streamed out, flapping in the wind.

I crawled over the bow to retrieve the loose end and standing on the seat, held the end up with my arms outstretched so that the wind would dry it more quickly. The wind billowed into the sleeping bag, making it curve, and immediately the boat picked up speed. Then I realised what I'd quite unwittingly done. I had made a sail.

To feel the boat surge along for that short minute was strange and exhilarating. No one rowing, yet we were fairly belting through the water.

'How about that then?' I yelled to Pete.

He looked up and realised what was happening. He said what I was thinking: 'It would be easy, wouldn't it?'

I tied the bag down flat over the bow and Britannia slowed down. I joined Pete aft and we had a smoke and a long serious talk, the outcome of which I wrote up in the diary.

Diary

With the use of a couple of oars lashed together and a bit of rope, we needn't have rowed at all. Out of the shipping lanes we could forge ahead without a thought of rowing in our minds. Both of us agreed that if we were on our own, the temptation would be drastically real and I think would take more resistance to overcome than either of us could muster. But with two of us constantly checking each other's actions and train of thought, there doesn't seem to be any great danger of not only deceiving everyone else but more importantly, deceiving ourselves. We set out to row round the world and that's what we shall do. I would certainly get no satisfaction at all from a deception.

OK, if a gale bounces us along for 40 miles without us being able to use the oars—as has happened—we are at the mercy of that wind be it in the right or wrong direction and we've got to accept it. If our course is maintained, that's good luck. If we're blown back or way off course as we were in the Straits of Gibraltar and off the Moroccan coast, that also has to be accepted as the rules of the game.

On the evening of 11th July, the sun had been down for only

an hour when a sudden unexpected wind swooped down on us. In another hour it had reached gale force and short sharp waves lashed angrily across the deck. We had donned oilskins earlier, and were bravely sitting aft, trying to ignore the savage gusts that ripped into Britannia. No matter how sophisticated the design of oilskins, the wave that hits you in the face will go down your neck. Waves burst over us frequently and both of us got soaked.

Before we crawled into bed (it had to be drier there) Pete began to fill up the gallon jerrycan with water from the main tanks. The first few strokes of the pump brought up a steady flow but then it started missing and a hideous belching sound emanated from the pump.

'Bloody air lock!' shouted Pete above the noise of wind and sea. He pumped harder and faster, the odd spurt of muddy water just dribbling out. Then nothing.

'Oh no,' he muttered.

'It's got to be an air lock, man.' I tried to sound convincing. 'We've got gallons left.'

'Well, we can't fix it in this sea,' he countered. 'Come on!'

We stripped off our oils and clambered under the dodger.

As soon as we lay down I could feel the boat's head respond to our weight. At this stage, as stores and water diminished, Britannia was becoming very buoyant and a bit top-heavy. It was time, I thought, to take on seawater ballast. I cursed myself for not thinking of it earlier.

With her bow lower, the sea immediately took advantage of Britannia's disability. Twenty-eight stone of flesh had its disadvantage and as we lay there waves cannoned across the deck and exploded on the spray dodger, shooting jets of water through the air holes in the top and flooding over the deckboards at the bottom. After a while Pete said:

'Can you feel a list on my side?'

'Yes, I can.'

'Well, I think that's our water,' he said triumphantly. 'It's not getting out of the port tank for some reason.'

'Problem solved then,' I said, but wondered, 'Is it really?'

Log: 12th July

1535. A dreadful night. Gale and a hideous cross-sea which still hasn't abated. Difficult to write this. Had to sleep with flaps down, sweating was horrible. One in twenty waves crashed in and all is wet. No work today but surfing down waves is hairy and at least we are moving. A sea bird was calling earlier, a wheezy whistle. Another Man-of-War on deck. A tin of precious peanuts had blown—rusted in spite of varnish. Very sad to dump it but we opened another.

2135. Gale is increasing. Because of the wind bearing the boat over when she's beam on and we are trying to sleep forward, we've decided to do four-hour watches tonight so that two of us are on the same side of the boat, one sleeping, one awake—to counteract the dodgy list. Watches commence at 2200 hours.

Worried about water—still can't get it flowing satisfactorily. Air lock or what?

May be prudent to watch anyway tonight, according to my calculations we should have been going through shipping lanes these last few days.

I put the log book away in its pocket and picking up the radio and a flashlight, went aft. I pulled my hood up and leaned hard against the starboard side. Even with both of us on that side, I could still detect a slight list. I hoped it was our tankful of water.

Two long cold hours to midnight and then it was the 13th of July. I felt a superstitious twinge. Hallo—I thought I saw a light. Probably phosphorescence. It was so long since I had seen anything else on the horizon except horizon that I didn't suppose I'd recognise a light. But when I stood up I saw very definitely—it was a light.

'Are you asleep, Pete?' I yelled.

'Not after that.'

'I can see a ship, boy,' I sang.

'You're kidding.'

I began to feel excited.

'No—straight up—no bull—as the artificial inseminator said.'

'How far is she?'

'Can't really tell. I can only see a mast light so far—hey—' then in my best German Mike accent: 'You don't vould believe.'

'What's happened?' Pete stuck his head out of the dodger.

'Another ship!' I was laughing. 'It's like the Solent, man!'

Pete scrambled out of the rathole dressed only in his pants.

'Looks like a tanker,' he jabbered excitedly. 'We're going through a lane!'

'What a pity it's dark,' I said quietly. 'We couldn't possibly attempt to go alongside one in this gale.' The wind was now at least force 8. The tanker, I saw, was passing directly in front of our bow—about one and half miles away. The first ship was, I thought, hove to, as she hadn't seemed to move much. Broken down perhaps? We might be able to row down to her and get in her lee. But the wind gusted to remind me that rowing would be very difficult.

'Maybe if I fired the gun or a flare—she would come to us! It would be so easy. No more water or gas worries. And Maggie and the folks would know we were OK . . .'

How tempting it all was. But I knew that if for some reason they saw us but could not get to us, they might put out an alert. We could have put a lot of people to a great deal of time and expense, and possibly danger . . .

The ship was moving now. About a quarter of a mile away and with her red and green lights showing. She was coming straight for us.

'Swing the tiller arm over, Pete.'

I sat on the bow seat, untied my oar and began to row. Pete, I saw, was shining the flashlight at the ship's bridge. Though upwind, I could hear her engines throbbing.

'She's seen us,' said Pete.

I glanced round, just noticing her head turn before a blinding spotlight picked us out. I stared at the strange vessel. She was a factory fishing ship. The hundred yards of sea that lay between her and us was monstrously magnified in the flood of light. Even a ship as big as that could plunge up and down waves as recklessly as we could. I stared at the amazing sight.

'Look! People!' I gasped.

There on the deck, Oriental seamen worked hard handling nets, lines and pulleys. They were concentrating on their job, ignoring us. Only the three figures on the bridge stared in our direction.

I displayed the thumbs up sign and they returned it. The ship chugged on into the gale, black sea breaking savagely and solidly, then lashing back as a billion pure white droplets. At 300 yards the mountainous waves began to obscure all but her mast lights. Then she was gone.

'It's funny,' said Pete miserably, 'you pray for a ship as hard as you can and when they actually come that close, you pray for them to go away.'

'You know,' I said, 'they may report us to Lloyds, so something good may have come of it. It wouldn't be a waste of a ship.'

I left Pete arranging himself in the galley entrance and returned to my pit. It suddenly dawned on me that the ship would have hit us had it not been for my being on watch at the time. All those nights spent without a watchman, and the first in ages—a ship on a collision course. Spared again by Providence. How many chances had we got left? I wondered, not for the first time on this voyage.

I thought about luck. Our own miraculous escapes from several situations. But was it luck? Was life out here governed by the same law of chance that applied to our poker dice, for example? Was our destiny as vague, as mechanical as that? That surely would mean that life is not mapped out for anyone; that we all of us just drift along waiting for the next shake of the dice. I couldn't believe that. I had been brought up in a Christian family, but after the teenage rejection of beliefs, which is normally a brief aversion, I never got back on the road at all. God was there all right but what He was and what He did was a complete mystery. Often in tight spots I prayed—to what, I didn't know. But it gave me a glib reassurance and if I got out of that problem that was fine and I'd have probably got out of it anyway, without God.

I could only relate God to emergencies of life and death proportions. But I could never sense God being around when I was walking down a country lane or having a pint in a pub. My god was a limited version. Not the All that we are told; a god of convenience.

As I lay in the rathole, the odd wave lapping under the deck board and wetting my hair, my god's credibility rating was on a downer suddenly. I remembered Maggie's message. She had written it on the endpaper of a Bible she had given me. It said :

'God brought us together
God will keep us together.'

So God had mapped out our lives—not chance. So a simple faith. That once I'd done all I could, I'd let God take over. It was going to work. I felt happy and, strangely enough, excited.

I wondered if Pete was thinking the same as I was; maybe his God was still in the convenience stage.

Another heavy wave toppled into the boat. I heard Pete gasp and splutter as the water drained off the deck and Britannia settled upright again. I listened for him to say the usual 'I'm OK' after waves hit us like that and when he did, I sank down into the sleeping bag.

I began my watch ten minutes late. As we exchanged places, Pete mentioned that he had seen nothing else. Half-way through my stint, the first flash of dawn showed through dark rolls of cloud. Steadily, the grey light spread and the lower stratus cloud took shape as yellow edges formed. In the brightening light I scanned the deck. Swilling about in the water left trapped were half a dozen flying fish. I crawled on hands and knees and tossed them back.

'Now if there were a couple of dozen they'd be worth cooking,' I said to myself.

It was a funny day. The weather was squally and black clouds pouring out life-giving rain were totally wasted as they all missed us. By mid-afternoon the wind dropped and the air became sultry as the sun shone weakly through the clouds. The sea remained very choppy, so work was hot. Already I had used my daily ration of water. I began to suck barley sugars as my throat was burning.

Pete's diary: 8th July
The calm's again making Derek restless. I make the effort to cheer him up.

Pm. I had a strange mania for cutting things up this afternoon. I had a small growth on the bridge of my nose caused by glasses chafe—had the thing for years but lately it's been getting on my nerves. With my trusty Swiss Army knife I had a go at amputation. First with a blade, not a success, then with the scissor attachment—snip, snip, off it came. A lot of blood for such a small incision. Encouraged by my prowess with the knife, I cut the sleeves off an old sweater, trimmed my toenails, trimmed the lamp wick and cut up a pair of old plimsolls. When I'd run out of items to destroy, I asked Derek if he need anything cutting.

'Only your vocal chords,' he came. If Derek lands with a high voice, I accept no responsibility.

Started Sartre's *Reprieve,* looks promising and it should keep me occupied for a couple of days. Took only two hours to read Clarke's *2001*—enjoyed it though.

Derek, with glowering expression, is writing furiously in his diary—he's just had a dig at me—sly one too, probably leading up to something. We haven't had a decent argument for ages.

The expected confrontation didn't come. Rather, we slipped into a state of euphoria, as rowing in that heat on our reduced water intake was out of the question. We read, talked and listened to the radio, Radio Surinam by day, and to our amazement Radio Luxembourg by night.

Derek filled the Tupperware containers with water in an attempt to counterbalance the water trapped in the port tank. As he did so, I made a mental note to find a way of pumping out the precious water locked away. As we had seen a couple of ships the previous night, we kept up our watches.

The next day at 0930, whilst at his ablutions, Derek spotted the factory ship again, five miles off our port beam. Our unanimous decision was to fire a flare, until I thought a little about it and said to Derek :

'Hold on a bit—let's have a discussion—she's not moving.'

We talked about the pros and cons for five minutes. Did we really need to? If we didn't now, and later on really needed help, it would cause more trouble for our would-be rescuers. Would it endanger the lives of any on board the fishing boat? No, but to leave it might well place future rescuers in danger. Conditions then were ideal for going alongside a ship. Yes—we would fire a flare.

Derek unwrapped his prized possession—the Very pistol presented by German Mike's English partner. The polished brass gleamed excitingly. I knew then he had been dying to use it. He fired three times, the red flares arching up 150 feet and with a pop, fizzling out. No acknowledging flare from the fishing boat—no sign from them. We waited, looking around as we did so, noting that the grey sky and sea were ideal for picking out flares.

'They're moving away—they haven't seen us,' said Derek quietly.

'Then I'll try one of the big fireworks,' I said.

We had acquired a number of parachute flares with a ceiling of 900 feet. They were kept only for dire emergency. They were three years out of date, and having heard nasty stories of people losing arms and heads with old flares, I couldn't imagine ever using them. All this went through my head as I rummaged through the flare bucket, and Derek's 'Are you sure about this, Pete?' didn't deter me.

I whipped off the wrapper, reading the instructions aloud as I went.

'Remove top tube A—remove lower tube B—lift exposed trigger and let go—hallo, the trigger looks a bit duff.'

'Whoosh!'

The lower tube, which I was supposed to be gripping firmly, shot down, embedding itself in my naked foot while the business end took off, missing Derek's head by inches. In stunned silence we watched the projectile shoot off on a course parallel with the sea, to expend itself ten feet above the surface.

'It bloody near took my head off,' said an angry Derek.

I was too busy attending to my fiercely throbbing foot to console him.

As the fishing boat chugged off over the horizon I set about repairing my wounds. A red hole half an inch in diameter stared up at me. Fortunately it wasn't very deep. I dunked my foot over the side for a saline wash. A voice inside me said simply 'Sharks'—so out it came. A dollop of Savlon, then gauze stuck down with a plaster. Vain as ever, I noted how well the white bandage showed up my tanned foot. It was a new sensation; something different to look at. Strangely, the pain felt nice too; just as a child, having grazed himself, cries until Mother bandages the wound.

I made breakfast, three-quarters of a cup of cocoa. Better late than never.

A pretty depressing situation, yet both of us were happy. I had no idea why. Derek mentioned that he had never seen me looking so healthy. I thought we were both very fit, if thirsty. We convinced ourselves that the water tanks were not leaking, and that it was simply an air lock in the piping preventing flow. Silly of us not to have worked out means of obtaining water through the filler inlet. A bend in the inlet pipe prevented anything but a very long flexible straw from getting through. Needless to say we didn't have a long flexible straw. Once the four gallons in the deck jerry had gone, I decided I would drill a hole through the deck, through the insulation and through to the tank top. A conservative estimate of our water situation was thirteen gallons total, and what we could make from the stills. Prospects were grim.

If there was any one particular day of the week when I thought mostly of home, that day was Sunday. I knew just what everyone would be doing at any time during the day. Brother Tony at the pub, Mum at church, the smell of roast beef wafting from the kitchen.

Sunday. 1745. Derek was clattering around the galley preparing a risotto. I saw him look up, vexed at the chore. He said very calmly :

'There's a small ship dead on our bow.'

'You're joking.' I looked round and sure enough, there was our elusive fishing boat parked just one and a half miles away.

'Let's go, Dereko!' I shouted as I grabbed the oars. We were two different people now.

'I'll just finish cooking this.'

Derek steered, cooked, cleared the deck and yelled encouragement to me.

'That's our ship—they've seen us—they're waving. Not much further.'

Derek took over the rowing as I filmed. As photographer, I dreaded these encounters. The photographer in me wanted to film but being a crew member I had to work the boat. A conflict of priorities which fortunately Derek understood.

Britannia neared the small grey ship. I could see the shapes of people running around and hauling lines over the side. Then I saw in black lettering the legend 'Ho Chung Eng No. II'. Closer still, I could really judge how rough the sea was. With nothing to compare the size of the waves with, this rolling ship soon dispelled any pleasant thoughts of an easy going-alongside.

The fishing ship was too small to have much of a lee and once we actually drew parallel with her, the two vessels were going up and down on alternate waves. It took an agonisingly long

time to fight to heaving line distance. The men on board shouted
and smiled and tried to sling lines. Then one bright spark attached
a rope to a javelin and flung that. It missed Derek's stomach
by inches.

At last Derek grabbed a floating line nearby and we pulled
ourselves closer. The swell became frightening. Britannia lurched
up and fell down. One minute I was looking into a porthole,
the next I stared down at the deck. As I threw jerrycans up to
the friendly Formosans, Derek fended Britannia off with an oar.
While two jerries were being filled, I shot a few feet of film of
the exciting event. I suddenly thought : 'We've got our water.
No more hideous rationing. Pints all round tonight.'

Derek spoke to the captain, whose English was very bad.
Derek's Chinese was even worse.

'What—is—our—pos—it—ion ?' asked Derek, pointing at the
chart.

The captain smiled and nodded.

'Have—you—any—food—to—spare—flesh—fluit—pot—at—
oes ?' Derek was making an effort. He rubbed his stomach and
smacked his lips.

The captain smiled and nodded.

'Could you leport us to Lloyds please.'

Captain as before.

By now Brit was taking a bashing from a projecting gantry
on the stern of the ship. Having taken on ten gallons, I asked :

'Two jerries be enough, Derek ?'

'Better have another two—you never know.'

As I passed them up, a seaman handed me a bag of broken
biscuits and on the next wave, a carton of two hundred
cigarettes.

The crew lined the stern and cheered us as we pulled away.

'What marvellous people !' was all I could think of to say.

We drank three mugs of water each. It tasted wonderful and
after our risotto, we indulged in biscuits and honey and a
cigarette each. At last I could produce a decent amount of pee.
In a happy mood we talked and joked until the early hours.

Diary: 15th July

With the water shortage and the bad feeling that goes with
it removed, I felt contented with my lot, until I realised I had
swapped my dreams from plain water to dreams of ice cream,

lager and strawberry milkshake. So I am just a product of the consumer society after all, and I thought I'd risen above all that.

Today's sight doesn't look very promising. It could be the wind switching South during the night. We struggle on however, taking long stints at the short rough weather oars. D's

Using the short oars

taken to smoking cigarettes like a duck to water—we grab at any pleasure. D told me yesterday that he had been feeling very listless lately due to lack of water. I had thought that he had at last got into the lie-back attitude that goes so well with this life. Now with a few pints of water inside him, he's as energetic as ever. Perhaps what one lacks the other makes up for. Our characters are poles apart but on most occasions we blend together, making a good team. Yesterday with the fishing boat, we both knew what the other was up to without even looking. Four o'clock—time for my row.

With no more reliable north-easterly winds, the tendency was for south-easterlies and the inevitable cross waves that went with them. At least, I felt as the trade winds lost power and direction, we couldn't have far to go.

Our gas consumption was now spectacularly low—down to
15 minutes a day! I tried to imagine any housewife coping with
only 15 minutes' cooking time. The Meta solid fuel tablets, cut
into four, boiled one-and-a-half pints. Derek also came up with
the brilliant idea of using surgical spirit and cotton wool. It
worked very well.

It occurred to me that we were leading a very slapstick life.
On one occasion I was reading *Akenfield*, happily lost in the
Suffolk countryside. I did not hear or see the wave, but certainly
felt it, breaking over my head. It was as if the sea were reminding
me of her presence. I was not to go too far away—she hadn't
finished with me yet.

The sea roughed a little more, taking conditions on board to
the ultimate of discomfort. Always one for my creature comforts,
I had a simple scale worked out rather like the Beaufort wind
scale.

Wind force:

0 — 1   Luxury—lazing.
  2   Comfy, ideal reading conditions.
  3   A bit wobbly for rolling fags.
  4   Getting the odd wave aboard. Still reading.
  5   Beware of spray—soggy pages.
  6   Able to read but keep book high off deck.
  7   Can manage a little writing.
  8   Reading has to be done in rathole only.
  9   Sleep.
 10   Try to sleep.
 11   PRAY.

'We have been at sea long enough mate!' said Derek, looking
up from his log.

10

Hatred

17th–24th July

Derek: from the Log:
1205. Another miserable grey morning began rudely when a ton of sea came crashing over us while we slept. Now the sleeping bags and foam rubber bits are drying on deck and we are working unwillingly.

Last night, half an hour after sunset, I noticed a largish tuna going after Pete's dogends and bits of silver paper that I flicked into the sea. I threw a shrivelled flying fish overside and he grabbed that. I put another on a small hook, well hidden, and let it out. BANG! The brute took off with a 50-yard run, stripping line off so fast it burnt my thumb. It was like hooking an express train. After a few seconds he broke free. Very upset about that—a good few days' fresh meat gone.

1717. From three position lines, our southing has developed into a marked northing. 16°55′ North, 47°11′ West. The wind is fast rising from NE and the sea makes work a farce. We've just stopped. Force 6 and going up. Damn. Even Albert's deserted us.

Just as I feared, a nasty gale pounced out of the darkening sky. Strangely, though the force was constant, the direction was vague and I noticed that the wind switched back and forth from North-East to South-East. Britannia rode the wild seas well. They were becoming confused again. Our brave little boat, now considerably lighter and putting up more windage, butted many grotesque-looking black humps of water aside. But for every wave cleared, a dozen hit her, hurt her, tried to cripple her. We helped the old girl by removing the rudder and our bight astern so that she could run beam on down the wind. I watched the

lamp, burning valiantly, being wrenched from its mounting by
a deck surge which savagely thumped the port side.

I was squinting out through a slit and could only jam down
the bottom of the flap against the deckboard as the brute stormed
towards me. A clap, a ripping sound and thunderous gurgles.
Pete shouting, 'Look out!' Solid weightiness as repulsively warm
as a huge animal smothered me. Pete groaned. Britannia
shrugged the water off her deck defiantly. I glanced out again
through the curtain of lingering droplets.

It was chaos in the rathole. John and Sylvia had aptly named
that pit. Water dripping down the side, swilling about under the
foam rubber; a hideous soaking tangle of clothes and bedding;
knees in crotches, elbows in faces; hot, dark; sickly smells of
armpits and foul breath. Wherever could the romanticism of
this adventure be? Certainly not in the rathole.

Neither of us could sleep. We lay there bracing ourselves,
listening to the fearful booms around us. Dawn came and we
were still wide awake. Shattered.

Log

The sea has humiliated me. Injured me. Turned me into an
animal. Look at me as I eat. Cowering over my dog bowl and
gobbling up food like the very creature the bowl was intended
for. Eyes always shifting—looking this way and that, watching
for the next soaker. I crouch, belch, pick my nose, spit, scratch
my salt sores. What am I turning into?

Look at Pete. The once tall, handsome lady's man—now
hairy and grimy, squatting there casting furtive glances around
him. He too is on the defensive all the time, suspicious of every
wave, every noise, smoking a fag cupped in his hand like a
schoolboy having a puff behind the playground wall. Fear has
been planted in his brain like mine. No chance of a smoke,
a movement, a meal, without first holding on, checking,
watching. And then after all that, the sea laughingly flings
itself aboard or sucks Britannia suddenly into a deep valley so
that our stomachs are left behind. The sea is trying to break
us—I wonder if it will?

Supper of beef mince and rice preceded a fishing session and
the same thing happened, I lost my fish. It wasn't that I was
losing my touch. There was an urgent need for the fish. It was

no longer angling—I had to catch fish for the meat. Dried beef
and chicken was becoming so boring that neither of us felt like
eating it. But fresh fish was there and it became my obsession
to keep trying. When I hooked the first dorado for days, I
panicked. Instead of giving him line and waiting for him to tire,
my instincts were to grab him quick, winch him in and not to
play him. This was no longer sport. I had to have that fish, and
as I reeled him in eagerly, the hook pulled. I felt like weeping.

'Don't worry.' Pete again. The saviour of my sanity. 'I'll tell
you about the bird who came into my darkroom while I was
developing pictures . . .'

Just before darkness, huge tuna, thickset brown fish eight feet
long or more, suddenly bolted out of the waves ahead of us. We
saw six of them charging through swarms of flying fish, scattering
them. There were pathetic little thuds and plops as some of them
hit Britannia and tripped on to the deck. Then a brief flutter,
and death. The great tuna pressed on. It was life to them. Just
as we caught fish to eat, they had to—that was the struggle of
the sea. I began to think that we too were part of that existence.
But what part exactly? Would there be something chasing us?

'Killer whales, of course,' I thought. The only beasts that could
complete the food chain.

'Killer whales,' I said absently to Pete.

'What! Where?' he had whitened.

'No—that's the only thing that can finish us off.'

'We gotta gun though.'

Ah yes, the trusty gun. I pinned all my faith on that gun.

Throughout the night, the wretched wind swung back and forth
and as the hours wore on, a cross sea grew so confused and shook
Britannia so violently that there was nothing we could do but
cling together in the rathole and pray we wouldn't be
overwhelmed.

Oh God. Haven't we suffered enough? We've had far more
than our fair share of hard times. And we've got through them,
no thanks to you. We've fought like cornered rats to stay alive.
You know we can't last much longer mentally. The torment of
knowing that the folk at home haven't heard from us for weeks.
The uncertainty of what's going to happen next. Come on, God.

Give us a chance. I listened the night out and around dawn noticed the hideous twisting sea begin to quieten.

For the seventy-first time since leaving Casablanca I got up and began the early morning ritual. Unlash the bucket. Stand up and hold on, one hand on the grab rope, the other on the rim of the bucket. Squeeze the reluctant drops out and toss the catchings overboard. Rinse the bucket. Replace. Look around. Well, what a surprise—nothing but sea! Grope a way aft and flop down in the galley hole. The sun is still low and in the shade that the blister makes it's chilly. Now the worst job of the day. Breakfast. What the hell is there? Well—fill the kettle first. Sixteen squeezes of the pump—I'll use a Meta tablet today to heat the water.

And so on. That time of the day never filled me with inspiration. There was no keenness to start a new day and all that. I hated that time, especially when Pete poked his hairy face out—like a ferret sniffing outside its lair. Then he would lurch up, and I would be compelled to watch him pee and see the yellow fluid trickle out of the bucket. His teeth-cleaning followed, the first of the five daily sessions. Why this masochistic performance, on his teeth of all things? Why didn't he row non-stop for twelve hours instead?

'Why don't you row for twelve hours?' I said.

He looked puzzled, then as he bent down to put his toothbrush away, I heard : 'Piss off.'

But once we had a mug of Ovaltine in our fists and the smoke was rising from our pipes, the day would begin to improve. Conversation, the sanity-preserver, followed. We would discuss what we had to do—apart from the day's rowing. Today it was deck scrubbing. The rotting corpses of flying fish trapped behind the liferaft and under the rowing seats were stinking like hell. And Pete had to organise his film pack, I had to check the rudder. It would be busy.

On the eastern horizon I saw a black smudge. It was a cloud and it moved towards us. As it got closer I could see no contrast between cloud and sea. Pete was staring at it too.

'Rain,' he said quietly.

'Action!' Our lethargy vanished.

We scrambled off the rowing seats and as I stowed the oars Pete dug out the polythene rain-catcher. While we waited for the squall to come, I doused myself in saltwater and soaped my body in anticipation of a freshwater rinse. The squall came nearer. I could feel the wind strengthening. Then I saw the white waves leaping along below the cloud. We stretched out the catcher. The sun had gone in and I shivered, as naked and wet, I felt the breeze creep over me. Any minute now.

Then the weather played the most malicious trick of all. The rain missed us by a few hundred yards. We watched angrily as it hissed down, making the flattened sea smoke with splashes. The sheet of dry polythene flapped in disappointment; Pete swore, and I stood there stark naked with grey soap slime quick-drying in the wind.

When the last of the water had drained out of the galley, I prepared a risotto and got our salad in soak. This was a special treat which I had discovered quite by accident. Runner beans and onion slices were being rehydrated ready for cooking when I thought that maybe they could be eaten cold. I made a vinaigrette dressing from oil, vinegar, mustard and seasoning and splashed it on. It was delicious. I thought about all the other Atlantic rowers and ocean travellers who steadfastly gnawed meat-bars and chewed obnoxious vitamin-packed stodge. Did they really have such a lack of imagination? Or did they really want to suffer? Do it the hardest way? The most unpalatable food to supplement their penance.

I told Pete what I was thinking and he mentioned Ridgeway and Blythe, the paratroopers who rowed from America to Ireland in 1966.

'I could never understand their idea of adventure,' he said, 'this idea of pushing themselves right to the edge of endurance.'

'I can't imagine why they made it so tough for themselves,' I agreed. 'They were doing something damn dangerous in the first place. Why treble the problems?'

'They were bloody soldiers, weren't they? Who the hell knows what makes soldiers tick?' Pete smiled. 'I can hear them now.' He put on his officer's voice. 'Come on Sergeant! Your row. I've just done my 20-hour shift and eaten my ration of salt and half a chocolate button. I'll sleep on my bed of nails now!'

I creased up, watching him salute and sing the Last Post.

Pete looked up at the sky thoughtfully. 'Ever since we started from Gib, I could never think of another ocean like the Pacific

with this one in front of me. I can only think one stage at a time.
It's too immense. My eyes are set on rowing the Atlantic—and
by God we're going to!'

Pete

I could feel the tension building up, Derek casting black looks
at me from under his shooting hat—funny how something as
innocuous as that hat could look so menacing. I sat puffing on
a cigarette, relishing it to the end. How well named they were
—Craven A—very apt. As I threw the butt end overboard
Derek said slowly: 'How about dividing the remaining cigarettes
between us?' I didn't answer directly, I was surprised. Derek had
never smoked cigarettes before—indeed, he had only started a
pipe with a purpose when the tobacco had arrived from Benson
and Hedges. As a certified and unrepentant cigarette addict, I
had smoked most of the 200 given to us by the fishermen. The
thought of dividing them equally knowing that Derek was not
a real addict and smoked less than me was preposterous. I could
imagine what I would be like when my half gave out and Derek
was still puffing away—I might even knife him in the back to
get at them. I could not use this in an argument against him.
Without the craving he just would not understand. Once all the
cigarettes had gone he could go back to the pipe, no problem.
So I had to win this point at all costs—hitting hard would be
the only way. The balance was on my side because I needed
them.

'I disagree—we didn't divvy all the B and H and you smoked
more of that in Gib than I have since we've been out here—
anyway, you've never smoked so many cigarettes before.'

Derek glared at me as he answered:

'We divide the water and biscuits, why not the fags?'

A good point—I had to turn it to my advantage.

'We don't always share everything. You used the trip funds
to drink in the Bat and Ball. I didn't and I still don't begrudge
you that.'

Derek saw red, pointing an accusing finger at me. He almost
shouted:

'You used trip funds for cigarettes in Gib.'

'Got 'im!' On a technical point, pouncing for the kill, I felt
guilty at the ease with which Derek had fallen for it.

'Not true—most of the money I spent in Gib came from my bank account in London.'

Silently we glared at one another—how petty; obviously Derek had been bottling it up all afternoon, watching me snap the lighter at a ciggy, inhaling deeply and with relish, blowing the smoke out through my nose and mouth (disgusting habit!). All this for forty cigarettes—I felt ashamed but I could not get too magnanimous—a generous junkie?

'How about you taking five and I keep the rest?' I thought the seven-to-one ratio about right.

'Keep the bloody lot,' replied Derek. Shrugging, he added: 'You put up a convincing argument, Pete.'

'You didn't do so bad!'

Photography kept me busy for most of the day—I must have got on Derek's nerves as I grumbled about my distrust of the light meter, in the same way as I got peeved at his mistrust of the navigation. The photography was important to me; after all it was visible evidence of our trip and it could be instrumental in helping to alleviate the depressing financial situation that we knew was awaiting our arrival on land. The thought of losing the film gave me nightmares—I became very protective about it, wrapping each reel in polythene bags with silica gel crystals, then placing it in a Tupperware and storing it in the driest hatch.

Our ritual mealtime chat that day was on the subject of the impressionability of children. These debates were started by either one of us in conversation. Once mutual interest was made clear, we would chunter on for hours and, as in this case, arrive at some sort of conclusion—children were highly impressionable, they just needed more to impress them. And that went for us too. We take too much for granted in our everyday lives, forgetting the ingenuity that went into everything we see and use.

Later on, Derek drew up what we hoped would be the last 10° before land—the approach to Barbados—scribbling on the plotting sheet the afterthought: 'What a little dot to miss!'

'Positive thinking,' I thought, looking across the water.

Suddenly a tuna fish leapt 15 feet vertically clear of the water: he had positive thoughts too.

The dorados had left us. The line came back with just the silvery lure, an empty hook and a few feet of tentacles from a

Man-of-War wrapped around the line. Derek retrieved the lure and weight, then cut the offending line as I filmed what I thought to be an unusual occurence. Then as I put the camera away, I felt little enthusiasm, only a feeling of wasted energy.

Derek announced our position : 15°55′ North, 48°33′ West. He was not pleased at the result. I told him 'Leave it.' And on that subject I wrote in my diary: 'Derek very disappointed— but I am fed up with telling him "It will take as long as it takes." He will have to learn to accept that fact.'

Assuming the Formosans had not reported us, it would be seven weeks since our families had heard from us. We knew they would be very worried, even with John and Sylvia to reassure them. (No news is good news.) With that thought in mind, I scrabbled aft for the radio and with Derek holding the aerial as usual, I began to transmit. Not a whisper from anyone. After an hour of trying, I disappointedly packed up. Derek, as a last resort, tried the small VHF transmitter, much to my amusement, which turned to amazement when the sound of an American coast-guard came through loud and clear. I thought they were calling us, but no—another voice, also American, came through. They gave no hint of their position but it cheered us to think we were within VHF range of somewhere.

Another attempt with the transmitter

The effort of trying the radios for two hours, far from being exhausting, surprisingly gave me fresh impetus to do something and get a positive result. Derek too was affected in this way. He pumped the starboard deck hatch which was full of water, as I filmed. We restowed its contents with gusto. Derek went on to remake the Mark II paraffin stove by punching holes in a large Kesp tin, then placing a smaller tin filled with paraffin and a rag inside the larger tin. It worked—just. The tins complete with full kettle were lashed to the aft daggerboard. It was a very dangerous operation, but necessary if we wanted to eat. The torches had become unreliable, so as Derek toiled with the stove, I got busy with a screwdriver on them—the problem was simply rust on the connections. Twenty minutes with emery paper solved it. Derek found some forgotten candles hidden away in a hatch. He had the bright idea of cutting each one into five stumps and the heat generated, when lit, would boil a kettle sooner or later. We tried it, but the great heat below the kettle melted the small pieces of candle into one little lake in which five pieces of string floated. 'Well, we do try,' said I.

Watching Derek fiddle with an assortment of stores reminded me indirectly, through Alec's still, about water. With some 600 miles to go, water would once again be a major problem. It would be now if Derek had not insisted on the extra ten gallons when we had met the fishing boat. Like a recurring nightmare, my thoughts of water refused to abate. I went over in my mind the event that had led to our last crisis—shortage of gas, with which we should have been converting seawater for weeks, the main tank's running out. The main tank's running out, I repeated in my mind. A bell rang very loudly—idiot! I admonished myself. With the water from the Formosans we had sat back and failed to apply ourselves to the problem—we still had a list to port, why? I stood up in a trance. Of course, the tanks were plumbed together with a common tap which had favoured drawing water from the starboard tank.

'I've got it.'

'Got what?'

I explained my theory.

'How to get the water out is the problem,' he said. 'But if we put our weight on the starboard side it should run through.'

'Why—the boat's been rolling back and forth for weeks—no, it must be more than that,' I said, looking down at the deck below which lay the tanks. My eye caught on the breather pipes. Another bell rang—leaning over, I put my finger over the breather to the starboard tank.

'Try now.'

Derek pumped—a cough and splutter, then a steady stream of water came through. The answer would be elementary to any schoolboy—simply to offset the bias to the starboard tank. We had to isolate it by blocking the breather pipe to that tank. We created a vacuum in it, effectively cutting it off from the system. We had an estimated extra ten gallons of water.

Tuesday 22nd July was a squally day with lumpy seas. I should have known better than to try boiling a kettle on a precarious paraffin stove made from old cans on an open deck in a force 7 ! Within minutes of lighting the stove and perching the kettle on this doubtful rusting can, a wave thumped Brit's side. The contraption keeled over, igniting the paraffin. A sheet of flame shot across the deck. Derek, sitting forward, looked on helplessly— nothing he could do. Brit was divided in two by a curtain of flame. Grabbing the extinguishers from the galley, I used two of them to put it out—it happened so quickly that the flames had not even scorched or melted the deck paint.

'Phew,' said Derek in relief. 'Can you imagine what J.F. would say if we returned Brit with a bloody great 'ole in her— Sorry John, had a little fire.'

I laughed at his remarks, but I was still shaking inside. If that fire had caught—it did not bear thinking about. Britannia was a fibreglass boat. She could have gone up in minutes. Our day ended with Derek muttering a position of 14°38′ North, 50°39′ West. I was thoroughly fed-up and made no comment, but shuffled off to bed in a bad mood, leaving Derek sitting aft. I turned as I slid into the rathole and looked at him—he was obscured by spray.

'Not far,' I thought. 'Barbados—dry land for a while, no more frights.'

Derek

I staggered into the glaring morning of 23rd July. Feeling wretched from so disturbed a sleep, I sat aft, scowling at the irregular pounding waves. My eyes then travelled back to the deck and I became aware of a dark shape, fairly large, among the litter of tiny dead flying fish. I reached over for it and was surprised to see a flyer of at least half a pound. He was certainly the biggest to come aboard. I had seen even larger ones in groups of three or four when we were still within 300 miles of land. Nowadays they were small, about three inches long on average, and their shoals must have been in the thousands.

Flying fish on take-off

I gazed at the fish : once a proud flyer, swift and beautiful. Now a lump of grey, dead meat. I thought of all the fun these fish had given us. They had provided us with amusement when we timed their flight from the moment they zipped out of the water to the moment they returned with an undignified plop. One I timed was still flying after 18 seconds before I lost him behind a wave. And another spent so long in the air that I thought he must have been a bird.

I made the morning drink and Pete was still below.

'Come on blast you,' I shouted, 'the drinks are getting cold.'

A sudden unreasonable touch of aggro. I heard his muffled voice, then he shoved his head out looking fierce.

'Listen mate,' he said angrily, 'if you can't sleep that's your problem but don't stop me from sleeping.'

'But I've got your rotten breakfast,' I protested.

'Stuff your bloody breakfast—you should wait till I get up.'

'We can't afford to boil the kettle twice,' I countered. I was getting mad too.

'Yeah, OK mate, so wait till I'm up. Don't give me the crap about boiling the kettle twice.'

'You're bloody lucky someone makes you a drink at all!' I was shouting with rage.

'Come on,' I thought. 'Have a go at me. I'll take you on, you swine.' Thankfully, Pete had the presence of mind to cut the stupid and dangerous slanging match there. He withdrew his head and left me wondering what on earth had possessed me to think like that.

'Hell man—I'm sorry,' I called out.

'Forget it. I am too.'

He came out, sat down next to me and we discussed the whys and wherefores of such an outburst.

'It's just your common or garden stress,' he declared.

'Aye—we'll have to be careful.'

As the sea was choppy, we took separate rowing stints in the afternoon with the nine-footer oars. I ground along, trying not to think of our problems. Suddenly Pete attracted my attention. He was pointing to the diminishing water slopping around in two of the jerries; the other pair were empty. Then he glanced at the deck jerries.

'Oh shit. We don't really know how much we have below, do we?'

Of course there is always something that one forgets to take or do. We had forgotten to instal an inspection hatch into the water tanks. We didn't really know if the tanks were leaking slowly or not. For all we knew, they could be empty. This fear gnawed at our brains. Every time we drew off a cupful—an airlock, then a spurt of dirty water, would make us shudder with foreboding. I began to dream about water. The terrible day when we discovered nothing at all in the tanks. When we would have to rely on solar stills which seemed so fragile—they couldn't last many days of tossing and bumping against the boat. Alec's still lying there impotently—no gas to fuel it. Pete and I eyeing each other suspiciously, accusing each other of taking an illegal sipper.

Our fear grew to phobic proportions. How would we take the stark reality of the announcement 'The water is all gone'? Those tales we'd heard about men's throats hurting with dryness so much that all they could do was madly drink seawater. The savage fights between thirst-crazed sailors to get that last drop of water. It was all too horrifying to talk about. Instead, our minds raced silently from one horror to the next.

Soon I thought I had the symptoms. Yes, my throat was tautening—I felt weak and dizzy. I looked at Pete. The deprivation was catching up on him too. He stared glassily at a fixed point on the horizon. 'We will not last long on this hateful rationing,' I thought. Something had to happen.

I crawled out of the scorching sun into the rathole. I felt for the gun under my sleeping bag and the dreadful thought crossed my mind for the second time that day: there would be more water for just one of us . . .

We got back to the oars. Pete was doing his stint when he brought a piece of branched yellow weed in on the end of his oar.

'Pretty,' he observed.

' 'tis, isn't it. Sargassum weed I think.'

'Lots of it about.' He pointed at big clumps of it.

'Must be in another strong current or an offshoot of the Sargasso sea,' I said.

I examined the frilly plant. Then I shook it, and a horde of little beasties dropped out on to the deck. I sifted through the livestock and found two main types. One was a tiny multi-armed starfish. The other was a maggot-like horror, with a brown fringe of legs or hairs dangling underneath it. These fascinated me and I thrust one of them under Pete's nose. He jerked his head back in disgust.

'Yeuk—you and your bloody creatures,' he spat.

As I couldn't share my enthusiasm at the find with my shipmate I gathered all the animals and the weed and returned them to their environment.

After supper—chicken and spaghetti flavoured with tomato soup—I thought that a tidy-up in the port galley hatch wouldn't come amiss, so I cleared the jumble of gear off it and just as I bent down, a little swine of a wave bashed the boat and jerked her over. I fell on to my knees and somehow twisted, landing heavily on my already damaged coccyx. I let out a great roar which brought Pete scampering out of the rathole.

'What's happened?'

'It's my back again,' I gasped.

Pete stepped over the deck jerries and looked at it.

'You must have landed on the tiller arm!' he said knowledgeably.

'I know what I landed on—can you see anything? Any swelling?' I pulled my shorts down.

'Only your spotty bum.'

'Strewth man! It's my injured back again. I might not be able to row.'

A worried look came over his face at the thought of doing all the rowing. He took a closer look and said, 'That's nothing to worry about. Can you stand up?'

'Of course I can stand up. I can't sit down.'

'Try it.'

I hauled myself up and he laid a cushion underneath me as I sat down. I felt pain only if I shifted backwards. Just the position I should be in for rowing.

I squatted uncomfortably, trying to take an interest in what Pete was doing. Earlier we had discovered that the lid of our fuel-saving pressure cooker had broken. Probably the spring had either corroded with salt water or had simply snapped. By pure fluke we happened to have Fairfax's pressure cooker, the same model as ours, in one of the hatches. Pete had found it and was pumping Plus-Gas into its innards to get it moving again. At last the knob freed itself and we were back in business.

Just before 2000 hours, Pete noticed a beautiful rainbow arching in the East.

'A promise of land in two weeks?'

How we hoped so. This existence was becoming unbearable.

I I

Misery

25th–30th July

A week or so to land? These last days are telling on our
general well-being. Physically we are still quite fit, though both
suffer from backache while we fight for sleep. Mentally we are
flagging a bit. Day-to-day jobs seem to take a long time to do
and we both lapse into vacancy during some chores, as though
we're robots. Rowing solo at the oars does kill time quite
quickly now, because we set our own pace and ordain our own
breaks and when to pack up. Much more flexible these days.

We're maybe becoming slightly more irritable but this is
difficult to detect as we have been living together so long and
have put up with such a lot from each other. We find petty
happenings usually leave a mark on each other's patience. For
instance, me watching the bread being divided and protesting
that one piece is bigger than the other—and it may only be by
a few crumbs. But the disputes are quickly settled. If we call
each other a bastard it makes no difference at all; nobody else
is involved or listening so there's no need to worry about a third
person's reaction (as with Carol), and that reaction towards
you.

This boat is a small, self-supporting world unto itself and I'm
sure we are thinking small to get into its way of working. However, as in any community whatever, survival and success all
depend on symbiosis.

I stopped my ramblings here; my elbows were stiffening up as
I leaned on them. Thankfully I turned over and lay flat out. I
turned the little light out and noticed that the sea had doused the
deck lamp. Darkness was total. Thick clouds had hidden the
quarter moon and the once spectacular phosphorescence was in

dim form. All I could see was the circle of illuminated figures on Pete's watch.

Suddenly, I became aware of a sound that wasn't wind or sea or boat. The hairs on the back of my neck prickled up and my ears strained. I thought it was a voice. A ringing, haunting, sweet voice drifting across the waves.

'Of course—a bird!' But what?

The song reminded me of a skylark's lilting and trilling, though it sounded even more pure than that. Perhaps a petrel. I had heard them at night in nesting holes in Ireland but they had sounded a bit harsher than this one. It was a lovely experience. The song lasted for about three minutes and it gave me a tremendous boost. If a little bird could survive out here and sing its heart out, then I was sure I could keep going.

Then the roar of the sea blanketed the warblings and I tried very hard to sleep.

I couldn't stand the damp steaming rathole any longer. My body felt hot and pulpy. The gale still shook Britannia. Pete and I rolled around and bumped each other despite the wedges of our sleeping bags. My back was hurting like hell and all it needed was rest. Gratefully I crawled out of the hole and the tepid blast of air blew some sense into me. It was nearly dawn. Light grey bands were making a show in the East. It was too rough to row or do anything much, but I was damned if I would go back into that hole. I shuddered at the terrible dream I had had during the few minutes' kip—Maggie in an air crash of all things. Horrible—why couldn't my mind recall pleasant memories or scenes? Why should I have bad times asleep as well as awake? I propped myself up against the empty deck jerry. I was scratching myself again—that awful rash of salt sores infesting my legs itched till it nearly drove me to despair.

Physically and mentally I knew I was flagging. I eyed the cause of it. Those four deck jerries, two empty, two half-empty. I carefully checked the slopping levels of the precious water—a stark reminder of our situation. Tenuous to say the least. If we lost those two we would probably die, for all our solar stills and condensers—they couldn't be used in a gale.

I dragged myself back to the galley and rolled back the dodger. With weary repetition I lifted the kettle out. The sun, barely showing through the shapeless clouds, looked unfriendly : a sly white disc sneaking behind grey banks. The sea always looked sharper and fiercer around this time of day. It was the weak dawn sunlight deepening the shadows in the troughs. I thought of the boring day ahead. Another same day. It turned out that I was wrong.

We did our rowing without moaning. Indeed, there was no reluctance as there used to be : just on with the job and get to land. We worked solo in shifts. Not a lot of talking, our mouths were too dry. I tried a couple of sunshots during the day but I couldn't get my balance for some reason. I worked out the position lines and they didn't cross, so I cursed and packed up. 'Who cares—we'll hit land some day,' I thought. A lousy day all in all. My back making me bad-tempered and the incessant pitch and toss of the sea—'Oh, thank God for supper time.' Afterwards I sat back on my usual perch and smoked. Pete came aft and smoked too.

'Look at that.'

Pete startled me. 'What next? I thought. I stood up and looked to port. A tanker one and a half miles away was just disappearing into a black rain squall. That fantastic sight immediately gave me the shakes.

'I'll get the gun.'

'Wait,' said Pete excitedly, 'look—she's turning. She's bloody seen us !'

The beautiful ship had swung slightly towards us by the time she emerged from the squall.

'She's seen us man,' I echoed with disbelief.

'Right, I'm going to pack the film up for a start,' said Pete.

'And I'll get the jerries ready.'

Pete

The rapid change between misery and happiness at sea never ceased to amaze me. There I was sitting puffing my pipe in the rain squall dreaming of creature comforts. As the rain cleared, 100,000 odd tons of tanker became visible, full of food, water, warmth, cigarettes, people. Most of all, we could get some news home to our families and the film to ITN. Strange how we regarded ships as being there solely for our needs. The fact that they had to earn a living was secondary to us. We were told by Alec Gardner of BP that for a tanker to stop and lose an hour on account of us could mean that towards the end of its journey, it could lose a tide, and with tanker charter rates at £9,000 a day, it made for a very expensive postal service. Still, we had not been heard of for two months—and it was only money after all. The thought of a hot shower rang through my mind as I rummaged in the Tupperware for the film.

Derek

Wide-eyed, I watched the great tanker describe a wide circle as she began to slow down. I was thinking of that water—gallons of it. I guessed she would be alongside us in approximately 20 minutes. I glanced at my watch. It was 2150 and the light was fading rapidly. Already she was over two miles away and trying to turn. I yelled a running commentary to Pete who was scrabbling furiously in the forward hatch.

'She's turning—gradually—moved a fair way out but—now, yes, she's bows on to us about three miles. Here she comes!'

I was trembling with anticipation. When she came alongside it would be dark—manoeuvring would be very tricky—we mustn't foul it up.

Remembering the black tanker, I clipped the flashlight to my belt. My brain began to race. Water, people, saying hallo to someone different, maybe fresh food, maybe bread and eggs. And yes, Maggie would be put out of her misery when we were reported. Thank God for that ship.

All around us were localised rain squalls where cloud touched the pulsing sea. I heard Pete moan as a wave crashed in just as he transferred the film from one box to another.

'Did it get them?'

'No—what's she doing?' His voice was muffled from the hatches.

I stared out. Another squall had covered her.

'She's in the muck now but she'll be out in a minute.'

I held my breath and waited for her to reappear. I gazed and waited. That was the last I saw of her. Darkness fell—I couldn't even see the lights.

'She's gone,' I croaked.

She couldn't find us in the rain and massive waves. I couldn't believe it. God had sent this ship to help us out and then snatched her away just as she was within our grasp. How could He torment us like that after all we'd been through? I could have wept. But I tried to cheer myself up like Pete. Clinging to a twig of hopefulness I said : 'At least they'll report seeing an orange boat with two men aboard.'

It was a savage blow but we could get over them quickly nowadays. Disappointments of this dimension were taken calmly. We'd get another chance soon.

While Pete repacked the film, I wearily stowed the jerrycans. I had pulled them out of the hatch and emptied their seawater ballast when we had the vision of fresh water. I sighed : 'Still, it shook us out of our lethargy.'

Another kamikazi fish, flying over, tripped over the grabrope and spilled on to the deck. I got him for the pan.

'Seeing as it's like Piccadilly Circus,' said Pete, 'what about watches tonight?'

I took the first. The night was black and I knew the moon wouldn't be out until Pete's watch. I snuggled down in the galley, wrapping the tattered dodger around me. Pete handed me the Sony and then went forward. I tried to forget the waves and plugged the earpiece of the Sony in. Luckily I got our religious station ('Always good for a laugh' as Pete put it) : Radio Paradise.

The minister preaching sounded like a Southern States redneck. He strongly warned his listeners to 'Whup yore chilren regular'. It was cheering me up already. 'Why,' he bawled, 'if ya don't they'll turn out like the one I saw the other day. From behind I saw hair half-way down the back—dirty raggy pants. Well, I didn't know whether it was a Jack or a Jill but it sure smelt like a John !'

That was what I needed. I folded up with laughter . . .

Pete scrambled in at dawn. We lay in the half-light listening to the gunshot cracks and hissing spray outside. Then we dozed for a couple of hours before the sun's heat drove us outside. I was pleased that the wind had dropped but obviously the sea had taken no notice and was crashing away as usual. Snow-white Tropic birds jerkily flew over us, their magnificent tails streaming out behind them. From a distance I couldn't see the two narrow

white plumes and the birds looked slightly ridiculous without
tails. But seen closer, they were superbly balanced creatures.

I searched the deck for flying fish. We'd had a bumper night,

Five-and-sixty flying fish   Pete's eye view from the rathole

65 of them. That's 32½ each—what a feed! I dug out a cupful
of flour and dunked them all, getting more flour over myself
than them. Reluctantly I had to use the Casablanca margarine
to fry them in. We had not intended to use this foulest of foods
for cooking, just as a barrier cream or for greasing rowlocks.
With the departure of the cooking oil, however, this was all we
had left. I scraped a fingerful of mildew off and dropped a clean
lump into the pan.

I enjoyed that meal. With lemon juice and cayenne pepper and
a little imagination, they could have been good old English white-
bait. Peter sucked a few and scowled. I knew he hated them. He
shuddered, then scooped all he had into my dog bowl.

'You're bloody welcome,' he said, and prepared himself for

the loo rope. We drained our ration of black tea, had a smoke and buckled down to rowing.

Pete's diary

Flying fish for breakfast. Like any sea adventure I've read, the tale would not be complete without them. The tale for me *would* be! They are terrible scrunchy bony things. I am sure they were the cause of my squits. It seemed my bottom was hanging over the gunnel for two days. It's OK for the Iron Cook to laugh!

Derek

After my stint I pumped another six inches of water from the port galley hatch. Pete said the leak must be around the rudder slot. I bailed out all the remaining stinking water the pump couldn't gulp and wiped the slime from the boxes.

Despite our valiant attempts to keep a decent course, the gales and predominant south-easterlies were inexorably knocking us north. My fix on 27th July was most disappointing. At 1530 we were 15°45' North, 53°37' West. A swell from the North-East and wind from the South-East collided and made the sea confused. Rowing became a farce. To add to the misery a tropical depression was setting in and the stifling heat and heaviness of the air quickly began to crush morale. Whenever the weather was like this, my fears of impending hurricanes grew even stronger. I felt really scared every time the glass took a plunge or there was a particularly spectacular sunset. It was our policy though to listen to every forecast, and so far no storms were brewing. However, never before did we need so much speed as now. The old temptation of the sleeping bag sail returned but we managed to subdue it. We were living with two threats : hurricanes and water. Of the latter, we had five gallons of tainted left. Now was the time to conserve it even more rigorously. Pete and I worked out a plan.

(1) We had to figure out a way of working the solar stills from the deck and not in the rough sea, and Alec's still on the open flame.

(2) We had to use all liquids left strictly for sippers. These were six litres of Biostrath (though this could only be used in

moderation); the vinegared plastic lemons ran to a dozen and a half and nearly made me sick, but they were liquid; the bottle of holy water that Mamma Lombard gave to Pete and that he said was for the use of Catholics only, not Protestants!; a small bottle of Venos cough mixture would be pressed into use if necessary. That was all.

(3) All our food which would require rehydration was to be eaten dry, starting in a week's time if we hadn't landed.

(4) The actual drinking of fresh water was to be one and a half pints per man per day.

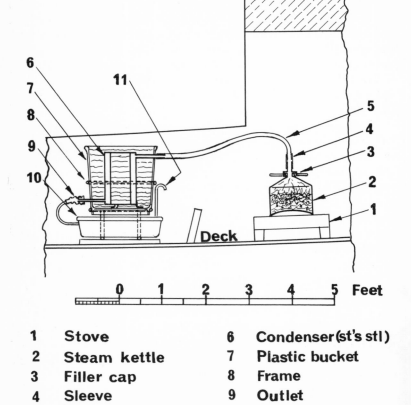

1	Stove	6	Condenser(st's stl)
2	Steam kettle	7	Plastic bucket
3	Filler cap	8	Frame
4	Sleeve	9	Outlet
5	Flexible pipe(st's stl)	10	Collector box
		11	Vent

Alec's still (salt water condenser)

(5) The barest minimum of water was to be used for all cooking from now on.

(6) The deck jerries must be covered with a cloth or something to prevent the sun's heat from spoiling the water any more.

These were tough measures to take but then we were in a very tough situation. My apprehension was heightened by another scare. I had found that my navigation during the week was becoming erratic. The rough sea and permanent clouds hiding the sun were the cause. I could only 'shoot' through a hole in the clouds if I was lucky, but I tended to treat these sights with scepticism. So with each passing day when I estimated our mileage rowed and applied it to the worked positions, the two points disagreed with each other more and more. If the navigation had been wrong all the way across then we might be weeks away from land. Another thought was that perhaps we were fighting a north-west current or maybe an eddy and we were losing up to 15 miles a day. I could not believe that the backbreaking toil on the oars each day realised only 20 measly miles. My spirits dropped like the barometer.

I lay on my belly in the rathole checking and rechecking all my calculations. I examined the sextant for error. I reread all the relevant material and still I couldn't find out what was wrong. My depression began to deepen. For the hundredth time I asked myself : 'Why did I get involved in this?'

Diary
A sultry close day. Both of us are listless, bored, miserable. The fix today denoting our 'unprogress' did nothing to dispel our gloom. Even our evening meal doesn't fire us with enthusiasm. We've been out here long enough—too long I reckon. We're showing symptoms of the infamous 'mental plonk'.

29th July. Never felt so miserable in my life. Wild sights and the whole plotting of our route seems in jeopardy. The last ten sights have all been wild. On top of this, water, food and fuel are all low and there's an untimely gale blowing. The sleep bags are soaked, our spirits also.

30th July . . . Things are getting on top of us.

A school of dolphin visited us just before dark. They were bold and came to within an oar's length of us. They splashed and chased round and round and it was wonderful to see them. I

suddenly felt happy as they chased off ahead of us. I cooked a
supper of odds and ends which included French onion soup,
cream of veal and vermicelli, and the last spoonful each of
honey. Not a lot for growing lads, I thought. I felt better that
evening while we smoked and chatted. It was amazing how
fickle my moods were—just like the weather.

As the light began to fade I saw three big cumulo-nimbus
clouds to the East. Below each one was blackness.

Pete

A painful night's sleep, perhaps doze would be a better word, as
the sea was rough and Britannia, now lighter with the lack of
stores, rode the sea in a corkscrew motion.

Diary

The wind now gusting 6-7, my bleary eyes peeping through
the canvas dodger as I lie in my damp sleeping bag—if the
waves don't get you, the condensation will . . . 'Get up Bird!
You lazy bastard,' I tell myself. I try this self-effacing technique
in an effort to get up, but I ought to know by now that it
doesn't work and never will. I watch Derek's legs as they wave
about from the after rathole. The rest of him, arms, hands,
head, is busy burying itself in pots, pans and tins as he gets the
breakfast going.

At last I make it. Now the race for oilskins before a wave
bathes me. What an effort! Now that ten-foot crawl 'n stagger
from bed to galley and I am knackered. After breakfast, in the
lee of the aft blister when the sun gets up a bit, we can remove
our oilskins and if the sea moderates, we can do some rowing.
It's all so much effort. We do tend to row when the mood takes
us but we do urge one another on. I must say the idea of
rowing alone doesn't appeal much. We have tried it and the
only argument in favour is that one can stop and start more
easily without thinking about one's partner. It's certainly more
work and I'm sure not nearly as efficient. We seem to be
making steady progress, no sign of a slow-up, we row without
thinking or feeling, like a couple of trained apes—only stopping
sometimes for bum breaks—and we are encouraged by our
latest position.

Derek looks a bit rough, fit but definitely rough. I don't

suppose I look that good but that's not as worrying as the mental side. We sit sometimes for hours saying nothing. It's all been said I suppose. What we do say is a repeat of long-ago conversations and ideas. I sit for a long time gazing at the sea. It never bores me but I do more and more think of wet, smelly London—I wonder how they all are?

The last day of July was upon us. I noticed Derek getting more and more short-tempered. It culminated that afternoon as he sat working out some sights on the plotting sheets, mumbling away to himself. I turned away back to the sea. Looking down into the water, I noticed a plotting sheet slowly float by, waving as it went in time with the waves. Looking up at Derek's grim expression, the sextant in his right hand, I really believe he would have thrown it, as he had the plotting sheet, had I not said something. We talked about the problems.

The last position had put us back a hundred miles. Up till now all the positions had been consistent with the last and with Dead Reckoning—so what had gone wrong? Had the sextant been damaged? Quite possible in this weather. How long had the sextant been misleading us? If we missed the Leeward Islands without seeing a ship, we should drift on into the Caribbean. With our water this low we could be in real trouble. We were also now well into the hurricane season. I thought Derek should leave navigation for a couple of days, have a rest from it. We would carry on using DR. So it was resolved for a while. We tried to forget it.

I decided to do a bit of cheering us both up : so out came the Jew's harp. While I was twanging away, I realised we hadn't done much taping and it was time to do some sound effects. So I played the third Brandenburg, on Jew's harp of course, and peed in the bucket, which when played back didn't sound a bit like the real thing. I also tried rowing effects—this sounded like someone opening and closing a door with rusty hinges. But at last we felt better, and listened to Radio Barbados coming through loud and clear. They were talking about Caricom, the Caribbean equivalent of our Common Market. I liked their approach—looking forward to the future with confidence and hope. I wished we in England had their freshness and will for the future.

I nearly didn't have a future that night and it would have been poetic justice too. From the day we left Gib, I had made myself responsible for the general maintenance of the boat and equipment. This wasn't a hard and fast rule. If for example Derek found a loose rowlock, he would find the appropriate tool and remedy it. I did, however, check equipment periodically in an attempt at preventive medicine. The most important item for these checks was the grabrope which ran either side of the boat, from the bow up along the blister through a metal ring, across to the aft blister, through another ring and down to a fixing point on the stern. The weakest point in this arrangement was where the rope went through the metal ring on either blister.

We had just finished our meal of the day. I had left my pipe forward, so lifting myself up by the starboard rope, I started along the 15 feet of open deck. I had only gone a couple of feet when a wave stronger and steeper than the rest hit us on the starboard side. The rope snapped at the forward ring. I was holding on to this useless rope as I began to go head first over the side. Halfway over the port rail I suddenly stopped with the weight of Derek on my legs. He had been standing up and when he saw me topple, he rushed over and with a flying rugby tackle saved me from going all the way.

I immediately repaired the rope, having discovered it had chafed through until it was just strong enough to hold my weight but not strong enough for the sudden shock of the wave and my weight combined.

The next morning I did a quick maintenance check of Brit—everything that could possibly have chafed, rotted, worn, I checked and checked again. I had learnt my lesson.

The weather was stifling, overcast and depressing. The barometer had dropped three millibars in one and a half hours. I hoped this did not mean what it indicated—a hurricane. We talked of the possibility of one. Our relations were now very good, even in this weather. A few months ago we would have found some excuse for an argument, but now we had been through too much together to get upset with one another.

Derek slowly polished the flare gun. Cleaning things can be good therapy. Nothing can be wrong when you polish, like knitting or washing your socks.

12

Priorities

7th June

And now a confession to the reader. On 7th June, nearly eight weeks earlier and four weeks out from Casablanca, we made a momentous decision, which we have not so far mentioned. In this chapter we explain how and why we reached that decision.

Derek and Pete

Derek

We had been analysing our motives for undertaking the expedition, after our escape from death by tanker screw. We both agreed on one point. As I wrote in my diary : 'Why should our personal search for exhilaration, or whatever we set out for, involve the most serious risk of all : our lives?' This very obvious thought struck me hard as I scribbled these lines down. I glanced up at Pete, scowling at the hazy sunset : what was it that he had said . . . 'It's not only me that I feel concerned for—and you of course', he added quickly—'but also my folks at home. I mean man, think about what they must be going through. Oh, I know we pumped them with our own confidence and reassurance before we left. But I know only too well they won't kid themselves.

'You see,' he had continued, 'just recently I have discovered that being loved bears a tremendous responsibility. It works two ways. You can't take love for granted and return nothing, can you?'

I shook my head. I'd never seen it that way. Of course, even my blunt instincts had told me that Mum and Dad, Geoff'n and Maggie, would no doubt be concerned about my rowing off. But that I should actually have a sense of duty, of obligation towards them because they loved me, never entered my head. My mind was too choked with the eyes-fixed-ahead image I had adopted to counter the initial cynical reactions to my plans. I had become little short of obsessive. Selfishly ego-tripping, I'd grown insensitive to other people's feelings while I promoted myself and the expedition. I'd been thinking of the trip to the exclusion of other essential things in life. Pete was absolutely right. Being loved is a huge responsibility.

Then my mind became disturbed. Fleeting thoughts of disconcerting logic came to me. 'Surely, having realised that love is like a game of tennis where failure to return a ball eventually ends a match, how can I justify myself by keeping the old chin up and bravely plodding on? . . . I may think it's fine to sit out on an ocean smoking a pipe and feeling patriotic, but looking at it rationally, what am I really achieving? Some vague notion about bettering myself? The glory? All that crap like "because it's there"? The need for challenge and man's basic instinct to accept it? But my challenge might kill me.'

My Irish voyage should have taught me that life was too precious to be put continually at risk. I had completed that voyage. Should I then have decided that that was enough? After what we'd been talking about, I thought the answer to that was yes. God had given me life. Why end it prematurely? I loved life.

But so what? Surely I couldn't just get out of this boat and start home on the next ship that we managed to stop? How could I possibly give up? The very obvious feeling, guilt, troubled me. Over two years of hard work, sacrifice and dedication had gone into the expedition. People had been asked for support and given it. Television and newspaper coverage was huge. I should be letting all these people down—and myself. I knew that public expectation was becoming a nightmarish pressure. And then I felt my personal pride beginning to shatter. 'The fellow who gave up' was a title I'd hate to live with. The gleeful chorus of 'I told you so', the sarcasm and jeering; my ears were starting to buzz already.

I knew Pete shared some of my thoughts—but was he too thinking of quitting? If he wasn't, maybe he'd try and convince me to stick it out. After all, we had talked about the question of being tempted to give up. Both of us had sworn we would try to talk the other out of packing up; we knew there would be times when such temptation occurred. But I felt I was so right. My life first. My reputation second.

If I told Pete that I wanted to give up, say when we reached the West Indies, what would his reaction be? Would he say 'But you can't, man. What am I going to do?' I'd feel terrible then. I'd be letting him down too. I did, however, actually discern that Peter might be having second thoughts. He was certainly still thinking about our going under that tanker. And his talk of responsibility did sound as though he was sorting his priorities out.

I wondered how, indeed if, I could broach the subject to him. Would he take it as a weak admission of failure or would he be relieved I'd mentioned it? The wind rose. A full moon played hide-and-seek as quicksilver cumulus blew past. Humps of black water ducked underneath us as Britannia reared up. Sometimes she didn't rise fast enough and a ton of water crashed over her. It was time to turn in. While I waited for Pete to finish cleaning his teeth, before I fastened down the dodger from the inside, I was working out what I could say to him.

Pete's diary
Derek says he is in love, but how, after getting engaged to the one you love, can you just go off rowing across oceans? Soon after his engagement all those months ago in Gibraltar, Derek casually said to me : 'If I don't carry on after Panama—I'd still want to keep an interest in the expedition, perhaps as PR man or agent of some kind.' Shrugging it aside I just said 'Yes.' I hoped that giving the cold shoulder to his statement would reduce its importance. I was sure it was a spur of the moment remark which he did not mean and would regret having said. But after the conversations of the last couple of days, I'm not so sure he didn't mean it.

Dawn broke into my fitful sleep. I arose to find my back ached

abominably. To move it anywhere away from the absolute
vertical sent a jab of pain down my spine. I stood holding on to
the forward blister, slowly straightening my back until the pain
eased enough for me to stagger down to the galley. Derek, having
made breakfast, handed me my dog bowl and said :

'The last of the Nido, mate. It's dried egg from now on.'

'Oh no !' I said. My conversations were never bright in the
morning, whatever the circumstances. The Nido was one of
Carol's best purchases—a malty cereal made up with hot milk.
It reminded me of baby food. I remembered that as a child,
having grown out of sloppy food, I still coveted and on occasion
even pinched a spoonful of Farex from my younger sister's plate.
Fond memories but now nothing to covet and much less to steal.

We sat clad in oilskins and wrapped, it seemed, in our private
thoughts. The white crests crossed and recrossed one another, rose
to a peak, then fell leaving a hiss of bubbles. Our worlds only
bridged when the common enemy broke on the stern sending a
shower of water over us, extinguishing pipes and misting my specs.
We cursed in unison.

Time, that was the problem. One year of this I could manage
quite well. Eighteen months was a bit much—two years was too
long and our estimated 29 months with stops bringing the total
time up to four years if all went well seemed impossibly long.
Added to that was the two-year preparation. A total of six years—
six years too long to be involved with one person and one idea.
The thought was not a new one. It had been with me for some
time. I could see problems looming ahead at each stage—waiting
for supplies which were always delayed, for example. I could not
see our finances improving very much along the route either.
Britannia too—how long would she last? Already we had leaks,
not much it was true, but for a glass-sheathed hull to leak would
mean serious problems later on.

The long silence was broken by Derek saying :

'I'm thinking of giving up.' He surprised me.

Turning to him I answered quickly : 'Me too.'

I could see I surprised him.

If anyone in Gib had told me that within two months Derek
would have said that, I would have called them a liar. Of all the
people I knew, Derek would have been the last to give up on
anything. The conversation that now unfolded gave the true
picture of our feelings. Derek, when he got engaged, had changed

from being a fiercely independent person who enjoyed his loner life to one of complete empathy with another. Excited by his new-found involvement, he had failed to take into account his own need and Maggie's to be together. He thought that their love would be strong enough to endure the separation. Instead, it was the love that made the separation unendurable. When I had met Derek for the first time he had had one priority—to row round the world. He hadn't given up, he had just changed his priorities.

I told Derek of my preoccupation with time. I had come to believe that to spend too much time with just one other person did not make for a balanced human being, however intellectually stimulating he might be. We talked on about why both of us, for different reasons, had arrived at the same conclusions almost simultaneously. Something to do with empathy after the time spent alone together?

Derek

We began to discuss what was to be done when we reached land. The first problem was our debts. Pete looked up from his diary :

'How much cash do you think we'll have?'

'I think we owed about £300 to the bank before we left. Our only revenue will be the money from what ITN screen and if the agency sells any pictures. Then there's the 10 per cent fees and all that . . .'

' "All that"—you mean the £700 we owe to Alec and my Mum,' said Pete.

'Yes, but hopefully that's long term. We need cash to get us back.'

'And the boat.' Pete mimicked Fairfax's accent. 'Where ees my boat you villains? What 'ave you done weeth 'er?'

I laughed. 'We could always row her back.'

'Like hell we could,' said Pete, not taking it as a joke at all.

'I think,' he said, 'that we must go into one of the bigger ports and look for a ship going to England. Then ask through their agents if we could beg a passage back and take Britoo as deck cargo.'

'Well,' I replied, 'in normal successful circumstances that would be easy. But I wonder how people will react to our giving up. Maybe they won't want to know us any more.'

'I'm sure BP or P & O would help if they could,' Pete tried to

convince himself. 'I mean, if we get to land, that's an achievement isn't it—blokes don't row boats across the ocean every day,
do they?'

'Well, I suppose it's all going to stem from the way we approach
it. If we admit defeat yet at the same time rub in the success part
of it—we may scrape some help up from some kind soul.'

I was now aware that the threat of public expectation was not
nearly as dire as I had originally thought. It was my life. So if I
did let sponsors down or other interested parties, if I lost money
and if my pride was injured—I'd still be alive. And I'd get
Maggie.

Soon I'd be home to my girl. Now everything was tangible
and I really could see an end to the project. With the reward of
overcoming my pride came a bonus. Maggie and I would be together within a matter of weeks rather than years. The prospect
really thrilled me. What, I wondered, would she think about me
giving up? I was sure she'd say : 'Whatever you want.'

Oh roll on land! I could hardly wait. Straight back home—
and I'd have my stag night in the Woodsman, then my girl and
I would be married. That was all I wanted. There'd be a job to
get, a mortgage to find, kids—these would be my new priorities.
Life was either that or this. The sea humped and broke heavily
across the deck, dislodging the oars. Roll on land!

13
Faith

1st–10th August

Derek

The last 24 hours were catastrophic as far as navigation was concerned. An estimation of our normal day's progress, 35–38 miles, was applied to the positions I fixed, but lately the figures were not making sense. Sights clashed wildly with the Dead Reckoning and I got into such a state of concern that I began to blame the sextant. How I wished Pete had a knowledge of navigation.

We could have been in the middle of the ocean for all I really knew. The last navigation check, from Gdynia II, had been, I reckoned, over two thousand miles back. The sextant could have been damaged and we could have been overestimating our mileage, so it was possible that we were not as near to land as we thought. Therefore rationing would be a hit and miss affair—well, everything would. Having almost decided that the sextant had an error of collimation (the collar holding the telescope is out of alignment and generally most of the angles work out to be more than they should be—adjustment should be done by professionals), I decided to give the Cruiserfix a bash.

This was a new gadget, quite ingenious really, but one I should have preferred to operate in calmer conditions. If the plastic protractor and movable pointer could be kept steady, it could show on a scale one's latitude at local noon when kept horizontal. Also if latitude and true North were known and a couple of simple sums done, one's longitude could be found too. It only worked in sunlight when a shadow was cast on the time scale.

But as the boat rolled and wallowed in very choppy seas, I subconsciously held the sun's shadow at what I wanted to believe, and with an average from five readings every so often, I read off the desired area; around the 58th Meridian. It was a doubtful affair. I couldn't really ascertain the latitude, and if that was wrong so too would be the longitude. And the good old noon shot with the sextant wasn't any use now that we had come close to the equator. Here, the sextant angle was becoming so close to 90° that it was impossible to take the angle properly. But I was still hoping that the sextant was right. At least it meant that the former consistency in sights applied to the DR was correct. But the sextant was giving fixes that denoted a mere 15–20 miles per day. Certainly, the way we had been working lately we were covering more ground than that.

I stayed up to 0500 hours on 1st August, hoping for some decent star shots, but cloud and squalls killed that idea. I did snap Polaris, putting him on a guessed horizon, as the moon had slunk away, but again I thought it was wild : 14°59′ West. And a stab at Altaire worked so amazingly way out that I thought my navigational knowledge was probably non-existent after all.

Diary: 1st August
How I envy Pete. I haven't let on that my navigation may be totally up the spout and he is sitting there fondly believing that we'll be in Barbados in a few days' time. Hell, I can't understand it. All around us we have coastal signs; green water, terns, gulls, rubbish floating and the sort of cloud that one sees over islands. The sextant says about 240 miles to go. DR and Cruiserfix say 60. No more than two days rowing.

I read through what I had written and felt a great sense of fraud. I should tell Pete—it wouldn't be as big a disappointment now as when he realised the situation in a few days' time when there was no land.

'Hey Pete.'

He looked up from his book.

'I'm going to lay all my cards on the table.' (I thought I sounded like James Cagney.) I told him about the very great possibility of the navigation being completely wrong—even so wrong that we could still be in the middle of the ocean, though I expressed my doubts about that. Pete was gazing out to sea, quite expressionless. Then when I had finished and was waiting for a comment, he turned his head. He was smiling.

'Don't worry mate. We'll get there one day. Remember Moriarty.'

'Good man,' I thought. I laughed and began the song. 'Moriarty solves all our problems.' Pete joined in and sang for a full five minutes. Having fantasies of land was not taboo so long as we realised that they were fantasies.

Diary: 2nd August
We fancy we see land all around us because we want to see it. But it's shadow and cloud base and we know it really.

I had been watching an attractive Noddy bird. He was fishing near the boat and wasn't having much luck.

Noddy bird on Britannia's hull

'Come and join us,' I shouted. And as he fluttered and dipped near the bow, he suddenly swooped and lo and behold, landed on the blister.

'Roast Noddy bird,' said Pete, eyeing the little chap hungrily.

'Got to catch him first.'

'Use the flare gun.' Pete sounded serious.

'What, kill him and cook him at the same time?'

He smiled. He was only joking after all.

'Why is he called a Noddy bird?'

'Dunno,' I replied. 'Actually it's a kind of tern ... Might be something to do with its white head.'

'But Noddy wore a blue hat,' Pete said knowledgeably. 'And a bloody bell.'

'Well then, his brown feathers.'

'But Noddy had a red shirt!' He was serious.

'By the cringe! Look, all I know is that it's called a Noddy bird. Don't ask me why. Probably because he nods.'

Pete peered at the bird who glared back indignantly through beady eyes.

'He's not nodding. Definitely not nodding,' he confirmed.

A hash of vermicelli and beef flavoured with oxtail soup was relished at supper-time. Pete sat back, picking the last shreds of meat out of his teeth with a matchstick. I was fiddling around with the radio, and for a change tuned into a Guyana station. There was a Bach evening in progress, and both of us, being fans, listened to the organ music in raptures. It was the first time I'd heard it played on a Moog Synthesizer. And to add extra atmosphere, the SSE wind brought the first smell of land since Casablanca. The exquisite perfume of blossom was blowing from South America and it was a reminder of everything I had missed.

Crackling atmospherics around sunset obliterated our concert and the beautiful blossom smell fizzled out too. We were left with the lousy sea swishing and cutting over us while we sat and smoked. My worries returned with the silence. That navigation ... were we rowing across a current, not with any more, but diagonally across? Of course! That would explain our reduced mileage and the sights that said too far North to be believed. After all, our attempts at a southing would bear that out. I got up and tottered forward to the rathole. I dug out the Pilot volume and thumbed through salt swollen pages. There it was! 'General surface current circulation July to October.' A diagram showed it plainly. There was a definite WNW trend in the flow, of up to 20 miles per day in the area I was checking. I jabbed an accusing finger at the diagram as I showed Pete.

'That's what the problem is.'

We had been struggling to keep a southing all day, and at night the current had undone all our good work.

'Well, we'll have to row all night,' Pete said gloomily. 'Keep the boat Barbados bound all the time.'

'The obvious,' I said, 'but look at the sea. You can't row in that at night.'

We stared at the steep choppy waves. Waves that though small, would crack an oar if it got caught under a breaker. I knew it was impossible to work in such seas, but it would be worth a bash with the short oars.

Pete lost at poker dice, so he went on first shift. He had scarcely pulled the boat into momentum when I heard an almighty thump followed by a screech. I peered out into the gloom and saw Pete's legs flailing in the air. Then came loud swearing which moderated into grumbling as he winched himself off his back and got on to the seat.

'Bloody crabs!' he murmured. He crashed away for another 20 minutes. Just as Britannia seemed to be responding to his effort, a guerrilla attack by a couple of nasty invisible sidesweepers catapulted the boat over. An alarming groan as the oar strained in the rowlocks when the boat tipped, then a curse. Creak, curse, creak, curse. It was hateful.

'Oh come on then, pack it in!' I called angrily.

We sulked, sitting in our usual positions aft. The wind was piping up, and I could distinguish the distant mad screaming of terns above the rumbling sea.

My thoughts turned to Maggie. I knew that she knew we had (or should have had) stores and water facilities to last 12 weeks since she'd heard from us via Gdynia. So I was certain she would not raise any alarm that would result in a search for us. Then I wondered about our promise to try 12-day radio transmissions. We had failed miserably on that score. Would BP issue any worrying statements, or would they accept that no news is good news?

'What about trying the radio tomorrow if it's calm?' I asked hopefully.

We knew, though, that it wouldn't be. To operate the set there would have to be a perfectly quiet sea. Not only for keeping the aerial upright instead of whipping from beam to beam as the boat rolled, but for dragging all the equipment out of the galley, so that one of us could crawl in and get the radio. And then there would no doubt be a fruitless morning—completely wasted. If no contact was made we'd have lost another 15 miles.

'When we're sitting in Bridgetown harbour, then we'll transmit,' cracked Pete.

The 3rd of August was our 86th day out of Casablanca. A hell of a long time to be bobbing around in a rowboat. It was beginning to tell on us. I looked into the broken shaving mirror and saw a completely different person from the one I had known three months before. My once dark brown hair was bleached yellow by the sun, and the pale English face a rich leathery brown. But my features startled me. I looked years older. My eyes had a deep staring appearance and lines on my forehead were more pronounced. Pete too had changed physically. His mass of matted curls grew into his ginger beard and he looked more like a tatty lion than the smart female fancier I used to know. Behind his glasses, tired eyes : eyes that had seen so much fear and uncertainty that they gave the impression of pleading for final defeat.

Yet both of us were convinced that we would make a safe landing. We had talked about it : of what we would eat, do, where we would walk, even composing our telegram to say we were quitting. These were not fantasies. They were, like all dreams of faith, concrete and real. Of course we would succeed.

Pete switched on Radio Barbados. Suddenly the air was full of music and encouragement. The calypsos were our carrot. 'Come on,' they were saying. 'Come to our beautiful island. You can make it.'

We rowed hard. The sea was short and choppy. A tropical depression, bringing stifling heat, nearly choked us with breathlessness. But how we rowed. We started getting new blisters in the palms of our hands and in the bends of our fingers. Fresh sores erupted in the sweaty creases of our buttocks. The sharp spray of the waves made them sting like wasps. But we kept at it. An endless cycle of in-out, in-out. Counting strokes, visions of trees,

beer and girls; glancing at watches; wiping sweat from brows.
At the height of that fierce day I rowed quite unconsciously.
Then mercifully the blazing sun sank a little in the hazy white
sky.

I handed Pete a plastic lemon. He poured a mouthful
down, his face grimacing. I emptied mine into my mug. Brown
vinegar turned by the sun, and laced with slimy threadlike bits.
Terrible muck, but it was liquid.

I balanced myself with the sextant in hand, then carefully
worked out the third position line of the day.

'Well, I must believe it now.'

I avoid estimating mileage rowed and drifting to check the
fix. Just accept what the sextant says. 14°35' North, 56°12'
West. Where have we to go for Bridgetown? 13°05' North,
59°37' West. Look how close it is on the chart : about 230 miles.
Look how far it is in practice : about a week of agony.

We got back to the damnable rowing. Although the wind was
freshening, the air was close and oppressive. The sky was
shrouded in a wispy veil through which the sun sank like a silver
coin. Flickering shapes of birds—always moving, always restless,
passing in front of the sunset sparkle. Another night coming. Our
last at sea? Our last on earth? No to both. We'll do it.

We ate supper in silence. Rice and beef lumps was nothing
to get excited about. What we needed was something interesting
to happen. Something that would take our minds off the situation. By sheer accident, I found the very thing. I upset the jug
over Pete's backside. Boiling tea scalded him, and he leapt up
bellowing every profanity there ever was. In a trice he had his
pants off and was splashing seawater over the offending area,
still cursing vividly. He thought I'd done it deliberately at first.
I had to convince him that it was the sea again. He sat down
gingerly and groaned each time the boat rolled him on his latest
injury.

'Damn this trip,' he muttered.

Radio Barbados once again saved us. Songs, news, discussions,
advertisements. It sounded like a real swinging island.

'Don't miss the barbecue and dance at St John's this weekend!' the man said.

'You going?' asked Pete.

'No,' I answered. 'I'm going to the dinner at the Yacht Club.'

'Well, I'll go anyway—I'll bet there's plenty of nooky.'

Night watch

As darkness fell, out came our pipes. The tobacco was beginning to dry out and it soon burnt through. Pete would reload
our baccy boxes every couple of days from the old Kesp tin
in his hatch. We had decided in Gib to empty most of our
hundred one-ounce tins into one big one because of compass
deviation. By doing this we risked it drying, or, more seriously,

if the sea claimed it, that would be that : no smokes. But if Pete was as sly as me, he had secreted a few unsealed airtight tins in his hatch and to hell with the compass.

I lurched on to the deck next morning, eager to realise our old vision of that thin line of land—again not today. The sea was still there, but—

'Hey Pete. Come here and look !'

He too leaped out of bed. (What was he thinking—land, a boat ?) We both stared at the water. It had gone back to its familiar oceanic blue. No terns. Nothing. Not even oil lumps or a bit of Sargassan weed. Here we go again.

'It must have been a bank or something we went over,' I said.

'Sure it wasn't that we've gone through the islands and we're into the Caribbean ?' asked Pete suspiciously.

'Look, I'm believing the sextant. You believe what you want.'

'But look at the colour of the sea. Bright bloody blue. Middle of the ocean stuff.'

The argument was unresolved.

At local noon (our watches read 0800 hours GMT) the clouds closed in. We had been rowing enthusiastically all morning, with a light flukey wind that seemed to box the compass. But it kept us refreshed and we weren't fed up so much until clouds covered the sun and any chances of sextant shots were ruled out.

The wind built up its reserves. By 1500, there was a full gale blowing. Very quickly the seas rose, and our spirits dropped.

Pete

A grey sky with grey sea—a grey day. The drone of an aircraft fitted into the scene perfectly. So perfectly that although we heard it, we weren't aware of it until an old Dakota crossed our bows flying very low. We could see the portholes clearly. Derek reached for the small compass—she was on a course 325° Magnetic from Guyana to one of the islands north of Barbados. The possibility that they had spotted us was an exciting thought. Brit's orange paint against the dark sea would show well. Surely they must have seen us ?

'Just think,' I said, 'they may even broadcast our position on radio.'

We made a point of listening to the radio avidly during each news broadcast. I pushed the on-button on the Sony and tuned to Radio Antilles. We heard the DJ's voice boom out loud and clear.

'When the sun is high in the Caribbean sky—Jeff Feyday takes over from three till six when the sun goes down.'

I liked the way he said 'Caribbean'. We spent a few minutes imitating Jeff Feyday until he announced that week's number 1, 'Don't rock the boat, baby'—very apt. The clear sound of human voices took us close to land, and I imagined the palm trees, walking again, eating fresh fruit, meeting people—talking to someone other than Derek.

Another thing that listening to local radio did was to help to adjust our internal clocks from the GMT we were accustomed to. We both felt it unnecessary to keep winding on a watch five minutes or so each day as we travelled westward. So we used GMT throughout the voyage. It was only strange when, at one o'clock in the morning by our watches, when we usually went to bed, the Barbadians would be stirring for a new day, around five o'clock their time.

Our existence in rough, fickle seas did have its funny moments. I was watching the Noddy bird perched on the bow when Britannia flinched and dropped into a trough. Noddy, however, stayed for a moment in mid-air, his wings still folded. Rather disconcerting for the poor bird to find himself in the air and not flapping! He made a good recovery though, and soon roosted on undeterred.

Our sleeping bags, clothes and mattress had been drenched so often they could absorb no more. It was impossible to dry them properly. The constant movement as I tried to sleep was the real bane of my life. I could put up with dampness, little water, rowing, anything, but doing it all without sleep was unbearable. To sleep in a small boat at sea, you have first to wedge in comfortably; then a feeling of weightlessness alternates very rapidly with a feeling of extreme heaviness as the boat lifts and drops in the sea. To the vertical motion must be added the horizontal rolling, and if whatever you have wedged against stays put, you can be sure that your body will not. The trick is to fall asleep before this happens and the aches and pins and needles begin. Derek complained of back pains more frequently than I did. The clammy conditions in the rathole were a contributing factor to the grievances of both of us.

I felt Derek's brooding over the navigation to be unnecessary.

It was either right or wrong. He should assume it was right as there was no other information. To worry was negative—though I suspected wrong navigation was as much a blow to his ego as anything else.

I was sure I could feel land nearby, though I felt a lot could happen before we sighted it. Sometimes it felt almost tangible, and at other times I felt more pessimistic than at any other time in the trip, like a grand prix driver on his last lap leading to becoming world champion hoping a tyre doesn't blow.

Even though the seas were short and steep, Derek decided we would have a special meal—devilled beef and rice. I've always been a lazy shoveller, an easy on the chewing eater, rather than a cut, squash on to fork, chew 29 times and swallow man. Beef and rice would be just the ticket. Derek hummed away to himself in the galley, the hums punctuated by the now obligatory curse. After half an hour or so, I moved to the cry 'Grub up'. Derek dished up a rich red stew which smelt delicious.

'It may be a little hot—I accidentally dropped the cayenne pepper pot into the pan.'

I dipped my spoon into the dog bowl and shovelled a good load into my mouth. The sensation was remarkable—I could not taste a thing, my mouth was numbed. After the anaesthetic had worn off I felt as though my eyebrows had been removed. So strong was it my face began twitching. We threw most of the stew into a pot with intentions of adding to it the next day.

Derek's navigation went to the wall with the onset of a force 7. It blew SSE, which combined with the current had destroyed our sweat-earned southing by early afternoon. The gale moderated enough for us to take turns on the short oars. We headed due South for the rest of the afternoon. Battling through that horrible sea our tempers flared—at the sea, wind, luck and at each other. As each took his turn, the relieved man flopped down and had the sick pleasure of seeing the other in purgatory. I could not see any progress being made. All we were doing was keeping Brit beam onto the wind and sea. My remarks to that effect during the afternoon provoked a few heated words. It seemed so futile—Derek struggling with the oars. Each stroke seemed to say 'I told you so—I told you so'. The waves too had a rhythm and told me the same. It was as if Derek was trying to prove something to himself, and I thought: 'I don't object to anyone "doing their own thing" so long as it doesn't involve me. A bit late for that now . . . though not for much longer.' I hoped not much longer as I watched our last six gallons of water rolling around in the deck jerries. There would be one gallon of reason-able-tasting water, then there would be the five gallons in the emergency jerry which until Casablanca had held paraffin, and still tasted strongly of oil.

Our preoccupation on the night of that unhappy day was the distinct possibility of missing Barbados. We came to this realisation reluctantly, only after we had sounded one another out on the idea, slowly digging out the hidden thoughts from each other; a process we had both become masters at. Our dream, our goal, had long been Barbados. We had read all we could in the Pilot book and listened avidly to the radio. Barbados had been firmly imprinted on our minds. But now, because of our failure to make a decent southing, it was becoming less of a possibility; we should more likely strike Martinique, St Lucia or St Vincent first. And the thought of landing and not having the money to send a telegram home was not a happy prospect either.

The 6th of August saw us starting the last five gallons of water. The heat of this muggy tropical weather accelerated our water consumption. Another contributory factor was that our time at the oars had increased dramatically. In a few days, if we hadn't landed, we would have to stop work and devote all our energies to the production of water. Our surprise position was a bright spark in the day. Laboriously worked out by Derek, it gave 15°25′ North, 58°01′ West; around 150 miles north-west of Barbados. As our westing increased, the unwelcome northing increased too. The next 150 miles would be the hardest—we set to with gusto, rowing hard in the now calmer sea. We were suddenly optimistic—we were gaining ground south.

Derek

I left Pete meditating aft at 0400 the next morning. Local radio stations were playing relaxing midnight music as I flicked around the channels. I lay on top of the jumble of sleeping bags, tucked the Sony behind my sweater and used it as a pillow. I struggled to get to sleep but troubled thoughts nagged me, making me toss and turn and thump down the lumps in my bed which had never bothered me before.

There was so much that could go wrong. Suppose that water made us ill? And what if it ran out? If we got to an island, would we be wrecked on a reef? Hurricanes. Oh no! So close to land, one could be fatal. How would we get back home, assuming we landed? What would folks say when we told them we were giving up?

I listened to Pete straining on the loo line, and when he had finished I heard the rustle of oilskins as he dressed up. My mind was thinking furiously. Where is my faith? It's no use me trying to instil confidence in Pete when I'm not even sure. But what to do? What else but pray? A simple prayer. No deals with God. None of this if you do so and so, I promise to go to church and so on. Ask for the lot, and more. And above all, ask for a bit more faith.

That prayer didn't last long. I believed that asking for just a safe landfall wasn't enough. If I was meant to be with Maggie I would have to get home quickly. Without funds, we should have to work maybe in the islands for our fare home. So, quick passage home too, for us and Britannia. I didn't feel it was asking too much. We had had a rough time. Why not ask for everything?

After that I felt reassured. Pete squeezed into the rathole later and found me still awake.

I said, 'I just asked God for a free flight home.'

'That's funny,' he said, 'I've just been praying for a free trip too. But I didn't specify flying!'

'Ah well! We'll see what happens.'

Through my dawn drowsiness I felt Pete crawling all over me. I opened my eyes and he was slithering forward, trying to reach the cameras.

'Will you move your mighty member,' he breathed, jabbing me in the crutch.

'What the hell are you doing?' I asked.

'I want to snap Noddy—he's sitting there with his head under his wing.'

'Really?' I replied, guarding my face from his knee as he backed out.

Diary

Nowadays there's no hanging around making excuses for not rowing. Get up on the seat and get going. Every mile we lose being swept north means an extra 1,200 strokes back into wind. So no quibbling about heat or choppy seas—get rowing!

The ghastly exercise reduces us to brainless beasts of toil by midday. Minds stuttering vague thoughts—completely disjointed. To us they mean so much. Fighting against mental fatigue. If you stop thinking you've had it. Come on. Anything. How 'bout a song? No? All right, a nursery rhyme. 'Row, row, row your boat, gently down the stream, merrily merrily'—damn it, who the hell is merry doing this . . . Merry? Merry Christmas and a Happy New Year . . . Snow . . . Lovely white cold snow . . . Falling gently . . . Like a parachutist . . . I'd like to do that . . . Cool breeze. Must be over England. Or Ireland. Rain there, gallons of life-giving rain . . . Makes the fields green. Good crops there. Potatoes! Beef and dairy produce . . . Cheese. Irish Blue cheese with a rare fillet steak cooked in butter! Good food . . . Cooking . . . Maggie cooking my supper—not Pete—Maggie. No waves over food. No sweat dropping from armpits into the tea. Keep going. Rowing. Rowing.

No matter how hard I pushed myself, my willpower would inevitably be broken. All because of my backside. Twelve hundred strokes an hour would not harm shoulders or backs or hands. But those two lumps of flesh clamped tight to a hot piece of foam rubber! The entire body's sweat secretions aiming for the cleft between the buttocks. Each time I leaned back on the oars the seat cushion chafed. In—out in—out in—out; rub, scrape, rub, scrape. My skin reddened—rawed—peeled—stung. Hundreds of pinpricks of pain—like flea bites; the sweat rolled generously over these, increasing the pain. Suddenly a cold wave swept aboard. Immediate impressions of relief, then agony when the higher concentration of salt swamped the sores.

I broke the rowing and stood up. Pete looked relieved that the pace had stopped and he leaped up. Both of us pointed our backsides into the healing wind, and while we heaved a sigh of contentment, Britannia was quietly being blown off course yet again. Back to the oars. Correct the course. Row again.

Later: 'Switch the radio on.'

'What, Barbados?'

'Yes,' said Pete.

'Good for the news, that station.'

I fiddled with the tuner and got Radio Antilles, Dominica and St Lucia. But no Barbados.

'Give it to me man,' Pete demanded. He twiddled the knob furiously. The signal had completely vanished. Not even a very faint sound. Yet the radio was working perfectly; all the other stations were loud and clear. St Lucia was getting stronger. But no Barbados.

'What d'you think's happened, Radio Officer?' I said sarcastically, knowing full well he didn't know really.

'Could be a mountain in the way.'

Of course. I was sorry but I didn't actually say it.

'Hey! You could be right.'

'What's the big mountain on the island called?'

'Mount Hillaby.'

'D'you know where it is in relation to the transmitter?'

I put down the oar and clambered forward to the Pilot book and chart. The island appeared to be bristling with radio masts but assuming the commercial station was in Bridgetown, Mount Hillaby was indeed right between us and the transmitter.

I showed Pete and he said: 'Well, that's it then—if we row within that radio silence space, we could home right into the island.'

'Yes—but look at the bearing and look at the sea.'

He turned his head in the direction we should go and felt the blast of wind on his left cheek.

'Hell—we'll be almost rowing into it.'

'Come on then man—not far.'

Back to the oars. For the first time in several days we rowed together with the 12-footers. The sea was really too choppy for them but once we were underway it didn't matter if we missed a few srokes every so often.

On and on. When is it going to end? Please God make this damned wind stop. Give us a break. Keep going. Blast the oars. No, keep going. I'm waiting for Pete to say 'Let's have a break man.' I'll take the break but I won't suggest it.

Pete must have thought that too—neither of us let on we needed a break. But I had one excuse. Navigation. After four hours of continuous rowing I put down the oar, lying that I didn't want to, but I had to take a sunshot.

For a few glorious minutes I wobbled about upright with sextant clutched lovingly in my hand. I decided to take longer, so I did a series of three shots to average them out. Then it was sitting back and working them out. I transferred the previous night's position lines from Arcturus and Venus and drew a little circle around the final position.

'About a hundred miles to go!' I called in triumph.

'Fan-bloody-tastic,' Pete yelled back.

Just before we got back to the oars, I suggested a drink. Pete eyed the last few gallons. 'Nav might still be wrong mightn't it?'

'I'm sure it's not... How about a sipper of vinegar, then Biostrath, then a mouthful of lemonade powder? That's always good.'

'OK, and perhaps a special three-quarter pint of drink tonight.'

'OK.'

We rowed off with lumps of lemonade powder dissolving in our mouths. I didn't know if the powder would be more of a dehydrant than a thirst-quencher, but it seemed to produce enough saliva to moisten the back of my dry throat.

The wind was blowing South-East and had moderated to a force 4. The sea remained choppy and rowing as always was difficult. We spent one hour rowing due South, the next rowing South-West and so on; we could feel the boat being pressed beam-on off the desired course.

At 2000 hours (four o'clock local time) Pete suggested another break. We had been assessing what water we should have left in the tanks below deck. Although the pump couldn't reach it, there must have been a further two to three gallons left.

I applied all my weight over the gunnel and trapezed the boat over, so that whatever water there was would trickle from the port to the starboard tank—the side where the pump was situated. We gained another precious gallon—very muddy admittedly, but beautiful water. To celebrate, I made a cup of black mint tea and after we had drained it—back to the oars.

Our refreshment soon wore off and presently we were sipping Biostrath every half-hour, a cloying thick liquid and again I wasn't sure whether it was the thing to sip when one was deprived of a normal day's water intake, but it seemed to do the trick.

Throughout the afternoon and early evening we rowed hard. Jeff Feyday on Radio Antilles came and went. The news was read: nothing about us. We presumed the plane hadn't spotted us at all. At last, feeling absolutely knackered, we stopped for supper.

The sun sank behind a grey band of cloud and the friendly Noddy came back to us and roosted on the bow. He was certainly very territorial. Another Noddy hovered nearby making landing overtures and our chap made some threatening squawks to keep him away.

Darkness in the tropics comes quickly : twilight is very short. With the sun down, the radio jingling out a steel band and the two of us smoking, life seemed tolerable again. Indeed, we were almost having second thoughts about the voyage.

'I think I'll miss this life,' Peter said quietly. 'Just think, tomorrow or the day after and we'll be on land. It'll all be over, man.' He sounded genuinely disappointed.

'We'll never get another chance you know,' I responded.

'Aye, I know.'

'Still not too late to go on,' I said temptingly.

He definitely hesitated before he spoke.

'No—I don't want to go on.' He was quite firm.

'Me neither.'

I snapped Venus, Arcturus and Polaris, and fixed a position. We were only 65 miles off North Point Barbados. But I noticed that despite our magnificent attempt at a southing, we were being taken a bit too far to the West. The easterly since early evening was clearly the cause.

Both of us slept until dawn. I leapt out, scanning the horizon for that lovely island, but no joy. Britannia was pointing North-West with the wind on her beam. During the night, wind and sea had played their usual tricks, and I hadn't a clue how far off course we'd been punched.

While Pete concocted egg and onion rings for breakfast, I took the first sunshot of the day. Feverishly I worked out the azimuth, then the intercept, then I drew in the position line. It was running well west of Barbados.

'I'm afraid, matey, we won't reach Barbados now—according to this.'

'Oh well—never mind.'

We sounded quite flippant, but I felt bitterly disappointed and I sensed Pete did too. We knew so much about Barbados from the last two weeks of listening to the radio. We were geared up to land there by the weekend, and now we were savagely swept away, just as we had it within our grasp, so tantalisingly close. To add insult to injury, Radio Barbados was ringing out loud and clear. We had moved out of the cone of silence—gone round the mountain.

But in another way it was reassuring. It was another pointer to the fact that my navigation wasn't so wrong after all. Certainly it had been consistent. The stars were accurate and I had relied on them a lot lately. The sea colour. Radio signals. Drifting sugar canes, old bottles and shoes. A definite 'coastal sea'. It was all figuring.

As I went forward for the Pilot book to swot up the coast of Martinique and St Lucia, I looked over the bow. There, about half a mile away, was something that looked like smoke, moving rapidly over the waves. Spray from a whale? A whirlwind? The shape constantly changed, flickering yet moving fast.

At last I realised. It was a familiar sight to me. A flock of small wading birds, zig-zagging and banking as one strange body. Land would never be far from those estuary and beach dwellers. I got excited and yelled to Pete, but he couldn't see them at first. You can only see them when they turn their bodies over and contrast with the background. I remembered the waders I used to watch on the Essex coast. Just like these. A long trailing flight of about 60 of them. The shapes of the flock kept reminding me of land. The group elongated and turned into a train. Then it bunched and there was a house—then a tree—then a motor car. Things that I would very soon see. I knew I would, I could feel it. The little birds vanished to the South-East.

Pete's diary: 8th August
Usually you could set a chronometer by Derek's toilet habits, but for the last few days there's been no sign of movement in that area. This actually makes quite a difference to my life. Unlike me, he has been so regular as to be boring—it usually annoys me as I know my tooth-brushing five times a day annoys him. I put his lack of exercise down to nav worries. I wish I had more confidence in it. With no evidence to the contrary, it's best to accept it fully.

After an awkward day at the oars—spent cursing at the

sea or at each other—Derek set to his loathed task again. After what seemed like two hours he emerged from the rathole. His grumpy face betrayed the nature of our position—14°09′ North, 59°00′ West. All our battling and sweat today seems to have been in vain.

Gluttons for punishment, we rowed again due South that night. The tantalising smell of land, real or imaginary, drove us on to further tortures until our aching backs called a unanimous halt to our task. Without a word we flopped into a peaceful sleep.

Early the next day (9th August), having decided to forgo breakfast for half a mug of water and orangeade powder, we set to South once more. The combination of hot sun and strong wind was exhausting. We carried on. Bum breaks were kept to a minimum—instead we yelled encouragement to each other.

'Think of the beer.'

'Remember Moriarty.'

Diary: 9th August
Both of us feeling the strain of being near land and the possibility of missing it with no food or water. D apologised for being snappy—must be the dual strain of nav and rowing. SE winds don't help us. Aircraft—707—seen at 9.30 pm (GMT) heading 130°. Looked to be climbing. Feeling a bit depressed—oh for water!—nothing more depressing than being thirsty.

At 0200 on the 10th, I stood outside on deck scanning the horizon for lights or the tell-tale illumination of a cloud above the horizon. I fancied I could see lights to the South. In the space of an hour I saw a ship a couple of miles dead ahead heading North, a large jet also heading North and another ship heading South. A hive of activity. I related all this to Derek by way of encouragement for a good position. A few moments later he burst out of the rathole looking very excited.

'Hey—it's hard to believe it. We've nearly been on top of Barbados.'

'Where are we now then?' I asked.

'We're 34 miles East of St Lucia—look!'

He pointed to our longitude on the chart.

'Whoopee!'

'I've taken another shot this time of Polaris for our lat—13°46′ North.'

I leant over his shoulder holding the torch as he drew the line in, straight to the middle of St Lucia. I decided to believe that position. I liked it.

'But I'm still not sure,' said Derek, adding, 'maybe we'll see tomorrow.'

We went to bed that night feeling very nervous and chatting excitedly, hardly daring to believe in what the morrow might have in store. I dozed briefly, it seemed, then felt Derek get up. Blearily I looked at my watch—0710. 'See anything?' I asked.

'No, it's completely dark and no lights,' came the answer.

Just another anti-climax—I fell asleep. Again disturbed by Derek momentarily, I slipped back into sleep, then heard him shout something again—probably breakfast. Still drowsy, I became aware of what he was shouting about: the sound of his hoarse voice—he wasn't kidding. He couldn't be kidding shouting that loud . . .

14
Reprieve
10th August

Derek

It was just like I'd ever imagined it to be. In the dawn light I could see quite plainly a thin wavy line of land. Grey and solid. So tangible that my fear of mirages or illusions completely vanished. It was there. Thank God. I gazed in astonishment for a few more seconds, then I had to cry out. The Noddy bird shot into the air in alarm.

'Land! Pete, get up—LAND! LAND!'

I have never let myself go so much. My voice was climbing to a near scream. Tears flowed down my face and I was trembling from the noise I was making.

'LAND! LOOK LAND! Oh fantastic!'

I noticed Pete by my side. He was staring with his mouth open. His tired eyes glinted at the realisation of what it all meant.

'We've done it,' we chorused, slinging arms round each other's shoulders.

'Oh fantastic, oh fantastic,' Pete repeated. He was jumping up and down. He ruffled my hair and said: 'Well done—well bloody done.'

I felt like kissing him but there was only his nose that wasn't covered by hair or grime or spectacles, so I restrained myself. I'd never seen Peter Bird smile so broadly.

'Well done you,' I yelled. I thumped him on the shoulder.

'What a navigator I am,' I said proudly.

'Oh you're incredible, man. Congratulations.'

Mutual accolades flowed generously for another ten minutes.

Pete

Never could a lee shore look so sweet as it did that morning.

After my initial elation had subsided I felt a bubbling sense of well-being. Though we were aware of the dangers that lay 15 miles ahead, we had travelled near on 4,000 miles and were not going to be beaten by a mere lump of land sticking out of the ocean.

A strange feeling came over me as I sat gazing into the sea just as I'd done countless times over the last few months. This wasn't right, looking into the sea—I had to force my gaze on to the land ahead. We had made it—the days of dreamy sea gazing were finished. I wanted to land but I knew I would always look back on this whole experience with great emotion.

Derek
The whooping it up died down by degrees. Land is always a problem for someone who has just crossed an ocean.

Land!

Suddenly it wasn't friendly land any more. Gone were the visions of food and friends. Instead an ugly dangerous monster loomed ahead. What would it do? I had no secure thoughts. I could envisage, even getting so far as we had, being smashed to pieces in pounding surf over a reef or against a cliff. I knew well what could happen : I had spent 113 days of my life fighting to keep my boat away from the treacherous shores of Ireland. We weren't home and dry yet.

So first, decide what island it is. It will be fatal to follow the Pilot's directions for the wrong island !

Navigation points to St Lucia. I do a check with the chart. See, there's an apparently detached, large rock at the southern end. As we're about 15 miles distant, the islet could be a high promontory. What does it say on the Pilot—'Moule à Chique is a precipitous headland'—729 feet high. Low ground connecting it to the rest of the island. Yes—I can only see what looks like a channel—go closer and the land will appear. And the famous Pitons on St Lucia—I don't need a Pilot description to tell me about them. I can see them : two slightly rounded spires of rock dominating the south-western side.

The day brightens. Small clouds are forming over the bluish grey land. Britannia is drifting north-west in a coastal current, and as I gaze hard at our reward, I see shadows form.

Pete films and I photograph him in his element of sheer happiness and relief. We slip in closer. Now, with the first rays of the sun striking the island, it glistens a bluey green as dewy vegetation is lit up. I can see the gorges, ravines, the great volcanic peaks, their tops buried in cloud. The most beautiful sight I've ever seen.

The Pilot says there are no dangers affecting our little boat in the vicinity of the south coast, as long as we don't stray to within a mile of the reef-infested shore. Around the cape there is a little town called Vieux Fort with a couple of piers where we could get ashore safely.

The island turns green.

Now we've got to tidy the boat and ourselves up and get all our valuables—letters, log book and diaries, film and so on—packed up in Tuppers and put in an easy-grab polythene sack just in case we get into trouble and have to jump.

I'm going to have a good wash. Hair as well. Splash myself with aftershave and put on my best underpants. I'll dig out my going ashore kit—white jacket and trousers. They're creased and damp but I feel so good in them. Use the loo rope—for the last time.

Pete

As we packed up the gear and dumped the suspect food overboard, my gaze fell on the line of jerry cans across the deck.
Only one had water in—two gallons. I reflected on the possibility
of missing the island with only six days of water left. Yeuk.

'What d'you say, Pete?'

'Nothing, just mumbling.'

Then it occurred to me I didn't feel very thirsty—for the first
time in weeks. It was enough to know that water was not far
away.

We dug the warps out of the hatches, shackled up the anchors
and made ready. The galley was cleaned out and any non-
essential item stowed. We needed clear decks for any emergency.

With a happy song in our hearts, we took to the oars, hopefully
for the last time. We rowed strongly across the lumpy sea. Every
few minutes I turned my head, trying to gauge progress. There
were the forests covering the lower slopes and the mountains
beyond! The Pilot book told us Mt Gimie at 3,117 feet was the
highest of them, 'the one capped by a cloud'.

'There are sulphur springs near there,' said my ever-
informative Derek, sounding like the guide book.

At nine miles we could make out the shapes of houses. At seven
miles smoke rising vertically from a fire in a wood. We hardly
paused in our work, just striving to cover more ground. Turning
my head once more I could make out the land bridge linking
Moule à Chique to the main island.

'Well m'boy, looks as though we've made it,' said I for the
eighth time that morning.

'Say that when we're jumping around on solid land,' said
Derek.

Rowing was a pleasure that day—for the first time we had a
visible goal. The choppy water told us of the shallowing ground.
'Only have to cross that rough water at the point, around the
corner and take the first right to Vieux Fort,' sang Derek joyfully.

I glanced at Derek's face as he got up to alter the tiller. He
was beaming. I felt the vibes to be so positive from both of us
that I began to think there now couldn't be any more upsets
or problems. The sighting of land was proof enough that we had
done all we could. A handsome reward indeed!

Derek

As we rowed, strongly and now with a great sense of purpose, I noted that both of us were looking over the starboard side all the time. Normally we'd have been glancing all around us for creatures or waves. But there was no need for that now. With eyes fixed on the island we felt that no more dangers existed. As long as we could see land, our safety would be ensured.

Then I had a slight change of heart. We moved into decidedly choppy water; the confluence of a current division, or simply rebounding swell, I couldn't say. But Britannia bucked and wallowed and we caught crabs, fell back off our seats and cursed, as in old miserable times.

Closer and closer. Soon there will be solid, unmoving dry land. And people. What will it be like to talk to someone other than Pete again? I wonder what will be the first thing they say when we tell them we are abandoning the trip? Will they laugh and sneer? Will they be sympathetic? Will they ignore us or talk with us? How will they react to two mind-maimed mariners who have been at sea for too long?

And forgetting the strangers for a minute—what about our folk? What will Maggie say? Will she be pleased or disappointed? She has lived with this project for almost as long as I have. Will she understand my decision to quit? Two sides to that : 1. She'll get her man back, but 2. She will have to live with the questions—Has he got it out of his system? Will he ever regret giving up the world for married life? It'll be no good if after a few months I say 'I wish I were back in the boat.' No, I'll have to find new challenges. Everyone has a challenge. It's just that sometimes they become warped or selfish like this one was.

Anyway let's get there first . . .

The magnificent jungle-clad mountains reared their proud heads into the sky. Looking north along the east coast, I thought the edge of the sea glittered in the sunlight like Christmas tinsel. Plumes of smoke slowly spiralled up from a dozen wood fires in the foothills. A tiny black and green sunbird, miles from his jungle home, fluttered over the boat. He brought the first of the many warm welcomes we were to have.

With long, relaxed, professional strokes, we brought Britannia towards the densely-wooded hulk of land, Moule à Chique. The masonry tower on which was mounted a light was clearly visible on its summit. So far we had heard no noises of land or even surf. Gulls and terns shrieked out laughter and abuse as we approached, but no human voices yet. I gazed down at our escort of strange pale sunfish and absently thought, like the hunter I had been these last 93 days, 'I wonder what they're like to eat?'

Two miles off Moule à Chique I turned my head and rising out of a trough between the waves I saw a little narrow boat coming towards us. Five black men were looking our way. The boat was very narrow and had a strange flat bow board which cleaved the waves as it skittered along driven by an outboard. The boat circled us; the men looked alarmed. One of them in a yellow plastic mac said :

'What happen, man?'

'What happen, man?'

They thought we were a lifeboat and two survivors.

'We're OK,' I cried. 'We've just rowed across the Atlantic.'

They stared in disbelief, then the helmsman swung the boat round and they putt-putted to about 200 yards away where they slowly followed us in. The boat was named Star of the Sea.

The little boat chugged along keeping a respectful distance. The men eyed us with not so much suspicion as deep concern for our mental welfare.

'They probably think we're a couple of loonies,' I decided. 'I don't suppose they meet many rowboats out here whose crew say they've just rowed from Africa.'

'Yeah—we must look as though we've done something like that—look at our appearance.'

Our hair was wildly disarrayed by wind and bleached by the sun; our deck clothes were in tatters, our skins were bronzed.

We gave Moule à Chique a wide offing. Closer in, we saw thick marker floats of sugar cane bobbing at an angle to the surface. No doubt they marked lobster or crayfish pots. And then we saw the sea bed. About three fathoms down lay pure white sand and neat round weed-draped boulders. I hoped it wasn't shallowing off too steeply.

The last piton to the West slid behind the promontory as did the spit of land on the east side. We were under the Cape. We had rowed for four hours and I reckoned another half-hour before we landed. The air was full of birds. They cried raucously and their voices echoed against the lower bare rock face of the cliff. Looking up it, above where the vegetation clung tenaciously, up to the lighthouse, I could see two black figures watching us through binoculars. I waved to them and they waved back.

Still no smell of land. Another narrow boat bounced out. Another picturesque name too—Precious Lord Lead Me On. One old man and two young boys came alongside, staring wide-eyed.

'You orright, man?'

We said we were and told them what we had done. The old man broke into a smile, flashing pearly teeth.

'Oh boy, oh boy!' he yelled in delight.

The two youngsters looked puzzled but smiled.

'Vieux Fort?' I asked, pointing ahead.

'Yeah—round the corner—'bout three-quarters of a mile—wanna tow?'

'No thanks,' I replied.

'You twot, you should have said yes,' said Pete.

'If we can get across an ocean without help, I'm damned sure we can do the last bit by ourselves.'

Pete scowled and kept rowing. Every so often he stopped and filmed, then took up the oars again when I complained of the boat swinging off course.

Brown shiny rocks peered malevolently out of the surf. We

were getting a bit too close for comfort. The old man in the boat
waved us away from them and we altered course and struck
out across Vieux Fort bay. I glanced to the South and saw the
misty block of St Vincent over 20 miles away, and I doubted then
whether we would have gone through the islands without seeing
them as I had originally feared.

Swimming gulls flapped out of our way as we forged ahead
round the promontory. Then we got into the lee of the land and
my sense of smell exploded. The most astonishingly powerful
odours, pungent sweet molasses, blossom, seaweed and rich earth
wafted over us. I'd never smelt anything like it. All those months
of breathing nothing but purity—a sort of nasal vacuum. And
now this onslaught of beautiful perfume.

We both stopped rowing and breathed in the new air. A landsman can never appreciate the smells of his land until he has spent
a time at sea.

'Isn't that superb,' Pete said quietly.

We didn't sit there for long imbibing gorgeous sensations. Wind
came hurling down the hillside and pushing us out to sea. We
grabbed up the oars again and Britannia lumbered off. We set
a course for the end of a concrete pier. There was an orange-
coloured freighter alongside, and a small collection of local craft.
To the right of the pier were customs sheds with tin roofs and
a strange white dome which could have had something to do with
the treacly smell of molasses.

Suddenly the wind gusted savagely and without warning. It
caught Britannia on her blisters and spun her round. I leapt up,
altered the tiller and shot back on the seat. We pulled short sharp
strokes to get her underway but the same thing happened. And
again.

'Blast this,' I said angrily, getting up to swing the tiller.

The wind hammered us steadily and with wilful force inched
us out of the bay. We fought back but we hadn't the strength.
Then a lull of a few seconds enabled us to gather momentum
and we beat out a fast rhythm. A buoy nearby gauged our
efforts. Yes, we were getting back. We rowed swiftly, and using
the last vestige of our strength, pulled the boat into a thirty-
stroke-per-minute sprint. The wind increased. Britannia quickly
switched round and all our work was wasted. She was swept
back again.

'Oh damn this!' I cursed.

'It's your fault—you shouldn't have refused that tow in.'

'Oh crap.'

'And to you,' Pete snarled.

Just like old times. We both realised it together and laughed. Our tempers cooled. Reason came back.

'Let's drop the anchor,' I suggested.

'Maybe that waterski boat will pull us in,' he said, pointing to a white streak close inshore.

I hurled out the Danforth and let go a good few fathoms of line. I felt the anchor grip, then I wound the line around a cleat.

The waterskiers saw us and zoomed out. While they splashed towards us, I noticed the little wooden town of Vieux Fort. Lots of trees, red roofs, a central church with a wooden spire, coconut palms along the beach, ranks of boats on stays, groups of black children on the white sand. Just as I dreamed it would be.

'Hi, you're great fellas!' said the driver of the speed boat. 'We know all about you—you're supposed to be dead.'

I stopped eyeing the four bikini-clad dollies on board, and looked at Pete. He had heard too. Supposed to be dead?

'How come?' I asked in bewilderment.

'Tell you later,' said Junior (as he introduced himself), 'I'll take these girls back and then tow you in, we'll have a beer.' He roared off in a sheet of spray.

'Supposed to be dead?' I repeated.

'Who's been putting around rumours like that?' said Pete. We pondered. Then Junior returned.

'Throw your line,' he called when I had hauled up the anchor. Pete tossed it to him, and Junior made it fast to the towing cleat.

The outboard, which had been burbling away, suddenly gunned into a roar and Britannia jerked into motion. We travelled 400 yards to the pier at the fastest we had moved for three months. Junior let us go at the end of the pier where the orange ship was now leaving. Following his instructions, we tied alongside the island hopper Pamard, where the skipper and a few suddenly arrived spectators helped us aboard.

Hallos and handshakes were strange as we passed them. We stumbled shakily onto the pier. Pete got to his knees and kissed the ground. I watched then took a step towards him. My legs just folded up under me at the feeling of unyielding ground. I crashed over and found myself kissing the ground far harder than I intended! What a strange sensation it was. So solid and firm and unmoving. And how unsteady I was.

I staggered up and joined Pete who was plodding in an undignified fashion up the pier, testing his legs—much to the delight of a score of ebony children who giggled at his spastic movements. My attempt felt even more ludicrous.

Pete called back : 'You look as though you've had a nasty accident in your trousers.'

It took me far longer to adjust to walking than it did Pete. It felt like the time when I had had a six-week illness which confined me to bed, and I virtually had to learn to walk again. I plodded out heavy and unsure steps, testing the ground before I put weight on it. Pete laughed at my deliberations, but then I was more sure-footed than he was on the boat. I reminded him.

Scores of people gathered around us and both Pete and I became nervous, not knowing what to do or say. Instead we just smiled and stuck close to each other.

The St Lucians seemed to know how we felt and tactfully left us alone. However, the Europeans pumped us with questions and wanted us to tell all. It was rather disconcerting. We had decided not to announce our termination of the project until ITN had first been informed. So until then we would act as though we were simply resting in port. Our reasons were of pure loyalty to ITN : they had been involved so much with us, we felt it our duty to tell them before any other news channel. If anyone was interested.

It so happened that interest was running high when we landed. The locals had, that very week, seen a press stunt we had made on the Thames on the current British Movietone News Feature at their local cinema. And suddenly we had arrived on their doorsteps. (Strangely, half-way through our stay in Gibraltar, we had seen the very same piece of film at a cinema there.)

But we were more concerned with the reaction of the British people there. And there were nearly four hundred of them on a package holiday at the nearby Halcyon Days Hotel.

But luck was still with us and we met the aircrew of the company who had organised the holiday and owned the hotel—Court Line. They invited us back to a party later that evening after we had seen the police and customs representatives. We looked forward to that and the thought of 'thirteen lovely girls'. But especially to clear up the horrible rumour of us being dead.

Pete

Once aboard the Pamard, Emanuel and Hilaris made us welcome with soft seats and coffee. After an hour of chat, Hilaris asked : 'You guys hungry?'

'Er, yes.'

'Well, you come along with us. We ain't got no money—but our credit's good.'

We wobbled our way after them through the shanty town of Vieux Fort to a bar. After a couple of the local rums as an apéritif, we tucked into a typical West Indian dish of chicken, bananas and peppers. We groaned in pleasure at each mouthful, and with Hilaris and friends shouting and yelling encouragement, we devoured the food.

As night fell Derek and I stood naked on the pier while Hilaris hosed off three months' accumulation of salt. The feeling was indescribable. Junior arrived and bundled us into his sports car, taking us straight to the VIP's chalet in the Halcyon Days Hotel where the crew of the Court Line TriStar were staying on a stopover. With Captain Peter Hogg, Danny Dufain, the flight engineer and Chris the copilot and with thirteen beautiful girls to look after us, the champagne flowed. Derek telephoned ITN, leaving a message of our safe arrival with a switchboard operator.

Pete Hogg offered us a free flight home in the TriStar, subject to government and Court Line appro. Junior Alcee had a word with someone at Geest Line and arranged a free trip for Brit in a banana boat which actually docked where Brit was moored!

Derek

Neither of us wanted to tell anyone our secret. All those inquisitive, questioning people at the Halcyon Days. They'd heard of us, wanted to talk to us, wanted to know when we would set off for Panama. To tell them we were giving up . . .

'You say something, Pete.'

'No, you start.'

'No.'

Each of us had to be helped by the other to finish a sentence, so used were we to communicating with each other by verbal shorthand and intuition, and so unused to communicating with anyone else. We remained in this condition for a time even after our return to England.

It was Junior we told first, after we had rung ITN and left a message with their reception operator to say that we had landed, were safe, and would terminate. Junior's face showed an expression of true disappointment. 'Are you sure you really want to? You could stay here a while, have a rest, think it over.' He was concerned.

'We've thought it over,' I said.

'Well, you guys sure have got guts. You know best.'

The word soon spread around the Halcyon Days. The British holiday-makers expressed many reactions. Some sneered— 'They've given up, no good'—forgetting the 4,000 miles we had rowed. Some commiserated—'You've done well. But I wouldn't like to do it.' Some were relieved to hear our news. One girl told us that when she had seen Carol leave the expedition in Casablanca she was full of foreboding for the two of us. Gradually we became accustomed to hearing diverse opinions. It was our decision and no one else was involved.

In the middle of that night I telephoned Maggie. It was a very emotional moment. I wanted to know if all our folks were alive and well just as they would want to know about us.

'When shall we get married?' I asked.

'October 26th—I bought the wedding dress yesterday.' She cried with relief.

'But how did . . .?'

'I read between the lines of the letter you sent via the Polish ship,' she replied to my unfinished question.

I knew it was right to quit then—completely justified.

Maggie rang the sponsors, ITN and our families. From the latter came total relief. Our folks hadn't heard from us for ten weeks. I was told later that my 86-year-old grandmother, very deaf but still lively, had reacted rather strangely to the news 'Derek's landed!'

'Oh Gawd! Oh No! Oh Gawd!' she wailed at my mother.

'But what's the matter?'

'Derek—lying dead!'

Peter Tappenden of BP was soon on the phone. I told him our decision. I could feel the disappointment 5,000 miles away. I was really sorry for the PR men at BP and our other sponsors. The wind had suddenly been knocked out of their sails. ITN's reaction was different. It was news. Eventful news too. It would still be news if we had died, but if we had gone on it would have lost its sensationalism.

It took a long while to re-civilise. To eat with both knives and forks; to use toilet paper; not to make those natural but rude noises in company. All the while I felt overwhelmed. People, noise, smells, solid unyielding land. I sat in the garden of the VIP chalet, smoking a cigar and drinking a beer. Green lawns stretched around me, tall coconut trees swayed in the warm sea breeze. Tiny gems of humming birds darted in and out of the flowers. I could hardly believe it—all these beautiful sensations; what a far cry from the small boat against the sea. And the incredible offer of a free flight home for us and transport for the boat. Unbelievable.

Pete

Court Line confirmed our flight. Geest confirmed the free ride for Brit, thereby saving us a total of about £1,000. We unloaded Brit, and hauled her up the beach to be left in Junior's care until the Geest Crest docked later in the week. There was a delay due to a hurricane!

Once again we were staggered by the kindness of our fellow-men. Since arriving at St Lucia, we had been so well looked after by our new friends that at times I became very emotional about it. Pete, Danny and Chris made a concerted effort to allay my fears of flying. Their holiday clothes were replaced by smart uniforms; we stepped aboard that great pink bird roosting under the floodlights on the tarmac. Our thirteen bikini-clad beauties were replaced by thirteen just as beautiful air hostesses.

A few hours later, one of the girls leant over and whispered in my ear, 'We've shut down Number 1 engine.'

One down two to go—I headed for the bar. We landed in Halifax instead of Gander, Newfoundland, for refuelling. I watched as Danny and the ground crew worked on the stricken engine. An hour later it was pronounced fit—we took off for Gatwick.

Nigh on half-way across the Atlantic: 'Funny,' said the man next to me, 'we seem to have turned round.' I went to look for Rosemary, my favourite hostess.

Back in Halifax we went with our friends to a hotel while the

Halcyon Breeze had some drastic work put into her Number 1 engine.

'Well, we've been to Canada twice now, Derek.'

'Perhaps we should have rowed home,' he replied.

The effects of all the excitement, time changes and the anticipated reunions took their toll on me—I passed out with eyes open on a bar stool. When I awoke Derek told me, 'Peter Hogg wants a chat with us.'

The scene in the restaurant was not a happy one; even in my dazed state I felt the gloomy atmosphere. Peter put us in the picture very concisely.

'I am telling you both this because we have come to think of you as part of us. As from midnight tonight, Court Line Aviation ceases to exist. The aircraft is ready and my instructions are to return to Luton as soon as possible.'

Peter could have left the aircraft and its remaining 350 passengers, and with the crew could have taken the next BA flight to Heathrow with no trouble. Being the man he was, the thought of abandoning those people may have entered his head but it certainly didn't last long.

Derek and I helped the girls clean up the cabin before the passengers boarded. For a tense hour, we all prayed that news of the Court Line crash wouldn't come through to the airport. There was little doubt that the host airline would immediately impound the £12 million plane because of fuel, landing and hotel fees which Court Line couldn't pay. I expected the security men to come aboard and prevent take-off any minute. The passengers (minus six who couldn't be located) mustered on the tarmac in the middle of the night. Many had been woken up. Sleeping kids were carried into the plane. Then she taxied down the runway and Peter was given permission to take off. I breathed a sigh of relief. I looked round at Derek who stuck his thumb out and winked.

Once in the air, Peter explained the situation over the PA. When he finished his sad speech, 346 people applauded. My neighbour suggested a whip-round and we collected £300. Halcyon Breeze continued happily on all three engines. Derek and I popped into the flight deck frequently checking the three rev counters, with passengers merrily gulping the duty-free— including us. Derek was greatly impressed with the navigation computer which flicked up the diminishing degrees of longitude on a digital dial.

'Must get one of these for the next trip,' he muttered.

As the 'Fasten your seat belts—no smoking' sign went on, I went onto the flight deck for the landing. I felt honoured at the privilege, not only because it was the last landing of a Court Line plane, but because I could see my friends at their professional best. As the wheels touched, a cheer broke out amongst the passengers and Derek leapt about kissing the weeping girls. I felt a lump in my throat. Amongst the photographers and crowds on the tarmac, I picked out some familiar faces.

Conclusions

Pete

Although I have sailed for some years in cruisers and dinghies I can hardly be said to be a 'hearty outdoor type'. I am happy propping up a bar, or dancing at a disco. I like automatic transmission, central heating and Château Latour—in short, all the creature comforts.

However, one needs a yardstick to appreciate good things both material and spiritual. On the ocean I was bored, elated, hungry, thirsty. I had memorable meals and memorable conversations. The confines of the boat seemed to concentrate my emotions. I was never just happy, but deliriously so—never unhappy but wretchedly so; but the good times outnumbered the bad and I am glad of the experience.

Derek was married to his Maggie and Carol to her Pierre. My relationship with Silla ended mutually. I suspect that I built an image of her that was impossible to live up to.

I am often asked 'Do you and Derek still speak?' The answer is yes—and we're on good terms—we both have telephone bills to prove it.

I don't think I have changed much—if at all. John Fairfax once commented, as I cracked a 'funny', 'You will soon lose your sense of humour out there.' Perhaps it is unfair to quote him now, but at the time it was fair comment and he made me aware of the danger. I still laugh.

Was it worthwhile? I can only say that the day three idiots rowed out of Gibraltar gave a few million viewers of News at Ten a chuckle and in these depressed times that can't be a bad thing. Anyway, I'm glad I did it. For me it was worthwhile.

Derek

Britannia II was the seventh boat, in recorded times, to be rowed across the Atlantic. She was the longest of the seven, and the only one to have been rowed across the Pacific. Here's the list :

Richard K. Fox	1896	West-East
English Rose III	1966	West-East
Super Silver	1969	West-East
Britannia	1969	East-West
Khaggavisana	1970	East-West
Q.E.3	1971	East-West
Britannia II	1974	East-West

We rowed non-stop from Casablanca to St Lucia 3,545 miles (calculated from the zigzag of weekly fixes) in 93 days 7 hours. I reckon that drift alone was responsible for 35 per cent of that. Our overall average was 38 miles per day with some days at about 48 and bad days around 18.

I found it rather strange to hear people's reactions when we returned. Some were most impressed with the physical aspect of the voyage. Others commended our 'courage to quit'. However, we found that some people took an entirely different view; they were disappointed; they thought us cons; they were very cross— they obviously would have liked to see us row off into disaster so that there would be a bigger and more intriguing story.

Was it all a rash proposition? I don't think so. I'm sure that if it wasn't for my falling for a girl, I'd still be out there rowing. A few months at each stopover to get fit and to forget. I might have made it round the world with Pete if he hadn't experienced the same feelings as I. So if we both had stayed insensitive, eyes front, ignored people and influence from home—we'd probably have done it, given four years. Someone will definitely do it. It will be a single-handed voyage by a man with all the time in the world and by himself, for himself.

I knew it was right to quit by the way Maggie cried with relief when I phoned her from St Lucia. Then, as I peered out of the porthole and saw her standing there on the tarmac, it was confirmed. It was the right decision. We both ignored the cameras around us as we held each other very close. I remembered that there were many times on the voyage when I feared I would never see this moment. Yet there were more times I dreamed it and this dream had come true.

But there was something disconcertingly undreamlike about the whole thing. Dreams after all are merely idle fancies in the mind, or at the most aspirations. My thoughts, however, had been so concrete and real that it was as though I had been willing myself to this day. I remembered all those moments of great danger and uncertainty when God had felt so near and tangible, and I had turned to him. I had no fancy agnostic ideas : just a crumb of faith. That was enough.

Sometimes we were faced with situations which, in retrospect, appeared impossible : the black tanker, the big wave, the gas shortage, our thirst—incidents that only heightened my belief that luck had nothing to do with our survival. Before the expedition I had never found it hard to believe in God; yet for most of my life I just hadn't wanted to. 'King can manage on his own,' I often told myself. I didn't need God. Except maybe for emergencies. I remember sitting in the garden in St Lucia wondering how on earth I had ended up there. A free flight back the next day and the boat already taken care of. And I had actually prayed for it to be !

I recognised God when I was rowing round Ireland. I came home and found that the life of a landsman, and a suburban one at that, did not include the God I thought I knew. No one followed me up to show me the God who would have as much relevance to my life on land as he did at sea.

I had always been impressed with Maggie's faith which had enabled her to wait for me. After we married, it wasn't long before I shared her faith and I was baptised as a Christian. A friend who officiated at the ceremony seemed to sum it all up in a poem he wrote for me (we quote it at the beginning of this book). The title was from the name of the little boat we saw off St Lucia, *Precious Lord Lead Me On*.